All But Six

ALL
BUT SIX

A MEMOIR

Terrina Troy

WOOL & YARD WIDE PRESS

IDENTIFIERS: LCCN 2023914282 | ISBN 9798988788928

Editor: Michael Sandlin

Jacket and Illustration designs by: Patrik Svensson

Interior design by: Stewart A. Williams

Photography (author headshot) by: Britta Van Vranken

Terrina & Terry March 1969

Terrina & Terry 1986

Contents

Author's Note

Some names of people and places have been withheld, instead I use a "title." I purposely chose not to include certain names, because I wanted to give that person as little recognition as possible. And in some situations I wanted to provide privacy for people on the periphery of this story.

Conversations and stories are portrayed as accurately as possible, and most are verbatim. One hundred percent are true as I remember them. For the sake of brevity, some are shortened, generalized or representative of the situation, or conversation. Journals, calendars, photos and memorabilia assisted me with the chronology.

This book is not about retribution toward anyone. The focus of this story is on all the touchpoints where my life intersected with my father's. I purposely kept the emphasis on those moments, rather than details about other aspects of my life. These are some of the stories that shaped my life.

My father didn't believe in turning people into saints after they die. Nor do I. The language expressed is this book is not intended for children.

Introduction

My father and I had a unique relationship. Our unbreakable bond was tested and battered. But it was the only thing left in the end. The truth is, it never really ended.

Courageousness, perseverance, independence, and mental fortitude were passed down to me like a hand-sewn quilt, each generation adding another square, making it bigger, better, stronger. Flippancy was taught not only as the cornerstone of good living but also the key to survival.

Even as a young child, I felt like I'd been given a crash course on the real definition of bravery. If fear could have filled my stomach, I would have never gone to bed hungry. Had there been such a thing as college degrees in chaos and self-reliance, I could have earned a doctorate before finishing high school.

Without my sense of humor, finding perspective and succeeding in the world would've been impossible. I ultimately realized that my father and I shared the belief that laughter wasn't just a coping mechanism; it was a soul cleanser, necessary for survival. And thankfully, perfect behavior was not a requirement for love and loyalty, otherwise our relationship would have been devoid of it.

Later in my father's life, he described himself as "a working man, a blue-collar, dying breed, a lucky bastard with no clue how he ended up with such a great daughter—just a nobody."

I would describe him as the most independent-thinking, fearless, funniest man I'd ever met, not to mention my greatest teacher. I learned more from him than from any book. Though some of the lessons were agonizing, I cherish them all. He taught me consciously, and sometimes accidentally, how to become the woman I am today. Without him, there's no doubt that I would've become "just a nobody."

PART ONE

For you Daddy

CHAPTER ONE

The Making of a Daddy's Girl

If someone had told me in high school that my father was going to live long enough to see seventy years old, I would've laughed out loud. I didn't know anyone that had a father like mine. He was certainly an original, and he lived his life fast and loose. Over the years, I thought a lot about how he might depart this world. I was convinced that I'd just get a call one day and be told that he was gone. But that's not what happened at all.

Terrence John Troy, was the first born and a fraternal twin. At birth he weighed over nine pounds. When I read that on his birth certificate, I wondered how my poor grandmother survived delivering nearly sixteen pounds of babies on October 29, 1948. That should've been her first clue that she had just given life to a couple of hellions.

My dad had an amazing memory, and fortunately he passed that gift on to me. The very first memory I have is Christmas Eve, 1970. I was two years old, it was dark outside, and Dad had just returned home from work. The fire in the living room was burning, the tree was decorated, and a few gifts from family members were scattered around the room. It was a fresh-cut tree because Dad believed "only Polacks owned fake-looking white trees." At the time, I only had one Polish friend, and Dad was right, her tree was faux and white. Terry would routinely come into my room in the evenings and kiss me goodnight. He always wore a flannel shirt with a pocket on the chest, and he smelled like diesel fuel, coffee, and cigarettes. On that night, he tucked me in, kissed me, and said, "Now get to sleep Honey Babe. Santa's coming tonight, but he won't show up if your eyes are open."

Christmas morning I ran into my older brother Tony's room and screamed, *"Get up!* We gotta get out there." I heard my parents in the kitchen, so I headed toward the tree without him. The spruce was engulfed in wrapped presents, and there was one unwrapped gift; I knew immediately it was mine. I'd been asking for a big baby doll, and there she was sitting in my child-sized rocking chair. I squealed with joy, ran over, grabbed her, and hugged her tight. She was nearly as big as me and had short dark hair and big blue eyes that blinked when she was propped back.

"Whatcha gonna name her, Honey Babe?" Dad asked with a smile while holding his cigarette and coffee cup.

"Honey Babe," I said without hesitation.

"Well, that's what I call you. Are ya sure that's her name?" he said with a giggle.

"Yes Daddy, that's her damn name," I adamantly proclaimed.

My mother rolled her eyes as Dad let out a big belly laugh. Clearly my resemblance to my father did not endear me to her. But I had already realized, by age two, that he liked it when I reacted strongly to his teasing.

I took Honey Babe with me everywhere, and it was a well-known fact that having her with me was crucial to my ongoing happiness. I was about three years old when we traveled up north to visit my father's side of the family, at the top of the mitten near Alpena, Michigan.

After we returned home from our visit, I realized upon awakening from the long four-hour car ride that my doll had been left behind. Terry had loaded me in the car when I was asleep. I screamed my head off when I realized the horror of her absence.

"It's okay Honey Babe, it's not your fault. Your mother should've packed her. I'll just go get her," Dad said, flashing my mother a dirty look.

He grabbed some coffee and headed out the door to save my doll. As he walked out, he said to my mother, "Well, I'd rather have you pissed-off at me than hear her cry all night." When I woke up the next morning, Honey Babe was in my bed. Dad had driven all night to retrieve her and narrowly made it to work on time.

Terry liked to push people's buttons. It was a form of mental entertainment. He'd always get a cute little smirk on his face when he was giving someone a hard time. His favorite targets were uptight, closed-minded, or snooty people. I think he came by that genetically, as his father did the same. My grandfather, Bob Troy, flew thirty missions in a B-17 bomber in World War II. He was a technical sergeant so it made sense for him to get training in repairing TVs, which he did after the war. Dad told me Bob would work on televisions for free if the customer was poor; but anybody he thought had money would be charged twice as much. Dad laughed hard as he recalled the stories. Having grown up poor with few resources, it gave Terry great satisfaction to stick it to conceited people who looked down their noses at the working class. He always rooted for the underdog and had a soft spot for the underprivileged, too.

When the movie about Michael Oher was released, Terry called and said, "Have you seen *The Blind Side* yet?"

"I did. I loved it."

"Yeah, it was great. That Sandra Bullock character reminded me of you," he said, laughing.

I knew he meant she was strong-willed, but I also recognized my opening to play with him.

"Oh yeah, so you think I'm a bossy bitch, eh?"

"Of course not honey. You just know what you want, and you always do the right thing," he said with a chuckle.

"Aw, thanks Daddy," I humbly replied.

"I have no idea where you got your morals, because you sure didn't get them from me or your mother," he went on to say with a slight giggle.

He continued with one of his favorite lines, "Like I told my brother Joe, if I'd been born a girl, there would've been a whore in the family."

My parents were both high school dropouts, each around the tenth grade. Their marriage was a rocky one, to say the least. Not too surprising when you consider my dad was only nineteen when I was born. Ten days later he turned twenty. Our October birthdays made it easy to remember his age since we were basically twenty years apart. My mother was a year older than Terry and had already led a tumultuous life. I'm not going to go into everything about my childhood; however, to fully understand what happened later in our relationship, a little backstory is required.

I was an astute four-year-old when I witnessed a huge fight between my parents, including my mother slapping and scratching my drunken father and then ripping his T-shirt off his chest. I remember running into the bathroom where Tony was taking a bath, and yelling, "They should just get a divorce. They'd be a lot happier." Tony was about four years older than me, and two and half years after I was born, my younger brother Ted came along.

Dad had been working since he was a teenager driving all kinds of trucks and equipment. I considered him the smartest uneducated person I'd ever known. There wasn't anything mechanical he couldn't fix, build, or figure out. Relatives had shared stories with me about how he'd repaired his mother's car when he was only ten years old. He was born with an old soul, and innately had numerous skills far beyond his years.

Because of Terry's various occupations we always had lots of tools, vehicles, and heavy equipment around our house. Sometimes he would recharge and maintain golf carts, or he graded the dirt roads near our home, and then he'd park the road grader in our driveway. Occasionally, he'd drive a tow-truck home when he was on call for his friend's towing company. I remember many winter nights he had to pull people out of ditches. A few times when my mother didn't come home, Dad loaded me up in the tow truck in the middle of the night and took me with him. I'd fall back to sleep on the bench seat in the truck while he helped the stranded. Once in a while he'd get to the scene of an accident before the police did. He hated finding badly hurt people, especially kids. Even when he didn't have a tow truck, he loved helping people who were broken down on the side of the road and often stopped to help or offer a ride. But a lot of times he would pop the hood, assess the situation, and just fix it on the fly. He never drove by a distressed single lady without stopping—that's for sure.

In addition to his vibrant libido, he had a tenacious work ethic. Growing up in an Irish family, he learned the worst crime you could ever commit was being lazy. His grandparents on his mother's side were demanding, especially his grandfather, Bernard Flynn. Bernie worked extremely hard at his 160-acre farm in Alto, Michigan. Dad and his siblings were expected to visit and do the same, even when they were small children. My father was one of a select few who could get along with him. Bernie was a bit of a bastard at times, and he wasn't known for hiding it. He and Terry understood each other; they respected each other's grit.

My parents had a traditional marriage. My mother's role was to manage the house and the kids while Dad brought home the paycheck. It was no secret that Terry would characterize his wife's profession as "Chief Spender" and "Soap Opera Expert." He rarely became angry with us kids, unless we did something that happened to be one of his pet peeves. I can remember getting my hand slapped as a small child if I didn't have good table manners, but I have far more memories of misbehaving and getting away with it.

One time when I was about five, my mom was inside our home, "watching us," while my brothers and I were outside playing. The boys had used their BB gun to kill a snake. When they showed me their "catch" I noticed it had a large lump in it. I went into the kitchen and grabbed the biggest butcher knife I could find. I crawled up onto the dirty flatbed trailer parked in our driveway and started cutting the snake in half. Dad came home from work and noticed me sitting way up on the trailer with the knife, covered in dirt and blood.

"Whatcha doing Honey Babe?" he inquired with a look of disgust.

"Well Daddy, I'm trying to cut through this snake to see what this lump is," I answered as I held up the large, bloody knife.

"I see. Would you please hand me the knife? Where's your mother?" he asked as I preemptively pointed to the house.

I never got into trouble for discovering snakes eat frogs, but my mom sure did.

Another time I was playing with Ted. We each jumped into the electric golf carts that Terry had been charging in the garage. I asked Ted if he knew how to drive them, and of course Dad had shown him. He told me what to do, and we both hit the pedal at the same time and flew backward, driving the carts completely through the fiberglass garage door. My mom ran into the garage, peered through the large holes, and found us in the driveway.

"You wait until your dad sees this mess!" she screamed.

Later that night when our father came home, I heard a lot of four-letter words as my parents yelled at each other. But he never scolded us for our lack of supervision.

Occasionally, we were lucky enough to have my maternal grandmother volunteer to watch us. We all called her Gram, and she was my second favorite person. She always made us tasty food like fried bologna and cheese sandwiches, or her famous potato salad. She had a softness about her that we all took advantage of; she could never hold a grudge when we acted badly.

One day Gram came to babysit right after she'd just purchased a brand new car. She wasn't into watching *Dark Shadows* or *Days of Our Lives*; instead she'd do the piles of laundry and clean the house. I am sure she was knee-deep in grime when Ted and I decided to jump into the road grader parked in our driveway. Dad never locked anything and had a habit of leaving keys in vehicles. I asked Ted to start it, and he said, "The key's in it, you just have to turn it and push the button." He was actually doing it as he taught me, and suddenly the grader lunged forward. We couldn't see out the window, but when we frantically exited the tractor, we learned the *crash* noise was Gram's new car.

"Shit! You damn kids are a bunch of wild banshees!" she yelled as she appeared on the front lawn with her hands on her hips, surveying the large dent.

That was one of her favorite lines when we were out of control, and unfortunately, she used it often. When Dad got home from work, we were scot-free. He believed tormenting our grandparents was one of our chores. I remember hearing him say, "Well Margaret, I guess you need to do a better job of watching my kids."

Terry was blessed with being a tall, thin, handsome man with a full head of dark, thick hair. People made comments that he reminded them of Clint Eastwood. He never worried about upsetting Gram because she just couldn't stay mad for long. He knew how to sweet-talk her; even when it was obvious he was laying on the charm, she fell for it every time.

Growing up with two obnoxious brothers, I had to fight for what I wanted and defend myself if I had a chance at survival. Dad always told me it didn't matter that I was a girl; I could do anything the boys could do. So I climbed trees, played hard ball, learned to shoot pool, peed in the bushes, and fought like a lion. My brothers enjoyed wrestling me to the ground, sitting on top of me with their knees pressed into my biceps, pinning my hands above my head and spitting into my mouth when I screamed. They thought it was funny, but only until I learned that biting, head-butting, and kicking them in the nuts was effective in self-defense. I also learned that bullies only understand their own language; fight fire with fire. When my brothers would complain to our father about how brutal I had treated them, he'd just say, "Stop acting like a pussy and leave your sister alone."

When I went to kindergarten, we were living in an apartment in town. It was in an old historical house that had been turned into a couple of rental units, just around the corner from my elementary school. Many nights I heard Dad loudly cussing, as he swatted ugly bats with a tennis racquet, which had entered from the attic.

On school days, I would walk to the corner and meet my friend Bridgette, who lived a couple of blocks away. My parents knew her parents from high school—one of the benefits of living in a small town. Bridgette lived next to a lumber yard that had a small parking lot across the street. Terry would frequently apologize to her folks because sometimes he came home in the middle of the night and would park his loud semi-truck in the lumber lot before walking home.

I didn't go to preschool so kindergarten was my first experience with public education, and I started at age four. During the first week of classes, Bridgette and I were playing on the carousel during recess. Three boys made fun of her, and she started to cry. I immediately chastised the little jerks and began beating the crap out of them until they all ran off whining. The principal sent me home with a note for my parents. I couldn't read it, but I was pretty sure it wasn't an invitation to join the PTA. I never mentioned it to my mother that afternoon. That night Dad came home from work and said, "Honey Babe, I understand from Bridgette's parents that there was a little excitement at school today." I figured that was an actual question, but I treated it as rhetorical.

"Her mom and dad met me at my truck and told me a little story. Apparently, you got in trouble at school for beating-up some pussies," he stated with his classic smirk.

"Well she's my friend, and they called her mean names. They deserved it," I snapped.

He agreed and was extremely proud that I showed such loyalty to my friend. He didn't have a lot of respect for crybabies, and he never punished me for fighting at school. In hindsight, his "let kids be kids" attitude and general hatred for rules emboldened me to become a button-pusher, too.

On June 10, 1975 my parents were officially divorced. That same month, my mother quickly re-married the guy she'd been dating, and the court awarded her custody of all the children. The hatred between my parents never seemed to diminish. As an adult Terry used to call me up and say, "Well Honey Babe, today marks the day of my divorce being final from that cunt-of-a-mother of yours." I chose not to remember the date and typically responded to him with some sort of smart-ass remark like, "Wow Daddy, what are we celebrating next, colonoscopies?"

My father eventually moved into his new girlfriend's house. Her name was Carol, and she had a couple of wild teenagers and a few older kids. She worked as some sort of an administrator at the local nursing home in town. Terry would frequently stop in to see her and drop off lunch. When I visited him on weekends, he'd take me, too. Dad would say hello to everyone and would memorize all the names of the staff, doctors, and nurses. People treated him like a celebrity; they would abruptly stop what they were doing just to get his attention. Dad would squat down next to the ladies in wheelchairs and ask, "How are you doing today, dear?" He'd usually give them a kiss on the cheek and tell them they looked pretty. Even the men would grab his hand and ask him about the latest newsworthy event. I think many of them used to see him at the local donut shop, where they'd shoot the shit and solve all the world's problems before heading out to their respective dirty jobs.

"Daddy, it smells like pee. Why do you like coming here?" I asked matter-of-factly.

"Oh Honey Babe, it's not that big a deal to make these people's day. And they love seeing your pretty face," he quipped.

I didn't mind sharing Dad with those old folks, because I understood it was something that made him feel good; his way of helping the "underdog."

After my parents' divorce was finalized, my life changed dramatically. It had been a horrible process, and everyone came out of it with deep scars. Sometimes Terry would show up to take us for the weekend, sometimes my mother had just moved us to a new address and he didn't know where we lived. Occasionally, Dad would say he was coming to get us and then never show up. I remember crying myself to sleep, slumped over my luggage, defiantly waiting by the front door hours after the agreed-upon time. Weeks would go by without a word from him or an explanation as to why he didn't come. Often, he'd refuse to pay child support when he wasn't allowed to see us. My mother would request the court to put a warrant out for his arrest, he'd get thrown in jail, somebody would bail him out, and he'd disappear again. It was a nonstop chaotic cycle.

I have a vivid, painful memory from that period in my life that sums up the divorce aftermath. When I was about ten years old, my mother and her new husband had rented an old dumpy farmhouse, less than a mile from where I'd lived with my parents before they separated. When we first moved in, I had a bedroom upstairs across the hall from Tony's room. But like a typical old house, insulation was nonexistent. So when the colder weather arrived, Tony moved downstairs and shared Ted's bedroom next to Mother's room. The house had a long rectangle-shaped, glassed-in front porch between the mudroom and the family room, which became my bedroom.

There was a door that opened to the mudroom that had a window in the top half. My twin bed was pushed up against the door, and the other end of the room was open to the family room. In an effort to keep the heat in, thick plastic was stapled to all the windows and the door to the second floor always remained shut. From my bed, I could look through the door with the window and see the exterior mudroom entrance door. It was a classic 1970s particle-board style with three small cascading windows.

One afternoon while I was in the kitchen, I heard some banging at the back door. It sounded like it was coming from outside. There was a house rule that kids could not open the door no matter who it might be waiting behind it. Tony ran past me and yelled to my mother that Terry was outside. My heart filled with anxiety as I ran through the family room and into my bedroom. I jumped on my bed, and I pressed my face against the glass in the door. I looked through the mudroom and through the small windows of the exterior door, where I saw Dad outside. Mother and her husband entered the mud room and were between us as they approached the door. Terry was about six feet away from me, but all I could see of him were his eyes and forehead.

"Let me see my kids. I want to see my kids. Open the fucking door," he growled, as he pounded his fists on the door.

"You're never going to see your kids again. Get out of here, you asshole. I'm calling the cops," my mother screeched.

Her husband was threatening to physically hurt Dad and trying to get the security chain off the door. Somehow through the commotion and chaos my mother pushed the door shut and demanded they stop.

"I want my kids. Let me see my kids, you fucking bitch. I need my kids. *Open the goddamn door!*" he screamed.

I felt his angry, desperate voice pierce my heart. My mother and her husband left the room to call the police, and I locked eyes with

Dad. I looked at him with tears rolling down my face. I yelled as loud as I could, "I love you, Daddy. I love you, but please go before you get arrested. Please!" I wanted to be with him more than anything, like the old days. For his own safety, I had to get him to leave. I watched his eyes become sad. He looked defeated.

"Don't cry Honey Babe. I hate it when you cry. Please don't cry, baby girl. I love you. Don't forget I will always love you," he stated emphatically.

"I will always love you, too," I muttered, choking back tears.

He was quiet for a second as he stared at me, seemingly trying to decide what to do next. He kicked and punched the door one more time, and then his face was gone. I ran to my window but couldn't see through the thick plastic. I heard his car door slam and then tires maneuver through the deep mud puddles in our dirt driveway. I fell to my bed, hyperventilated, and cried myself to sleep.

Both of my parents tried to make me hate the other. But I never hated Dad no matter what my mother said, or how many times he disappointed me. He let me down more times than I can count, but in my mind he was never purposely cruel to me; he always told me he loved me. I remembered how special he made me feel as a young child, and I held on to those memories during the years he was absent from my life. I knew my father was deeply flawed, but I also knew the person he had the potential to be. His tender side was extremely redeeming, but it could also be fleeting. I didn't speak to Terry from the ages of around ten to fifteen. I guess he eventually gave up trying to deal with my mother, the cops, and the courts. And perhaps he figured it would be easier on me if he didn't even try. I also think he felt defeated, but too stubborn or unable to change his behavior that may have improved the situation. Within all the chaos, I felt heartbroken, lost, and eventually numb. With Terry's absence, I stopped allowing myself to cry; I was honoring his request. I became deeply angry, and a professional at suppressing pain. I made a conscious decision at ten years old to close off my heart to everyone in my life. Everyone except Gram.

Terry was an alcoholic and a workaholic. For many years he was making a nice living as a truck driver. This was back when Burt Reynolds was starring in the classic *Smokey and the Bandit* movies, and truckers were being glorified as outlaws and fun characters. He loved the hustle of it, and he would drive as much as possible. He doctored his books, popped speed, occasionally snorted cocaine, and worked days and days without sleep. When I was much older, Dad told me they were all doing it, and it was no big deal. Hauling illegal, heavy loads and avoiding the scales was routine. He used to say, "They're pitchin' and I'm catchin'," which was his way of explaining he didn't make the rules, he was just playing the game. It was clear to me that "his world" was rooted in a very different reality—not rulebooks or traditional mores.

When the trucking industry became deregulated it was difficult for him to make the same kind of wages, even though he was proficient in the business games. Around that same time, the United States was experiencing an economic recession, so he stopped trucking and headed west to weld on the Alaskan Pipeline. I don't know too much about this period of his life because it happened during the years I didn't see him, in the mid-to-late 70s and into the early 80s. I admired him for being curious, adventurous, and free. When we were apart, I longed to be the same. I was fascinated with his laissez-faire attitude and lifestyle.

Terry was a loner, but he could also make friends easily and chat up just about anyone, especially female barmaids. He was never afraid to strike up a controversial conversation, even if he knew it would probably end in a bar brawl. He was no stranger to cracking a pool stick over a guy's head, or dishing out a black-and-blue shiner. He wasn't a large man, but he was scrappy and unafraid. Most of his life he weighed about 165 pounds and stood six feet tall. He worked all over the country, and when he traveled he was typically low maintenance. However, the absence of Busch beer or his preferred cigarette, were clear exceptions. Every vehicle he ever owned had blankets and pillows in it; always prepared to sleep on a jobsite, or in the bar parking lot if he didn't find a better offer.

He was usually up for any kind of adventure that blew his way, and really didn't operate on anyone else's timeframe. I used to joke that he worked on "Terry Time." Sometimes he was a few hours late, occasionally a few weeks late, and now and again he didn't show up at all. He always had crazy stories about the people he'd met during his travels. Some of the situations that he would get himself into were absurd but became quite normal to me. He used the old saying, "If I didn't have bad luck, I'd have no luck at all." But I knew that much of his "luck" was actually poor planning, procrastination, and a bad attitude.

The early years of my life engrained in me that I was a classic Daddy's Girl. However, I figured out at a very young age, that if I was going to protect my heart and maintain a connection with my father, I had to be the adult in the relationship and love him unconditionally. He never apologized for who he was. He didn't tolerate anyone trying to change him, and God forbid anyone criticize him. Without a doubt, he was going to misbehave, so I had to set and strictly enforce my boundaries, to keep myself sane. That became even more important as time went on, but it wasn't always easy to do.

CHAPTER TWO

Diamond Reo

Somewhere during the time that I didn't see Terry, he and Carol had a nasty break-up, and he moved out of her house. I think she kicked him out, but let's not get technical.

In 1983, I was fifteen years old and struggling to deal with my mother and her husband; apparently the feeling was mutual. Arrangements were made for me to go live with my father, and I was dropped-off at Gram's so I could be retrieved without my parents having a confrontation. I moved in with Terry and his new girlfriend, Peggy. She had a young son, and the four of us lived together in a small, old rental house in the same town I had been born in. My mother had moved me and my brothers at least six times since I had lived there; it was an added bonus to be close to Gram again, too.

It'd been so long since I'd seen Dad, I think he struggled to jump back into a father role. But he hadn't had much practice, so it was understandable. It was a little uncomfortable for me too, because part of him felt unfamiliar.

Peggy and Dad enjoyed entertaining, and our house was often the gathering spot for all their friends. The front door was never locked, and I didn't even have a key. It was pretty chaotic at times, with people popping over at all hours to smoke, drink, and party. It was a two-story house with three bedrooms and one small bathroom. My room was the only bedroom on the main floor, located off the living room. It was small, didn't have a door, and had just enough room for my twin bed.

My father's twin brother, Tim, was also a truck driver and a raging alcoholic. When he stopped by, things became especially wild. I remember one time I woke up in the middle of the night to the sound of banging on Dad and Peggy's bedroom window upstairs.

"Hey you son-of-a-bitch. Get up and fuckin' let me in!" Tim barked, while holding a case of beer under his arm, barely keeping himself upright on the roof of the bay window.

"You dumb-fuck. The front door is open," Dad's voice echoed through the metal grate in the living room ceiling.

When Tim would visit, the twins had a ritual of cooking steaks and sitting at the dining room table, drinking and smoking all night. On one of those occasions, I returned home from being out with my friends. From outside, I could see through the porch window that Peggy was sitting alone, smoking a cigarette and crying at our dining table. The window next to her was busted out and there was glass, a few broken plates, and some steak bones on our driveway. I walked in to make sure she was okay and found more of the same all over the front porch, kitchen, and dining room. Tim and Terry got drunk and started arguing about how to cook (or something equally stupid), and all hell broke loose. There was always that one beer that tipped them from happy, laughing drunks, to pissed-off, fist-throwing assholes. The tipping point was impossible to determine. Was it twelve beers? Thirteen? Or perhaps seven because they'd been chasing their hops with hard liquor. It was impossible to keep an accurate count because who knew when they actually started drinking? Let's not forget the best way to cure a hangover was to crack open another beer in the morning.

My old friend Bridgette was quitting her waitress job at the local malt shop/restaurant. It was located on the main drag in a historical row building across from the beautiful courthouse in town. She recommended me as her replacement and the owner hired me. I was excited to have a job and initially walked to work, and then eventually bought a used ten-speed bike from the line cook. Most weekends I had to get up at 5:30 a.m. to get ready, get to work, and serve breakfast at the restaurant. It took a long time to shower, blow dry my hair, use hot rollers, and drain a can of Aqua Net to achieve that perfect 80s hair. The music and frequent party guests were so loud that I often couldn't sleep. I complained a couple of times about the noise, but it just offended Dad. Nothing pissed him off more than feeling criticized, so I just learned to shut up and drink more caffeine in the morning.

Dad was working sporadically and going in and out of drinking binges. I was giving school a half-ass effort while working as much as I could. I soon figured out that I couldn't rely on Dad financially; I needed to become as independent as possible, and that required money. I didn't have a curfew, and Dad's attitude about school was ambivalent at best. He told me that I could do whatever I wanted as long as I took responsibility for my actions; if I got into trouble, I had to agree to the punishment. Seemed fair to me, so I figured out what the minimum requirements were that would allow me to graduate from high school, while making as much money as possible. They were pitchin', and I was catchin'. I was determined to master the game.

I signed up for the local drivers' education program the summer before I turned sixteen. Classes were held at the high school and usually taught by mentally checked-out teachers. My instructor was a grumpy math teacher who had been there so long I think he had also taught my parents. My two girlfriends and I used to drive around town until he fell asleep. Then we'd drive about forty-five minutes to tour Michigan State University and check out the college boys. Typically, I walked to and from class or caught a ride with an older friend, but one day Dad offered to come pick me up after my session ended. As the kids exited the school to find their rides home, we all walked toward the parking lot. It didn't take me long to locate *my* ride. Parked in the fire lane was Peggy's white Chevette and two police cars with flashing lights behind it.

"Don't you cocksuckers have anything better to do?" Terry growled with a locked jaw and furrowed brow.

I stood on the sidewalk frozen and confused. As the officers reached for their handcuffs, Dad threw the car keys at me before his hands were yanked behind his back.

"Drive the fuckin' car home and tell Peggy to come get me out," he demanded.

I worried that the cops would realize that I didn't have my license yet. But they had their hands full, so that small detail went unnoticed. I was nervous about my classmates witnessing me breaking the law, but I did as he asked and managed to get home safely.

Later, I would learn that Dad had parked in the fire lane, prompting the police to run his license and discover a warrant out for his arrest. Apparently, he'd received a Driving Under the Influence ticket about six months prior and didn't show up for the court date. He'd blamed his bad luck for his capture and lamented that he was only in the damn fire lane for a minute. He never discussed the details of his DUI, and I'm not sure Peggy knew about it before posting his bail. Dad was a private person and hated nosey people, so I was careful about asking for any details.

One day, after I became a legal driver, I drove Peggy's car home after running an errand for Dad. I approached the driveway too fast, and I accidentally ran over the mailbox. I was quickly reminded that it wasn't the big stuff that upset Terry.

"I'm so sorry Dad, I accidentally hit the gas instead of the brake, and I ran over the mailbox. I'll pay for a new one," I announced upon quickly entering the dining room.

"Well, where's the fucking mail? You ran over the box, and you didn't even bother to bring in the goddamn mail?" he asked, as he dropped the newspaper on the table and blew smoke out of his nose.

It was clear to me that it was felonious to be that lazy. Feeling like a criminal, I hustled back outside and picked up the mail that was scattered all over the front yard. He eventually fixed the mailbox, and I never walked by it again without checking it.

That same summer, one afternoon Dad left the house and told Peggy that he needed to go buy some cigarettes. Everything seemed copacetic when he departed, but he didn't return that night. Peggy called the jail and the hospital, but she didn't find him. The next day, we found his empty car. Peggy became distraught and was convinced he was dead. Knowing how much he loved her, I was totally confused and freaked out, too. I couldn't fathom him just walking away from her. After calling all the bars in town, she figured out which one he had stopped into. The bartender at Duke's Bar told her that he had been partying with "some truck driver-guy," and they had left the bar together. We would later learn that he and the trucker had gone to Chicago on a major drinking binge. When he finally returned, about two weeks later, he just showed up on the front porch. I begged Peggy not to take him back because he had put us through hell, and there wasn't an acceptable reason for not calling. He never apologized to me, but he must have to Peggy. She took him back, and their drama continued.

As I approached my senior year, things were getting more chaotic. Terry would occasionally borrow money from me to pay the rent and to buy groceries and cigarettes. His drinking binges continued, causing him to switch local gravel-hauling jobs several times. Unfortunately, the owners and managers weren't a good fit for his personality. There continued to be consistent stress with his twin brother and others. Basically, I was constantly walking on eggshells, and I just couldn't take the instability anymore, so I moved in with Gram. Dad was really angry with me and felt betrayed, but deep down he was probably relieved. I was in a safe place, and he could focus on himself.

I made a conscious effort not to ask anything of Gram. She lived in a single-wide trailer on a half-acre lot, about a ten-minute drive from my job in town. Luckily, my friend Glee, lived in the country about ten minutes past Gram's property, so she'd pick me up for school and drop me off at work whenever possible. Walking to work wasn't an option anymore, and on occasion it was hard to catch a ride home with friends. Sometimes I would wait after work in the parking lot for Gram to pick me up after she finished playing bingo. On school nights, I typically worked until about eight o'clock, but Gram didn't finish playing bingo until around 9:30. Dad disapproved of me waiting around in a dark parking lot alone, so he decided I needed a car.

Eventually, Terry found a vehicle that he thought would adequately get me around. After work one night, I saw my new ride sitting in the alley next to the back door of the bar, a few businesses away. It was a 1978 burnt-orangey-colored Pontiac Catalina. A huge boat with rusted-out fenders and dents all over it. Dad was leaning against the front of the hood with his arms crossed and cigarette hanging pinched between his lips.

"It'll get ya to work and back, but don't put more than five dollars in the gas tank at a time," he announced as he tossed me the keys.

"Okay, Daddy, but why?"

"There's a pretty big hole in the gas tank," he snickered with his trademark smile.

Terry enjoyed seeing my eyes turn the size of saucers while I laughed at his ridiculousness. I had no idea if the license plates were registered or if the car was insured, nor did I care. In my view, it was my ticket to freedom. Free as far as $5 would take a girl. And just like when I was a toddler and he saved my doll, Honey Babe, he was once again my hero.

At some point that same year, Peggy kicked Terry to the curb.

Initially, he was living in his car, but eventually he rented a room in a stone farmhouse owned by an old family friend. They lived about ten miles past Gram's place out in the countryside. Terry was gone a lot, but we stayed in touch, mostly over the phone. He had a deep, gravelly voice that was undeniably his, and our frequent phone calls would ultimately define a large part of our relationship. The time we actually spent together was rare and short; his habit of disappearing into a new job meant I received many calls over the years from steel mills, gravel pits, and truck stops.

Even though most of Dad's jobs were in dirty environments, he was super clean and fastidious. He ironed a strong crease in his Levi's and was very particular about how his laundry was done, which was something I learned when I made the unfortunate mistake of folding his T-shirts incorrectly. If he was feeling grubby after wrenching on a truck, he'd refer to himself as looking like "Joe Shit the Ragman." Our family used to joke that Terry had arrived late to my birth because he needed to take a shower before he would go to the hospital. He also took great pride in the vehicles he owned. He typically drove a junker, but they were always clean and organized. He used to tease me that I was just like him because he said I was such a neat and tidy little kid that I even folded my dirty laundry. Surely I did that just to impress him.

Dad eventually obtained an older semi-truck and started working for himself. His younger brother Joe gave him the truck so he could find some independence. He was much happier being his own boss, and he was so proud of his new wheels. It was an old Diamond Reo, cherry red with lots of chrome and cool pinstripes. Everybody knew it was my father's because he had a name plate that read **TERRY TROY** under the steps of the driver's door, and the words **LADY TERRINA** painted in white, above the back window.

I'd been dating a boy I met in high school who was a year older than me. It wasn't a secret that his mother was extremely overprotective and controlling. She was also a strict Catholic and used the "guilt card" on her children often—just the kind of person Dad enjoyed messing with. Having been raised an Irish Catholic and former altar boy, Terry felt he had a lot to rebel against. One night during my senior year, Dad was in town and had parked his truck on the side street behind the bar. The next morning he called me at Gram's.

"Well honey, I found a note on my truck windshield this morning from your boyfriend's mother. Apparently she wants to talk to me and didn't have my pager number. What should I know before I call her?" he asked with a snarky tone.

I told him the truth and explained that I thought she was upset about some events that had occurred on my boyfriend's recent trip home from college. He basically said he wasn't in the mood to deal with "that bitch," so he'd call her later.

I was on pins and needles waiting for him to call me back. I knew this was probably not going to be a "Leave it to Beaver" type of call. Later that night, deep into happy hour, he called me back from a payphone outside the bar. I could tell by his tone that he was quite proud of himself.

"Well honey, you were right, she's pretty pissed off," he said with a chuckle.

"She said that my daughter had snuck over to her house when she was out of town and had sex with her son," he laughed harder and continued with more of his response.

"I doubt my daughter would have shown up without an invitation; she has better manners than that," he sarcastically claimed.

We both started laughing and he continued.

"Then she screamed, 'I found a rubber floating in the toilet.'"

"Daddy, what did you say?"

"Well, I just whipped it on her and said, 'You should feel lucky he's not fuckin' gay!'"

"Oh my God, Dad, what did she say?"

"Well, let's just say it was a short chat," he replied in his typical smart-ass tone.

He didn't have a problem with gay people. We have several gays and lesbians in our family whom he adored. He figured out pretty quickly that she was closed-minded and uptight. He wanted to push her buttons enough that she wouldn't dare complain to him about me ever again. I think he also viewed it as a teachable moment on "how not to take anyone's shit and the proper way to pierce an ego." She wasn't the first lady to hang up on my dad, and she wouldn't be the last.

On Sunday, June 8, 1986, I narrowly managed to graduate from high school. My ancient government teacher, Mr. Badura, told me he was only passing me because the thought of dealing with a Troy for another year was more than he could bear.

Dad came to the commencement ceremony, and I remember him saying, "Well honey, school was never my thing, but I'm glad you finished. Nobody can ever take that away from you." He sat with my boyfriend, who had just completed his freshman year at college. Dad's mother Margot and Gram also attended, along with a few other relatives. I was the first grandchild to graduate from high school on either side of my family because my older brother had followed in our parents' footsteps.

Even though I knew Dad probably couldn't afford it, he insisted on taking the guests who attended my graduation out to dinner that night. I appreciated his efforts, but these kinds of situations typically made me nervous. Terry always operated with cash and didn't respect financial institutions. It made me sad to see him pick up the tab just to save face, knowing he didn't have a savings account. I held my breath when he paid the bill. As he counted out the cash, I was praying he had enough. I had my graduation money ready in case he needed it, but he was well prepared and paid with hundred-dollar bills. I was proud of him, relieved and happy that he could hold his head high after we all had a nice, fancy dinner together—drama free.

Eight days later on June 16, Terry asked if I could do him a favor. He needed a ride but didn't mention to where. I met him in town at the usual bar parking lot.

"How come it smells like gas in here?" he asked, laughing as he jumped into the front seat of my car.

"You forgot to tell me not to park on a hill and some of it leaked out," I snidely replied and flashed him an annoyed look.

As he lit up his cigarette, I looked at him like he was nuts.

"Oh honey, we'll be fine; I'll keep my ashes in the car," he said flippantly.

"Yeah, right. Where am I taking you in this ticking time bomb?" I asked, rolling my eyes.

He hesitated for a moment, and then said, "Well, Honey Babe, Daddy's been a bad boy. I need you to drop me off at the jail."

I was taken aback, but I didn't say anything and just slammed the gearshift in drive. On the five-minute ride, he explained that he had to serve a ten-day sentence for his DUI offense. I felt sad for him, but at the same time, I was angry that he frequently drove drunk. I thought it was so stupid, reckless, and dangerous. But I could tell he was embarrassed and didn't want me to be upset about it, so I just sat there in silence. When he finished his cigarette in the parking lot of the jail, he knew I was worried. He gave me a hug and a kiss and tried to comfort me when he said, "Oh, it's no big deal honey. I'll be fine. And since I'm serving consecutive days, I'll get out after five days—if I behave," he explained with a giggle.

I was horrified at the thought of losing one's freedom. I tried to imagine what it was going to be like for him in that environment. It hurt my heart to see him shut my car door and walk away. But I quickly reminded myself that he was a firm believer in taking the punishment for making poor choices.

Later that week he asked me to pick him up in front of the jail. I figured he must have behaved himself, or he sweet-talked some female guard to let him out. As I dropped him off at the same place I had picked him up one week prior, he handed me a plain white envelope with my name written on the front. Inside was a four-page letter written in pencil, on blue-lined notepad paper that read:

June 17, 1986

My Dearest Darling Honey Babe,

I know I will never be able to find a graduation card that will even begin to tell you how much you mean to me, or a gift that will even begin to be adequate for such a precious little lady that you are.

I stood at your graduation and thought back on the last 17 ½ years. My first thought was the day you were born. I was the proudest young man in the world. I thought about the nights I would sit up and rock you in the rocking chair when you didn't feel well. For some reason you never wanted anything to do with your mother when you were sick. I thought about all the joy and laughter you gave me when you were learning how to walk and talk. I will always remember how neat and clean you were as a little girl. I then thought about all the years that were robbed from me because of the divorce. I remembered the anger and despair that grew in me. I remembered how hard some of the decisions I made were. Right and wrong ones as it turned out.

I then thought about the day you called me on the phone in 1983 and told me you were ready to come and live with me. I was as happy that day as I was the day you were born and just as <u>scared</u>. You see I hadn't had much experience being a father. I didn't really know what to do and so I tried to think back to when I was 15 and be the kind of father I wanted at 15. I probably didn't do a very good job I can see now things I could of done to be better. I only know that since the day you were born you *have given me nothing but joy and proud moments every single day of your 17 ½ years.*

I want you to know that every day of your 17 ½ years I've loved you more than life itself. I also know that in a lot of ways I haven't done a very good job of showing you just how much I did and do love you.

I hope in the future I can do a better job of actually showing you how precious you are to me.

I want you to know that I feel that you have had to do everything all by yourself, and you have done an excellent job. You are a fine young lady in every aspect of the word. I love you with all my whole being.

Your Dad
Terrence John

PS. Its been a long long time since I have written a letter so please excuse the spelling.
Love Dad.

I have many cards from him over the years, but this is the only letter he ever gave me. I'd kept it tucked away in the same plastic bag that held my gold high school graduation cap and tassel. After everything we went through together, it feels like a huge gift from him—almost like he knew I would need it years later.

The man who wrote me that letter while being reflective, sober, and forward-thinking, was the man I knew he wanted to be. But as I watched him slip into the back door of the bar, my heart felt heavy, knowing that there was a high probability that he would soon be far less eloquent.

CHAPTER THREE

Armpit of America

D uring my senior year, I had worked for class credits as an office assistant to the vice principal of the high school. It was just an opportunity to avoid taking a serious class, and I felt lucky to get selected. One day Mr. Okie asked me about my plans after graduation. I told him that I would probably just keep working because I couldn't afford to go to college. I was basically supporting myself, and it was all I could do to save up for prom, spring break, graduation photos, my cap, gown, and normal costs of living.

"Terrina, you are way too smart not to go to college. I'll give you some information and point you in the right direction. You gotta go," he insisted.

It was that conversation that led me to apply to Ferris State University in Big Rapids, Michigan. That was the only college that I applied to, and I chose it because my boyfriend was enrolled there. I really didn't think I would get accepted, considering my GPA wasn't exactly stellar. And when I had taken the ACT test earlier that year, I totally blew it off. What was the point? I remember being in the testing room nursing a hangover and drawing Christmas tree shapes with the answer dots of the multiple-choice questions. But despite these pathetic details, I was accepted into FSU and would start college in August.

When I told my father that I'd been accepted to college he was surprised but not excited. He managed to congratulate me and say he was proud of me, but I knew he was concerned about what I expected of him financially. Following my announcement, I quickly stated, "Don't worry Dad, I'll figure it out. I won't need anything from you." I could tell I hurt his feelings, but I didn't want to paint him into a corner where he'd offer to help and then fear disappointment if he didn't come through. I told him that I would work hard all summer, get a job at school, and my current boss also agreed I could still work as many weekends and vacation breaks as I wanted. He was concerned that I wouldn't have enough time to focus on my schoolwork. And he also pointed out that my car was probably not going to last much longer. He had his doubts, but that just made me even more determined. Nothing motivated me more than to have someone tell me I couldn't do something. I'm pretty sure I inherited that trait from him. But even though I felt he was skeptical, he still said, "Well honey, like I always tell you, there isn't anything you can't do if you try hard enough and never give up."

A few weeks later, I was driving into town to work the dinner shift, and my Catalina broke down. It just wouldn't go any further, no matter how many times I tried to start it. I thought maybe it was out of gas, but I'd driven it much closer to empty than that before. So I left it on the side of the road and walked the rest of the way to work, where I could page Terry. Nearing the end of my shift, he called me back and told me to call Johnny Howell's shop and ask for a tow. Dad had worked for Johnny when I was a child, and he knew they would help me and let my dad settle up with them later. I'm not sure he ever did, but that was the last time I drove that car; it had a bad alternator and wasn't worth the money to fix it.

Eventually, Dad managed to find me another car and said it was my graduation present. It was a maroon 1979 Ford Thunderbird, all tricked out with tape pinstripes, chrome wheels, and what looked like big garage doors on the headlights. There was a button on the floor that controlled the bright lights that I remember searching for with my foot. That car had all the bells and whistles my old car didn't have, including a big gas tank—sans the hole. After the surprise wore off, I felt guilty that he would spend so much money on me. I offered to pay him for it, but he wouldn't hear of it.

"Honey Babe, if I could've bought you a new one I would've, because you certainly deserve it. But this is just the best I can do," he said in a humble tone.

We both went back to working as much as we could. Dad had started a business where he welded tread back on the steel wheels used to crush gravel at large commercial gravel companies. He designed and built an automated system that was integrated into a large trailer that he hauled behind his Diamond Reo. He traveled around to gravel pits and would work for weeks at a time in one location. Later that summer I went with him to one of his jobs at the Holloway pit in Ann Arbor. I enjoyed discovering it was so different than what I'd imagined. He was so proud of the system that he had engineered and built all by himself. But as with any mechanical device, it had its breakdowns and frustrations. He made a lot of money, but he had a hard time meeting deadlines, even though he would often work twenty-four hours straight, sleeping at the pit, only leaving for dinner at the local bar. I think he'd burn himself out, get behind on deadlines, and then lose business. He also had a lot of overhead costs with diesel fuel, maintenance, and repairs.

When Terry wasn't welding on gravel crushers, he hauled steel coils on a flatbed trailer, usually between Chicago, Illinois; Gary, Indiana; and Detroit. I took a few days off from work before I went to college that fall and joined him for a steel run. Everything about his world was foreign to me; I was totally intrigued. Since I hadn't spent a lot of time with my dad in person, it was normal for me to feel nervous when I was with him, I never knew what would happen. I told him I had to be back at work in four days, so we couldn't dick around. He promised me he'd get me back home on time.

He picked me up at Gram's in his semi-truck, and we headed to somewhere in Detroit to get a load of steel. He quickly and easily maneuvered through traffic with his long flatbed behind us, like we were in Peggy's little Chevette, instead of his huge truck and trailer. I had total confidence in his driving ability; I'd seen him drive just about every type of vehicle there was. It was commonplace for him to curse at anyone that got in his way. He hated incompetent drivers and wasn't shy about flipping someone off, or rolling down his window to scream obscenities at them.

After arriving at the pickup location, Terry tried multiple times to back the trailer into place. On the final attempt, he ran over the curb, broke a big section of it off, and smashed a large bush. I could tell he did it on purpose after several attempts to avoid it.

"Oh shit, Dad. Are we going to get into trouble?" I asked.

"Fuck no. They should have done a better job of putting that road in."

I was a little worry wart, and for some reason felt the need to follow rules, unlike Dad. Whenever I would get stressed out, he would always say the same thing:

"Fuck 'em all but six. Save those for pallbearers."

He didn't mean screw people over. He felt being a people-pleaser was a losing game and that life was too short to worry about other people's judgment. He believed I should be my authentic self and let the chips fall where they may. I admired his ability to truly not give a shit what anyone else thought—trust me, it wasn't bravado.

As he weaved his way around all the official scale checkpoints, I asked Dad if he was worried about getting caught and he said, "Nah, it's not my first rodeo." He knew all the backroads and workaround routes. I considered him a freaky "map savant." When he gave directions, he always knew the exact mile marker. I never second-guessed his directions; they always turned out to be correct. We both loved maps and could spend hours studying them. To pass the time I would quiz him on cities, states and freeway numbers. We drove all night and eventually made it to Gary.

"Welcome to the armpit of America!" Dad announced.

"So this is Indiana, eh," I said, surveying the industrial park.

"Pull out that map of the mill, honey," he said, pointing to the glove box.

I was captivated by the size of the steel mill; it even had street signs. We took several turns at multiple stop signs, it seemed like fifteen minutes before we found the correct off-load bay. Once we arrived we were signaled by a man to pull into the building. It was dark, dingy, and smelled of diesel fuel and grime. Dad pulled out his paperwork and rolled down his window as the guy with the clipboard approached. I couldn't hear over the truck engine and loud noises of the mill. But whatever the worker said, it set Terry off.

"You lazy motherfucker. Cocksucker. Union asshole. You can't process me before you take your fuckin' break? You lazy son-of-a-bitch!" he shouted.

"Daddy, calm down. He's gonna call the cops!" I yelled over the mill racket.

"Just shop talk honey. He's used to it," he said, flashing me his famous smirk and giving me a quick wink.

Unfortunately Dad's little pep talk didn't motivate the man to forgo his break. We sat there for at least forty-five minutes waiting for someone to process his load. When the guy finally handed Terry the bill of lading, he yanked it away, pulled out of the dark bay and yelled, "Fuck you!" My heart was racing as I scouted for a cop, but apparently that was just a normal scene in steel country.

"Honey Babe, are you hungry?" he asked, trying to switch gears.

"I'd love to get some breakfast if we have time," I replied.

"Well, we'll make time, I could use some coffee, too."

He drove us to a nearby truck stop where we could eat and get fuel. Terry always flirted with the waitresses and whipped a few of his one-liners on them to see if they'd bite. If they were witty, he'd give them a wink and a big tip. He used to say, "I tip a lot more now that my baby girl is a waitress. I know it's a hard job."

I held my breath when our food was delivered. There was something about food not being cooked and served properly that really pissed him off. I'm not sure if that's an Irish thing, or a Troy thing, but it definitely ran in the family. If the plate showed up with a hair on it, all bets were off. Dad never held back his thoughts when it came to food. If it didn't taste good and the waitstaff asked how the meal was, they definitely got an honest answer, but not always a nice one.

One Thanksgiving Day when I was still living with Terry, we drove up north to his mother's. Grandma Margot had been working for days to cook a big meal for all of the family. She had five kids, three stepdaughters, and lots of grandkids, so there were gobs of people there. Terry was not a fan of her cooking but would usually bite his tongue out of respect. Before dinner was served, Margot asked me to pass around some appetizers. They were little sandwiches with the crusts cut off that she had made ahead of time and stored in the freezer. Then she'd microwave them, just before serving. They appeared to resemble cucumbers and Velveeta cheese stacked between Wonder bread. Terry was relaxing on the recliner when I reluctantly offered the platter to him and braced myself for a shit-show. Dad took one off the plate and bit into it as he grabbed a napkin. I can still visualize the look on his squished-up face.

"Oh Jesus Christ! That's terrible. Go tell her that fuckin' thing's still frozen in the middle," he muffled as he spit it out into his napkin.

I turned to walk back into the kitchen, accepting that I had become the bologna in their nasty sandwich. I saw Margot with her bright red-dyed hair, rushing around the kitchen wearing her apron over her dress, tea towel draped over her shoulder and brown, ortho-pedic shoes.

"Um, Grandma, my dad said to tell you that it tastes like shit, and it's still frozen in the middle," I reported as I cautiously approached her gourmet workshop.

She grabbed the platter with her famous one-eyebrow-arched-high look and lips pursed tight, accentuating the wrinkles around her mouth.

"Well, fuck him."

We both laughed at the absence of her standard proper persona. It seemed she needed, and maybe even welcomed, the release from the meal prep stress.

"Dolly, you go tell him what I said while I microwave these damn things some more," she ordered.

Dad felt content knowing he'd broken up a rather mundane day with a dish of humble pie. For a moment, I got a taste of what it must've been like growing up with Terry: siblings playing poke-the-bear. He knew his comments would piss her off, but they both acted like it never happened, reestablished decorum, and finished dinner together. That's something else the Irish do. Pass the cookies, look away—there's plenty of time to hold a grudge after you leave the scene.

Sitting at the truck stop diner in Gary, Dad used the table-top payphone installed in our booth. He placed a few calls to some dispatchers and tried to line up a load to haul back to Detroit. When he finished he said, "Looks like we've gotta head across town and pick up some steel. Ya never wanna dead-head back honey, it's a waste of fuel." We took a short, two-hour nap in his semi-truck and then drove to get our load. After we picked up the steel, he pulled into a bar, parked his truck in the back, and left it running. We had to wait around again until the scales closed, so we grabbed some dinner. I tried to imagine being a truck driver. It seemed like a lonely, stressful job to me. I asked if he ever got nervous going into some of the bad areas he had to work in.

"Honey Babe, I've worked in ghettos all my life. I'm used to it. You just have to know how to play the game," he said with a sigh.

On our drive back he explained how the trucking industry has changed over the years. He was an independent driver and felt like he only got the crappy jobs that the big players didn't want to haul. He talked about all the costs of being a trucker: maintaining equipment, fuel, road-use taxes, license plate tags and insurance. He was always amazing with numbers and could figure out his costs by the mile in his head. He was like that with everything, whether he was talking about the price of oil or a bushel of corn. He used to say, "This country would starve if the truckers quit working. People don't have a fuckin' clue."

After returning to my reality as a waitress and future college student, I scrambled to figure out all the hoops I needed to jump through to get ready, and I managed to fill out all the paperwork for my summer orientation class. A friend from high school was also going to FSU, so we agreed to be roommates. I drove the two of us north to Big Rapids, where we stumbled our way through the process. Neither of us had parents hovering over, guiding us through all the decisions. I still couldn't believe I was actually going to be able to move into the dorm, come August. I promised myself I would just focus on one quarter at a time and surely I could figure it out financially. I was beyond excited to move onto my new college life—much to the dismay of my boyfriend's mother.

CHAPTER FOUR

Maggie

Before my first quarter in college, I was notified that I had been awarded a small grant. I couldn't get any other financial assistance because that required both my parents to provide their taxes and other information. It would have been easier to achieve world peace, so I didn't even try. I had no idea how to tackle the process of getting declared "legally independent," and I figured it would cost too much. Despite all that, I managed to save up enough money to pay the tuition, room, and board.

Late August, Dad offered to deliver my furniture with his pickup truck to college for me. Even though freshmen weren't allowed to have vehicles, I had to take mine because I needed to travel back home to work. I felt lucky that I could park the Thunderbird at my boyfriend's off-campus apartment complex, for a small fee.

We decided to meet at Peggy's place the morning I left for Ferris. Terry and Peggy had remained cordial, and she and I had stayed in touch. She lived in a trailer park that was on the route to the highway, so I wanted to stop and say goodbye to her. My roommate and I met my father there; immediately my gut delivered a message that the day would not turn out to be about me.

Peggy was known for her cute little belly laugh and great sense of humor. She was a taller, big-busted, bleach-blond with long, permed hair and big blue eyes. She always wore black eyeliner that emphasized the twinkle in her eyes when she smiled. Even though sometimes her life was a hot mess, I looked up to her because she was loving, fun, and didn't judge me. Peggy liked it when Dad would light her cigarette and entertain her with his wit. Her real name was Margaret, but Terry called her Maggie—when he was trying to get something he wanted. I concluded that they still had a lot of physical chemistry when I heard Dad call her Maggie and she responded with her nervous, staccato giggle. I believed she had moved on with her life; I couldn't imagine her making a U-turn and driving back to the chaos and toxicity of their past. It was apparent to me by all the flirting, Terry was in denial about the limits of his charm.

After a short visit, my friend and I were getting antsy. We wanted to get on with our long three-hour drive to Big Rapids, and it was already late morning. Dad told us to go up to the gas station near the freeway on ramp, fill up my tank, and wait for him to join us; he'd be there in a few minutes. I said goodbye to Peggy and headed up the street. I put some gas in my car, parked facing the street, and watched the traffic drive by. My roommate and I passed the time by chatting about how nervous we were to meet our suitemates and other small talk. It seemed like it was taking him forever, and I started to wonder if he had passed us and hopped on the freeway without us noticing. We had been sitting there watching for him for well over an hour and a half. I didn't want to drive back to Peggy's for I feared he would take a different route, and we'd miss each other. I decided to leave because I thought he couldn't possibly still be at Peggy's. I stopped several times along the way to page him with the payphone numbers at each stop. I called Peggy, too, but she didn't answer. He never called me back, so I kept driving. We arrived at the dorm, and I instantly knew I was in big trouble when I didn't see his truck. I tried to process how he could keep us waiting at the gas station for almost two hours. We unloaded the items we had managed to jam into my car and waited for him. He had all the larger things—our wooden loft, my loveseat, and kitchen table and chairs.

As dusk was settling in, I looked out our dorm room window and saw him pull into the parking lot. I'd been paging him over and over all day, and he never called me back. We ran down to the parking lot to greet him. He wouldn't look at me. He just got out of his truck and started unstrapping the load.

"Dad, what the hell happened?"

"Where the fuck were you? I told you to wait for me. I didn't even know which fuckin' dorm you lived in. I'm lucky I spotted your car. What the hell were you thinking leaving without me?" he snapped.

"Dad, I was afraid you passed us, and I somehow missed you."

"That's bullshit Terrina," he barked as he cut me off.

He never called me "Terrina" unless he was extremely unhappy with me.

"Well, where the hell have you been?"

His breath smelled like beer and cigarettes, so I knew exactly where he'd been; I expected his silence. The scenario that I imagined was that he and Peggy had a good romp. She let him know she had a good time but wasn't interested in taking him back. I truly believe he considered Maggie "the love of his life." That was not the ending he had hoped for and being pissed at me was a great excuse to go to the bar and avoid dealing with his broken heart.

Once he calmed down, we started moving my furniture into the dorm. Everyone else had been there all day with their parents setting up their rooms and hanging out. My suitemates had gone to high school together, too. They seemed really cool, especially Jill. I felt a kinship with her immediately. Her mom and dad were there getting her settled and putting together the loft she inherited from her older brother, Brian. It was so large it took up most of their room, and there was no way they could have done it alone. Her father Fred, a big, handsome guy, full of energy, seemed like he wanted to get his duties wrapped up. Her mom was tall, pretty, and seemed laid back. She was cracking jokes and holding a beer and cigarette when I walked in with Terry. I looked over at him and watched his face light up when he saw Jill's mom, Suzanne. He introduced himself to both of her parents and made some polite conversation, alluding to himself as Father of the Year. Then we walked into my room, where the adjoining bathroom was approximately six feet away; both bathroom doors wide open.

"Now she's the kind of lady I could have a good time with," he belted out.

He sounded like he'd found "his people" and wanted to get the party started. Just another sign the net result with Maggie hadn't satisfied him.

"She's married. You just met Jill's dad. What the hell is wrong with you?"

"Well that's not a problem for me," he said with a smug look.

Mortified, I quickly shut the doors and flashed him a look of disgust. We were racing against the clock to get everything piled inside before it was pitch dark outside. When we were all done, our room looked like a bomb had gone off.

"Well girls, I've gotta get going. I hope you have a great time at college. Don't forget to say, 'fuck it' once in a while, and have a little fun," he said, after surveying the pile of rubble.

As I settled into college life, I focused really hard on balancing work and school. But work had to be the priority because without it there would be no school. It was hard to find a job in the small town of Big Rapids, with so many students looking for work. Thankfully, my fees were partly reduced by a campus work-study job that I did during the week. When I drove home on weekends to work, I'd give other students rides home for a small fee to help cover the gas.

I didn't have enough money to buy the books that the teachers listed on their syllabuses. I noticed that most of them were authored by my professors. I thought forcing kids to buy their books, in addition to the course book, was shameless self-promotion, and they were ridiculously expensive. I had never spent a hundred dollars on a single book in my life. I made the decision not to buy any. I also discovered that most of my instructors were lazy or burned out and would simply repeat everything they wrote in their books. So I tried not to miss any classes and took good notes. Once again, they were pitchin' and I was catchin'.

I didn't get a call from Terry after he left the dorm that day, until he called to wish me happy birthday on October 19. I didn't put too much energy into worrying about it because I knew he'd surface eventually. I was getting ready to leave Gram's house, after working all weekend at the restaurant. She was headed to bingo, and I had students waiting on me to give them a ride. Just as we were walking out the door, I heard her yellow rotary phone ring.

"Hello," I said, dropping my bags and grabbing the receiver.

"Happy Birthday Honey Babe, it's Daddy."

He asked me how Gram was, what I was doing for my birthday, and a lot of other questions that kept the conversation off him. He told me he was planning on driving by Big Rapids in a few weeks because of a job and wanted to visit. I asked him if he would make time to attend a few classes with me, and I was surprised when he agreed to do it.

"Well honey, I know you're busy so I'll let you go," signaling the call was over.

It pissed me off when he said that because I was never too busy to talk to him. But his mother dished out the same line. Perhaps it's an Irish thing.

A few weeks later, he met me at the dorm early in the morning, and we walked to my first class. Terry had just turned thirty-eight and had never attended college, so I think he was curious if he'd missed out on anything. He was kind of a morning person, at least when he wasn't too hungover. I was definitely not a "Chatty Cathy" in the morning. He used to wait to call me well after ten and start by saying with a giggle, "Good morning honey. Have you had your Diet Mountain Dew, yet?" My first class was some sort of sociology course about different religions. Thinking back on this, I probably couldn't have picked a worse class to take him to. He used to say, "When you're dead, you're dead. That's it. It's over. All that shit they used to hammer into me at Catholic school was just a bunch of bullshit."

This particular classroom was on the smaller side, with only about thirty students in it. As we walked into the room, the teacher was standing in front of the wooden podium; students were finding their seats. The professor was a middle-aged, frumpy-looking guy, with shoulder-length hair and a big bald spot on top. He had an unkempt beard and some nasty, crooked, yellow teeth. I didn't care for his teaching style because he just rambled about things that didn't have anything to do with the curriculum. While I turned in my homework assignment, Dad carried his Styrofoam cup of coffee to the back of the room to the last seat in one of the middle rows. I sat in the small desk directly in front of him.

"Boy, he's a real lady killer," he said, baiting my insecurities.

"*Shhhhhh.* Dad," I said, snapping my head around, flashing him a pissed-off look.

He gave me his trademark mischievous smirk and then slurped his coffee. As time dragged on, I could feel Terry fidgeting behind me as he bumped the back of my chair. I heard the *snap-snap* sound of a lighter and an inhale-exhale noise, as I was engulfed in smoke. I turned around to find him leaned back in his seat, one leg crossed over the other, puffing on his unfiltered Pall Malls.

"Dad. You're not supposed to smoke in here. This whole building is a nonsmoking area. You need to put that out." I quickly whispered blushing with embarrassment.

"Oh, fuck 'em. He can ask me to leave," he said, simultaneously blowing smoke out of his nose.

"Please Dad. Put it out before I get in trouble," I pleaded.

After flashing me a look of disappointment for my rule-following demand, he finally threw his cigarette into his coffee cup. By the time the bell rang, I had never been so happy to get out of class. As I pushed through the crowded hallway racing toward the exit, Terry shouted over the student noise, "How can you stand listening to that asshole? I know I only have a tenth grade education, but I know bullshit when I hear it!" I made the decision that fifty-five minutes was all the higher education Dad needed. I skipped the rest of the school day, and we headed to a restaurant for some breakfast.

After our meal, I took Terry back to my dorm and reintroduced him to my suitemate, Jill. We had become close friends and had shared a lot of laughs, tormenting our dorm supervisors and professors. We got Dad all caught up, and he was amused with the stories of us prank-calling our professor and our other bad but benign behavior. Our teacher had it comin' after making us study Dante's *Inferno*.

After Terry took a nap on my couch, he suggested that I call my friends and arrange to meet up at a bar. I knew instantly that this was probably going to be one of those nights I'd either regret, never forget, or both. My boyfriend, Jill and I, and about six other kids all took Dad to the local hangout called The Alibi. I was only eighteen, so I could enter the bar, but I couldn't legally drink alcohol. But this was back when things were much more relaxed when it came to checking IDs. Besides, Terry walked in like he owned the joint; the bouncer just waved us through. Dad ordered several pitchers of beer, and we all enjoyed a few rounds. The bar was filling up with students when Jill noticed one of the guys who walked past the bouncer was a jerk named Brian. He had a major crush on her, but she wasn't interested. She was taller and pretty and he was short with stubby little hands and a big mouth. I guess because he felt rejected, he used to yell, "Jill's a bitch!" every time he'd see her on campus. Whenever I heard him verbally attack her, it brought out my old, fighting spirit.

I had bumped into him a few days earlier on my way home from class. He was walking with three other guys from the Tau Kappa Epsilon fraternity. Brian wasn't a member yet; he was still pledging. They were informally called "Tekes," and known for being trouble-makers. Their parties frequently got out of hand, resulting in the cops shutting them down. I had planned on ignoring him, but as we were about to pass each other on the sidewalk, he said, "Your friend's a bitch."

"Get over it. She doesn't like dickheads." I quickly snapped at his pitifully small frame.

"Are you going to let that girl talk to you like that?" one of the frat leaders barked.

"Fuck yeah he is, he's a pussy," I said, as I stopped to face him.

Brian knew I had a large, buffed boyfriend; messing with me was probably not going to end well for him. He just stood there, frozen, stuttering something unintelligible.

"Eat that piece of gum off the sidewalk, right now!" screamed the head thug as he pointed toward the ground.

Looking defeated, Brian hesitated for a moment, but then he pulled up the wad of old gum and started chewing it. As I walked away from the disgusting scene, I shouted, "Leave Jill alone, douchebag!"

That night at the bar, Brian had noticed Jill at our table and started heckling her from across the room. Dad wanted to know who he was, so we shared the stories about our previous confrontations. Terry took a big swig of his beer and set it down on the table. He quickly stood up, briskly walked over to Brian, and got right in his face. He repeatedly jabbed his large index finger into Brian's chest, shoving him up against the wall.

"Listen, you little cocksucker. If I ever hear of you fuckin' with my Jill again, I'll knock your dick in the dirt. Got it, motherfucker?" Terry schooled him.

Brian must have taken good notes because he quickly exited the bar. As Dad rejoined our table, he winked at Jill and said, "Don't worry honey, he'll never screw with you again." I was not shocked, but my friends looked flabbergasted and thought it was hilarious. I laughed too, because I certainly didn't have any sympathy for Brian; I pegged him as a slow learner the second I met him. The only thing that was surprising was that Dad's impromptu "master class," didn't end with a broken pool stick and a ride with a cop.

The next day Terry took my friends and me to breakfast before we parted ways. He'd only been there about twenty-four hours, but that was long enough to leave his mark. He hugged all my friends, and kissed me goodbye before he climbed into his semi-truck. As he pulled out of the parking lot, with his cigarette pursed in the corner of his lips, he smugly said, "I love ya, honey. You girls have fun, and don't let any pricks give ya a hard time."

The rest of my freshmen year went by quickly. I managed to complete a full load of courses and passed them all with at least a C or better. Some of the girls in our dorm didn't cut it and dropped out after the second quarter. They missed home, their parents, and couldn't handle the stress of getting good grades. I thought they were lazy and whiners because my only stress was financial. Just like high school, I didn't have a home with parents hounding me with rules or major expectations. I considered my report card my private business.

I had spoken with Dad sporadically throughout the school year, usually about once a month. But unfortunately he was out of town working when I packed up my dorm room at the end of the year. Luckily my boyfriend had an old van and helped me move my stuff back to Gram's.

My Thunderbird was still running well, but I couldn't afford to renew the registration. I did manage to keep it insured, but I was running low on cash. I couldn't work nearly as much as I needed to, being away at school. Dad told me not to worry about the license plate tags. He explained to me that if I got caught, there's a ticket and a small fine. He said, "Sometimes I don't buy tags because I figure if the fine is less than the cost of tags, I'll take my chances." I was always impressed with how well he understood the law; he understood how far he could push it.

The very day I moved home from college I had to work the dinner shift at the restaurant, so I dumped my stuff and hustled to work. Gram came home from bingo a few minutes after I returned that night and said, "This place is a pigsty." I knew her complaining was really her way of letting me know she was glad I was back.

I spent the next few months working as much as possible and trying to gather up some more furniture. In the fall, I was moving into a four-bedroom farmhouse with three other girls that I had met at the dorm, and two guys I knew from high school. The six of us had to share one small bathroom, but it was okay with me because it meant my rent would only be $80 a month. Only the girls signed the lease, but we agreed to let the guys share our glassed-in front porch as their bedroom. Moving off-campus meant I would need a bed and some other furniture, so I started collecting what I could from garage sales.

Occasionally, Terry would stay at his rented room out in the country, when he wasn't hauling steel. In July, he stopped into the restaurant and asked me for a ride out there. I agreed to meet him a few doors down at the pub, after I finished work. I hadn't seen him since I'd eighty-sixed him from college, back in November, so I welcomed the chance to catch up.

I finished my shift and found Terry socializing with the bartender and the other people sitting at the bar. He introduced me to his new friends and pulled out a stool. "Have a seat Honey Babe, while I finish my beer."

Everybody knows you can't leave a beer half-empty, so I obliged.

Thirty minutes later and a few more beers I was getting annoyed. "Dad, let's go I'm tired."

He reluctantly flipped a couple twenty dollar bills on the counter, and we headed for the back door.

"I need to stop and get some gas; then we can go," I said, grabbing the car door handle.

"Oh, shit no. We ain't got time for that. I promised my friends I'd be home for dinner hours ago. Let's just go, we'll be fine," he insisted.

Dad was in a great mood, laughing and telling me funny stories, so I drove on. As I passed Gram's place I noted the trailer was dark, so she was probably still at bingo. Shortly thereafter, I turned right on a sharp curved road, which headed into a small town. There wasn't much there except an old general store with a couple of gas pumps out front. I'd been in there a few times with my friends looking to pass off fake IDs in hopes of scoring alcohol.

"I'm gonna stop and put some gas in," I said, as we approached the pumps.

"Oh no honey, we'll make it. Just keep going," he insisted.

"Dad, if we run out of gas, I'm gonna kill you."

He laughed and continued telling me another story about other times he'd pushed vehicles to their limits. He was relaxed and enjoying himself, but I kept looking at the gas level drop lower and lower, as we weaved our way around the curvy two-lane road. There was nothing but farmland and an occasional house; I knew there weren't any gas stations for miles. We got about two minutes down the road and my car started to slow down. No matter how hard I pushed on the gas, it kept slowing down. Terry fidgeted in his seat and leaned over to check out the gas dial.

"Dad. I can't make it go!" I yelled in a panic.

"Just pump it honey. Faster. Pump the gas pedal fast. Now slam it to the floor and hold it down," he ordered while he held back his laughter.

I followed his instructions as quickly as I could. And then the car came to a stop. I had nowhere to pull over because there was a long ditch that ran along the roadside, with weeds three feet tall and no shoulder. I looked over at him and he was laughing with an expression like he knew he was in big trouble.

"What the fuck are we going to do now, smart ass?" I asked.

"Just stay here, I'll be right back," he said, jumping out of the car.

"You better hurry up. I'm in the middle of the road. I'm gonna get killed!" I shouted as I watched him in my rearview mirror hustle up the road.

"Yes, Dear!" he quipped.

I sat in my car feeling like a sitting duck, worried that some creep might take advantage of the desolate location. Luckily it was a slow night because not one car passed. About twenty minutes later I saw Terry in my side mirror, jumping out of a pick-up truck with a can of gasoline. He poured it into my tank and jumped into the passenger seat.

"Well, now I have a good excuse for being late. I can tell 'em my daughter let her car run out of gas," he announced, snickering at the convenient opportunity.

"Yeah, right. What did you do with the gas can?" I asked unimpressed.

"Oh, I just left it on the side of the road for the next dumbfuck that won't let his daughter stop for gas," he answered with a cringing grin.

That was as close to an apology that I was ever going to get. In that moment, I fully understood that this was a man that just floated from minute to minute, and somehow always figured it out.

CHAPTER FIVE

Red Satin Sheets

S ummer flew by fast and when it was time to go back to college, Dad volunteered to not only transport all my furniture, but he also insisted on going to pick up all my roommates' stuff, too. I told him that wasn't necessary, but he swore it was no big deal since his trailer would have plenty of room. He only needed to help my three female roommates because the guys were moving in later.

His plan was to use his Diamond Reo semi-truck and one of his long trailers that had red wooden side panels that matched his truck. It was open on the top, but he had a large, black tarp he could strap down to provide cover. I agreed to his plan and was grateful for his help, but it was not without trepidation.

He arrived at Gram's at about seven o'clock that morning; we loaded everything I'd collected over the summer. He explained that he would make the two stops in Plymouth next and then head down to his last stop in Detroit before hauling the load up to Big Rapids. He made all the arrangements—this was his show. He figured he'd deliver the load about five o'clock that afternoon. I kissed him goodbye, finished loading the Thunderbird, hugged Gram and drove north.

I was the first to arrive at the old farmhouse, but one by one, my other roommates started pulling in. They told me what happened when the big red semi rolled into their neighborhoods. Sounded to me like everything was loaded okay and all went well, at least from their perspectives. So we cracked open some beer and waited for Terry to show up. I knew driving a big rig took longer than a car, but I figured he wasn't too far behind their arrivals. I nervously looked out the window for him and checked the clock. I started getting anxious as each hour ticked away. When eight o'clock came and went, I was in a full-blown panic, envisioning explaining to my new roommates that their shit had been impounded after my dad was arrested. I tried paging him repeatedly, but he never called. It started getting dark, and my roommates were phoning their parents. There were suggestions about calling the hospitals, but I knew it was way too soon for that. I didn't want to tell them that I feared he'd just been "sidetracked."

Around ten o'clock, I heard the sound of Dad's chrome smokestack rumbling. I ran out the side door to greet him, but I could barely see him. The truck's motor was really loud, and I was sure all the neighbors on our city block were viewing the scene. I stood at the side of the driver's door looking up at the truck cab; I noticed the window was down. "Hi Dad!" I yelled over the motor humming.

He didn't answer as he climbed down to the ground. He pulled his pants higher and put his fists on his hips. I noted the usual smell of diesel fuel, cigarettes, and beer.

"Don't even give me any shit about being late. Not one of your fuckin' roommates' parents offered me any gas money, and they sat on their lazy, goddamn asses while I loaded their kid's shit," he barked at me.

"Why didn't you call me? Why are you so late?" I asked, ignoring his bark.

"Because I've had a long fuckin' day and I stopped at a bar for dinner. I think I earned that," he snarled.

While he unwrapped the trailer I asked my roommates to turn their car lights on and start laying on the charm. I handed him a longneck Molson and he disparagingly said, "I see you girls haven't learned yet that the highest alcohol content is in Busch beer," breaking the tension.

My things were unloaded last, since I had been his first stop. Unfortunately, Terry had to carry most of the heavy stuff. My roommate from Detroit had a large armoire her father had apparently made from lead. As we all tried to help Dad carry it up the stairs somebody slipped, and Terry got pinned on the landing. He yelled short or breath: "You girls are bustin' my fuckin' balls tonight!"

By the time we got everything off the trailer and into the house, it was about midnight. My bedroom was one of the three bedrooms upstairs. The fourth bedroom was downstairs off the living room. My room was the largest, but it didn't have a formal closet. There was a small alcove that I'd planned to jerry-rig with a cheap hanging system. I couldn't put any of my clothes away without installing the white wire unit, but Dad was exhausted, and he didn't like reading directions. He took one look at it and said, "I'm really not in the mood to do this shit right now. I'm too tired to deal with a box full of parts. I'm going to sit down." I didn't want to seem ungrateful, so I just let it be. He went downstairs to rest on the couch and grab another beer.

About ten minutes later I heard wood being moved around below me. I went to see if anyone needed help, but as I stood in the living room, I overheard Dad and one of my roommates exchanging dirty jokes and laughing in her bedroom. I stepped into her room; they were setting up her waterbed. He was undoubtedly enjoying all the flirting from my trashy roommate. She just wanted her big bed put together so she could invite her boyfriend over as soon as possible. Terry looked at the angry expression on my face and knew immediately that I was about to rain on his parade. I restrained myself from wrapping her red, tacky, satin sheets around both their necks, and I turned and walked away. I went into the kitchen, and he quickly followed.

"What the fuck did I do this time?" he barked while holding his beer.

"You don't have the energy to help me, but you can put her fucking waterbed together?" I scolded.

I didn't wait for his response, I just stomped upstairs. A few minutes later I heard his truck engine start up. I looked out of my window, the streetlights slightly illuminating his trailer; he was rolling up his tarp. I stormed downstairs, through the kitchen, and out the side door, slamming it behind me.

"Go ahead and leave me, just like you always do. You can't come talk to me? You gotta run away? Who gives a fuck about me? I never ask anything from you, and the one time I ask for your help, you'd rather help some other girl. Give me a fucking break, Dad!" I screamed with tears pouring down my face, staring up at him.

"You ungrateful little bitch. I busted my balls today for you and your friends. At four miles to the gallon, this wasn't a cheap fuckin' trip," he fired back at me.

"I didn't ask you to be the big hero and pick up all their shit for free. That was your big idea," I barked.

"I oughta come down there and smack your ass," he growled through his locked jaw.

Without a second's hesitation, I screamed hysterically, "Go ahead big man! Give it your best shot. You think you scare me? You think you can hit me any harder than I've been hit before? Do it!"

He turned, walked to the other side of the trailer, jumped off, and climbed into the cab of his truck. I knew he would never hit me, so I went for his jugular. My heart was pounding as I wiped the snot and tears from my face. I turned and walked back into the house, slamming the door behind me. I went up to my bedroom and cried myself to sleep.

When I woke up in the morning, I looked out the window and saw the semi-truck was still parked outside with the engine running.

Somebody made Dad a cup of coffee; he looked like he was just waking up when I passed through the living room. I guess he'd slept on my couch all night. I didn't know what to say, so I just walked by him, and grabbed a Diet Mountain Dew out of the refrigerator. He came into the kitchen and asked if he could use the phone. I just pointed and nodded. He must have called a dispatcher because I heard him mention a load of steel. He hung up, lit a cigarette, slipped his boots on, and walked out the door, without saying a word. I watched him through the window get into his truck and pull away.

I knew that I could've handled the situation better. I was disappointed in myself for letting my emotions get carried away. I was so stressed out when he was five hours late and didn't even bother to call, that it didn't take much to push me over the edge. I felt worried, embarrassed, and disrespected. But it wasn't just that day that I was upset about. It was all the other times that he didn't call. All the other times he didn't show up. All the other times he didn't help me. All the other times he made me feel unimportant. And all of the times other people were more important to him, and I'd bit my tongue.

I felt terrible that I hurt his feelings, and I knew I probably wouldn't hear from him for a long time. But I didn't regret what I said. I felt it was necessary to remind him that I would stand up for myself. If I'm totally honest, my heart hardened just a little bit more that day. I was a "Daddy's girl," but I was also human, and I had my limits.

Just like my freshmen year, school was getting off to a bumpy start, but I jumped right back into my routine of going to class and working at night. I continued to drive back home to work at the restaurant, but business was slowing down, and I wasn't getting as many shifts as I used to. There was a rumor going around that the owner was trying to sell the place, so I figured my days were numbered. I started looking for another job at school, but most of the waitress jobs were at bars. I interviewed for several opportunities, but I was always told I didn't have "the look" for serving cocktails.

I knew what that meant, but I was unwilling to dress like a stripper to get tips. I worried about saving enough money for the rest of the year. I used some of my tuition money for living expenses, which put me in a tight spot.

I didn't hear from Dad on my birthday that year. I was still on his shit-list. He didn't have a phone number where I could call him, so I sent his birthday card to his post office box. A month later, probably after he received his card, he finally called me. He said he had one more welding job he needed to finish by the end of the year, and then he was just going to focus on hauling steel. He used the excuse that he was at a busy truck stop to cut the call short.

Christmas break Terry reached me at Gram's. He asked if I could do him a favor. I was hoping he didn't need another lift to jail. He explained that he was working up north, somewhere near Traverse City, at a gravel pit and needed a special part to repair his welding outfit. Without it he couldn't finish his work; he said he needed it right away. I would need to drive about thirty minutes away, fetch a large part, and then drive it up north near my school. I knew it was important, so I switched shifts at the restaurant and agreed to do it. He gave me very specific directions; he said it wouldn't take more than four hours to reach him and that he would be waiting in his Diamond Reo at a certain exit, off Interstate 131.

"Dad, what if something happens and I need to get ahold of you?"

"Oh, nothing will happen, you'll be fine. I guess if you get into trouble, just have the cops come find me," he answered, blowing off my concern.

I rushed to grab my purse, keys, directions and hustled out the door. It was already late in the afternoon, and I wanted to get there before dark. I found the commercial business building where my contact person, Mr. Kennedy, loaded the heavy part into my trunk. Traffic was light, and luckily it wasn't snowing or sleeting, but we were having a pretty bad cold spell. The kind of cold where it felt like your lungs would freeze when you took a deep breath. I glanced at the thermometer on a bank marquee; it read in the negative territory. I was grateful for the heater blasting my feet as I pushed the speed limits.

The ride between Grand Rapids and Big Rapids was fairly desolate and was a divided highway with two lanes going north, two going south and a wide median in between. About thirty minutes after leaving Grand Rapids, I noticed my headlights started to dim on and off. I looked down at the speedometer and saw that I was losing power. I had plenty of gas so that wasn't the problem. I tried desperately to pump the gas, hold it to the floor, and anything I could think of to keep it moving. But my car was dying, and I was forced to pull over onto the shoulder. I tried to restart it, over and over, but I just heard a clicking noise; the engine refused to turn over. I figured the problem was the alternator, just like my Catalina.

I didn't know if I should stay in my car and hope that a cop would drive by, or risk catching a ride with some pervert like Ted Bundy, who might murder me. After weighing my awesome choices, I decided that it was too cold to get out of the car. I hadn't packed a winter coat or gloves, just a thick Ferris State sweatshirt over a turtleneck. I was freezing after the first fifteen minutes. I remembered Dad's Christmas present was in the back seat. I'd bought him a quilted flannel shirt and a Ferris State T-shirt that had a picture of a bulldog and poodle fornicating, with the caption, "Ferris State Bull Dogs Do It Doggie-style." I was sure he would wear it with pride. I ripped the wrapping paper open, sat with my legs crossed under me, and draped the shirts over my lower half and feet. My toes were freezing so I used the pop-out lighter to warm them, but eventually it stopped working, too. Periodically, a car would drive by, but nobody stopped. I sat in total darkness, frozen, wondering if Terry was pissed that I was late. I kept looking at my watch and praying I wouldn't have to stay there all night. I cursed myself for being so stupid to do this alone.

Around eight o'clock, I saw a car slowing down on the south-bound side. Then a shining spotlight blinded me from across the four lanes. As it sped up and continued south, I noticed reflective letters that spelled "K-9 Unit." A couple minutes later some police lights pulled up behind me. The officer walked up to the driver's side; I cracked open the window. He shined his big flashlight in my car as he approached. He asked if I needed help. I explained that my car had died.

"Well, why didn't you leave the hood popped open so people would know you were broken down and offer you a ride?" he asked, pegging me for a bimbo.

"Look sir, I don't need to deal with some nutjob. Can you please give me a ride?"

"Sure, just get out of the car on the shoulder side," he replied with a chuckle.

Shivering and stiff, I rushed to grab my things and get out of the car. The cop opened his back door and I happily jumped in. Right when I sat down I heard a loud bang against the metal partition behind the seat and an angry, growling bark. I let out a girly scream. I had never been in a police car before, and even though I was innocent, it made me nervous and uncomfortable. I told the officer of my father's grand plan and he said, "Well, I can drop you off at the gas station at the next exit, you can call a tow truck." I asked if he could go find Terry, but I could tell he thought my story sounded sketchy. He reluctantly agreed to call another officer in that area.

I felt uneasy being at the mini-mart all alone with random strangers. My first concern was about how Dad might respond to seeing a police car show up. And then I quickly worried that he might get arrested. He probably had beer on his breath, and it was possible that he was totally drunk. Another scenario that crossed my mind was that he might not even be there. Or, the cop might have blown me off and not even bothered to find him. I told myself to stay calm and focus on the right solution. Was Dad going to come get me? What do I do about my car? What kind of a trail could I leave if I ended up being murdered by some psychopath passing through the gas station?

I decided to page Dad from the payphone, and leave him the number to the mini-mart. Then I called Gram and left her a message on her answering machine, so she knew exactly where I was. I tried to reach my boyfriend, but he was still at work and didn't answer. About an hour later I finally saw the big red trailer-less rig pull into the parking lot.

I ran to my dad and jumped into his arms. He hugged and kissed me—I'd never been happier to see him.

"Well, Honey Babe, I guess you've had quite the adventure, eh?"

"I'm sorry Dad. I know you needed that part."

"Well, you know what they say honey, if it's got tits or tires, it's gonna give you trouble," he said with a grin.

"What did you think when you saw the cop pull up?" I asked with anticipation.

"Well, I was getting worried, but I just figured you got a late start. I lost my buzz pretty quick when I saw that cop car. I was afraid he was going to tell me you had been in an accident. I'm sure glad you're okay honey."

Terry had my car towed to Big Rapids and then he dropped me off at my rental house about midnight. He said he needed to get back to his jobsite to make sure everything was okay. I was scared to stay alone in that big farmhouse, especially when the town was empty of all the college kids away on Christmas break, but I had to suck it up.

Unfortunately, I found out the next day that it would take a few days for my car to get fixed, so I called my boyfriend and asked for a ride. It was one big, terrifying cluster. But I learned to push through my fear, stay calm, and keep focused. I didn't know then how much I would need these skills later.

CHAPTER SIX

Spring Break Down

A fter Christmas break was over, I went back to my usual school grind. Ferris was on the quarter system, so midterm and final exams came up fast. In January, Dad called and said he was back to hauling steel full time, somewhere in Illinois. In the course of the conversation, he asked me about my plans for spring break. I explained that I couldn't work at the restaurant anymore and that the rumors were true: it sold to new owners, and they didn't need any extra help. I lamented that I'd be looking for new work, but I'd rather go see Glee, who'd been attending college in California.

"That's a great idea, why don't you go? You deserve a break."

"I can't, Dad, I barely have enough money to pay my tuition, and it's due right after break is over in February."

"Well, hell, I'll pay your tuition. I haven't paid anything toward your schooling, and you girls deserve to have some fun."

I wasn't sure how to respond. On one hand, I wanted to jump up and down and call Glee immediately. But on the other hand, something in my gut felt like this was not a good idea.

"That's very sweet of you, Daddy, but I know how hard you work, and I don't want you to have to do that. I'll see her this summer when she comes home to visit."

"No, no, no. Just get your ticket and cover your spending money, I'll take care of the tuition," he said, sounding annoyed.

"Dad, really that's too much. But thank you so much."

"I'm gonna pay your fuckin' tuition! How much is it?"

"I already have my rent money, so I just need about $400 for the school fees."

"No problem. When you get back from California, I'll have a check waiting for you."

Despite my hesitancies, I did buy a plane ticket to northern California. Chicago was as far west as I'd ever been, so I was excited to check out Glee's world. I allowed myself to cut loose, soak it all in, and had the time of my life.

When I returned to reality, I immediately started fretting over my looming tuition payment. I'd spent virtually all my money on vacation, except for my rent funds and a few more dollars. I think I had about $120 to my name.

Before I departed Gram's for school, I tried to reach Dad several times, but he never answered my attempts to page him. I arrived at my rental a few days before classes started and got settled in. I continued to try to reach Dad, but to no avail. I was nervous because I knew I didn't have anyone else to borrow money from. Gram didn't offer it; I knew she didn't have much anyway. It seemed everyone in our family borrowed money from her; I refused.

The days passed, and so did the tuition due dates. Even the late fee deadline. It was over. I was no longer enrolled at Ferris State University. And because I was technically considered a dropout, I lost my campus job. I couldn't stop the freight train of reality squashing me to the tracks, and I couldn't wrap my head around the word "dropout."

My boyfriend couldn't relate to my situation; his parents paid for all of his school expenses and gave him plenty of spending money. My roommates only cared about the portion of rent that I could no longer pay over the next quarter. I knew I couldn't get a job in Big Rapids, so the only option left was to pack up my clothes, leave the furniture for later, and drive back to Gram's. It was the longest, most miserable drive of my life.

About a week later Terry finally surfaced. I was so pissed at him, I didn't even want to hear his voice, but I wanted some closure, so I took the call.

"Hi honey, it's Daddy. I've had a pretty shitty week, but I've got your tuition money."

"It's too late, Dad." I snapped holding back tears.

"What do you mean it's too late? Why can't you back pay it?"

"No, Dad. I can't. It doesn't work like that. I'm not a student anymore. I lost my campus job, and I can't work at the restaurant anymore either. I'm fucked!"

"Oh, Jesus Christ. I didn't know," he said, sounding contrite.

"And where the fuck have you been for the last ten days? I've been trying to get ahold of your ass!"

Crickets. Nothing but dead air for about ten seconds. And then finally he fessed up.

"Well, let me tell you how fucked *I* am. I was coming out of Illinois in a snowstorm, hauling a trailer full of steel coils when the tires grabbed the side of the road and rolled my whole truck and trailer over—several times. I landed in the ditch upside down."

"Oh my God. Are you okay?" I said with a gasp.

"Well, it scared the shit out of me. I had to kick the windshield out to get outta there. It was snowin' like a bitch and my truck was totaled."

"I'm sorry about your Diamond Reo, Dad. I know you loved that truck, but I'm glad you're alive."

"It is, what it is. I'll figure it out and you will, too."

I found some old pictures of the red truck, with me standing on the step of the driver's side door back in 1987. I texted my Uncle Joe and asked him if he remembered what ultimately happened to the old Diamond Reo.

"He sold it for parts up here in Alpena, after the accident," he texted.

"The wreck in the snowstorm, right?" I asked.

"Yeah, he was coming out of Chicago hauling steel coils. He ended up in Cook County Jail, and it wasn't a social visit."

At the accident scene, he was arrested for another DUI. Thirty-two years later, as Paul Harvey would say: "Now you know, the rest of the story."

I was nineteen with no job and no plan. But I didn't have time to have a pity party, I needed money. Within a week, I had landed a job as a hostess at a popular Greek restaurant in town. It paid an hourly wage, but the waitstaff shared some of their tips. I worked as many shifts as I could and started to dig my way out of my financial crisis. After I dropped out of Ferris, my relationship with my boyfriend was strained. I began some honest soul searching and decided I needed a change of scenery.

Glee was getting married in August in California, and I was the maid of honor. I figured since I had to buy a ticket to attend the wedding, I would capitalize on the opportunity and find a fresh start. I was sick of the weather in Michigan, bored with my job, and the constraints of small-town life were stifling. I started telling people that I was leaving Michigan, even though I didn't have all the details worked out. When I told my boyfriend of my dreams, it didn't go well. He wanted me to stay there and wait around for him to graduate from college.

I decided my future wouldn't include repeating ancestral cycles, being uneducated, struggling, reliant on a man. That was definitely not my kind of gig, but that would have been the safe thing to do. Every fiber of my being was shouting, "Get the hell outta there."

CHAPTER SEVEN

California

E ven though my boyfriend and I had broken up, we remained friendly. He was kind enough to help move my furniture back from school. Gram and I organized a garage sale so we could get rid of all the clutter I dragged home. With the small proceeds from the sale, I managed to buy my bridesmaid dress for Glee's wedding. I told Dad that I wanted to sell the T-bird to fund my trip. He didn't want me to go to California and would have been happier if I was within driving distance from him. But my name was on the car title, so I was pitchin'.

I put my car up for sale for the price Terry said it was worth, but as summer dragged on, it wasn't selling. I told Dad I needed to lower the price, and that's when he fessed up that he had a new girlfriend named Michelle. They were living together in Indiana in a trailer park. She worked a paper route and needed a better vehicle, so he wanted to buy my car. He promised by the time I was ready to leave for California, he'd pay me. I felt relieved that I could stop showing the car to strangers by myself.

I managed to save enough to buy a one-way ticket for my trip, but not much else. I didn't even own a suitcase. Gram had an extra one that she said was broken, but I could duct tape it shut and throw it away when I arrived in California. It was an old gold Samsonite with broken chrome latches. I didn't care, I was grateful that things

64

were falling into place.

Dad came to Gram's to transfer the car title and exchange the keys and money. He brought his new girlfriend with him to drive the T-bird back. Michelle was a taller, big-boned gal without a stitch of makeup. She had long, dark permed hair with straight bangs and a nice smile. She seemed quiet and insecure; I noted she didn't look me in the eye when she spoke. I thought that aside from her large bust, she wasn't Terry's usual type. His other girlfriends were a bit feistier and more outgoing, but perhaps he was looking for something new this time. I was grateful that he kept his word to get me the funds for the car; I thanked him profusely and then hugged and kissed him goodbye. I could tell Dad was sad, but I was too focused on escaping to care; I had no plans to come back—burning the breadcrumbs on my way out.

I packed the old suitcase with my paltry collection of clothes, hot rollers, and a few framed photos. Gram helped me duct tape it nice and tight. When it came time for me to leave, she looked me in the eyes, tapped my cheek with the palm of her hand, and said, "Be careful kid, and call me when you get there."

"I will Gram. I love you," I said, as I squeezed her tight.

"Love you too, Terrina," she replied in her squeaky voice, as she grabbed her lucky bingo bag.

For a moment I felt sad, I would miss her a lot. But I shoved those thoughts aside. Again, I was too excited to blow dodge. No other family members came to say goodbye to me. Several of them told me I would fail and ultimately return; it was perfect fuel for my fire. I had a guy friend from high school drive me to the Detroit airport, which was about an hour away.

I was nineteen years old with a one-way ticket to San Francisco and $1100 cash in my purse. I called Terry from the airport to say goodbye and boarded my red-eye flight. As I looked out the window, I saw the luggage handlers were loading all the bags on the conveyor belt. I noticed a large gold suitcase lying on the ground. It was popped wide open with the contents falling out all over the tarmac.

"That's my suitcase. Oh my God, my hot rollers are rolling under the plane," I said to the young guy sitting next to me.

"No way, that's hilarious," he said with a big laugh.

"Yep. That sort of represents how my life is going right about now. Let's order some beer."

I stayed with Glee at her Aunt Donna and Uncle Jerry's house when I initially arrived. But it was a mad dash for me to get my act together because Glee's family was arriving from Michigan for her wedding in five days, and they needed the space.

The first day I opened the newspaper and called on some jobs. Glee helped me with some suggestions and drove me around to apply for as many as I could.

The next day I called on rooms advertised for rent. I found a nice Midwest girl from Iowa, looking for the same. She was a petite gal with platinum blond hair named Cheryl. She told me she was going through a divorce and wanted to rent to someone quiet. She also had a stinky cocker spaniel named Romeo that clearly liked to poop on the light blue carpet. I didn't care. She seemed safe and had a bedroom and hall bathroom that I could rent for $400 a month. It was a big stretch from the farmhouse rent, but California was a different world.

On the third day, through a contact of Glee's, I got a hostess job at an upscale fish restaurant. I was paid an hourly wage of $5, but with tips I could average $8 an hour. It was a great start, but I knew I needed to find additional income quick.

On the day before I had to move out, I bought a brand new red Ford Festiva. I was adamant that I wanted a new car because I could not afford to break down and not have anyone to call for help. I didn't want to be a burden on Glee and just wanted the peace of mind that I had reliable transportation to get to my jobs. Since I didn't have any credit history, the sleazy car salesman suggested we put it in Glee's name, and then I could change the name on the loan later when I was more established. That loan detail turned out to be a lie, and I totally overpaid for the car. But I wasn't buying a car, I had purchased freedom.

I moved into Cheryl's and slept on the couch for the first week. Then I bought a used waterbed that I found in the local classifieds. It had drawers in the foundation, so I didn't need to spend money on a dresser. I didn't have much, but I felt content.

After Glee's wedding, I started working with her and her husband at the café her mother-in-law, Priscilla, owned. I used to open up the café around 6:30 a.m. and work until about two o'clock. Then I worked every night shift I could get at the fish house. The café also offered services for catered private events, so I was able to learn how to be a caterer as well. Eventually I started cleaning Priscilla's house, and Aunt Donna hired me as a housekeeper, too. I never turned down a job and worked almost every day. My plan was to get California residency and start college the following year.

I had spent all my money just getting set-up with my car and apartment. When Dad bought my T-bird, he told me he wanted to help pay my first month's rent, because he knew it was going to be hard for me to accomplish everything I needed with just $1100. I called him and asked if I could take him up on that offer; I only needed $300 because I would have saved $100 by the first of the month. He assured me that he would send me the money before my rent was due.

The night before I had to pay Cheryl, I still hadn't received anything from Terry. My calls were ignored. Ultimately, I was forced to borrow the money from a guy I had started dating named Ben. Technically, he borrowed it from his younger brother who reluctantly agreed to lend it, but not without sharing, "Tell your girlfriend to get her shit together." Demoralized, I promised to do just that.

When I finally got Dad on the phone about a week later, he was not happy with me, and we fought. I hated being ignored, and he felt that I was unappreciative of his past efforts, all of which he thought entitled him to a pass. The bottom line was that he didn't have the money. I told him that I would figure it out and not to worry about it, which only made him angrier. I felt like a fool for relying on him again. It's a hard pill to swallow when you feel like your parent leaves you "hung out to dry." I wouldn't have been so mad if he had just called me ahead of time. But thinking that he valued "planning ahead" was just me being naïve. Terry used to say, "Wish in one hand. Shit in the other. See which one gets filled first." Even though it seemed both my hands were full, a few weeks later he wired $300 in Western Union funds.

I worked every hour I could and still lived paycheck to paycheck. I didn't buy anything that wasn't absolutely necessary for many, many months. I learned that it was helpful to work at a restaurant—I always knew I could eat for free at least once a day. And my little Ford would go forever on a tank of gas. I was promoted to a server position at the fish house and started making some healthy tips. I could make a hundred dollars on a slow Monday, so I took as many shifts as I could get. Having the extra money allowed me to buy some clothes and better work shoes, but I would struggle financially for a long time.

Even with the trials, I was happier than I had ever been. I felt footloose and fancy-free with a deeper understanding of liberation. I thought 1988 was one big roller-coaster ride. Little did I know that I would soon find myself on the mother of all rides.

CHAPTER EIGHT

Mother of All Rides

I had settled into a nice routine of working hard and hanging out with friends. I was starting to learn my way around California and really enjoyed the mild winter weather. I felt like things were finally starting to settle down a little bit now with a few months under my belt.

One January morning, I called Dad, and he said something that kind of stunned me.

"Hey Honey Babe, I was thinking I'd like to come out for a visit and check out California."

"You want to visit me?"

"Yeah, would that be okay?"

"That would be great. I just need some notice so I can get some days off work, so we can hang out."

It had been a long time since we had spent any time together, and it made me happy that he wanted to see where I lived. I had to work the day he arrived, but I managed to get most of the weekend off. I lived in the East Bay, which was more than a sixty-minute drive away from the San Francisco airport, and it could take much longer during rush hour.

I was so grateful that he was willing to fly out to see me that I wanted to do something special for him. I couldn't pick him up when he arrived, so I paid for a limousine service to meet him. I told him a driver would be meeting him and to look for his name on a sign. He thought it was just a car service; he didn't know it was a limo that would be waiting for him.

The Friday he was due to arrive, I had the morning shift at the café. I had enlisted my friends to help me entertain Terry over the weekend; we were all anxiously awaiting his arrival. I figured he should be getting to the café around the time I was getting off work at two. When my shift ended, I grabbed my things and sat down on the curb in the parking lot of the café. I watched the traffic go by and imagined how fun it must have been for him to get a limo ride. I had never been in a limousine and thought it sounded glamorous.

As the time ticked by, I was starting to get worried that the limo driver had been in an accident. It had been four hours since his plane had landed. I called and checked on his flight, and it had landed on time. I called the limousine company on the payphone outside the convenience store next to the café. I told the guy who answered the phone that I was really worried as to what could have possibly happened. He put me on hold for about five minutes, which seemed like an eternity. When he came back on the line, he said, "They are on the way and will be there soon." I said, "What the hell is going on?" He didn't have an answer and said he would look into it after he spoke with the driver further. I hung up the phone and resumed sitting on the curb. I had been there so long that the café had closed for the night.

At about seven o'clock a sleek, silver limo pulled into the parking lot, five hours after it was supposed to. I knew immediately what the problem was; Dad was sitting in the front seat and the driver was a blond, older woman. It all made sense now. I instantly felt sick to my stomach. Of all the damn drivers in the world, his had to be a woman. As she parked the limo, I noticed the windows were down, and they both had cigarettes hanging from their lips. I stood by my car waiting for him to get out of the passenger side. As they opened their car doors, I was literally speechless. The driver opened her trunk and placed Terry's bag near my car tire. Dad staggered over to me and gave me a hug. He could barely stand up; I fought to hold up his dead weight. I helped steady him for a minute and was immediately overcome by his hard liquor breath. He was so inebriated his eyes were going in different directions.

"Hi, Dad. I've been waiting for you. Why are you so late?"

"Well, I talked the driver into taking me to the bar. Right, baby?" he slurred his words as he spoke.

"What?" I stood there confused.

Then he walked over to her, presumably to say goodbye, and started French kissing her.

"What the fuck is going on?" I shouted.

He slowly stopped and struggled to reach into his pocket for his money clip. He pulled out some loose cash. This pissed me off even more.

"Dad! I already tipped her on my credit card." I flashed the driver a nasty look, and she started to get back into her car. She'd been drinking, too.

"Well, she's a fuckin' slut anyway," he said, slurring more words.

If I hadn't been so mad at her, I would've apologized for my father's misogynistic comment, but I didn't. I was reminded of the saying I'd heard Terry say in jest a hundred times, "I never went to bed with any pigs, but I sure woke up with a lot." Now I understood.

As the limo pulled away, I loaded Terry's bag and helped him get into my car. I put his seatbelt on and told him to stay there for a few minutes. I walked over to the payphone and called Glee.

"Glee, Dad is wasted, and I can't take him back to my place. Cheryl will have a fit. I don't know what to do," I said, feeling desperate.

"Just bring him over to the condo and we'll figure out what to do next."

She and her husband were there when I arrived about five minutes later. I managed to get Dad to their front door, and Glee helped me get him on their couch. He started to wake up a little bit, but then he'd pass out again. While we all sat in the living room, I explained what amazing luck I had to get an old and drunk blond hag as his limo driver.

Terry was starting to settle into a nap with his arms crossed and his head bent over resting on one shoulder. He was slumped over, half sitting up, half lying down. Then with a quick adjustment, he pushed his feet straight out and kicked the coffee table over, Glee's things went flying everywhere. The loud noise and activity must have woken him up because then he announced, "I gotta piss." I grabbed him by his arm and led him to the bathroom. I had no idea how he was going to actually pull this off, but I was not about to help him urinate. I stood outside the door and overheard him talking to himself. I leaned closer and heard him say, "Listen you motherfucker. I'm gonna whip your ass." And then there was a loud crash and a bunch of banging noises. I ran into the bathroom and found him pissing in the bathtub. He had grabbed the shower curtain to stabilize himself and yanked the whole rod down. The curtain was situated on the floor and the rod had come to a rest in the middle of his piss stream in the tub. I waited for him to finish, then barked at him to zip up his pants. I was angry and embarrassed that he was being disrespectful of my friend's home. I helped him back to the couch where he slept for a couple of hours.

Later that night, Glee packed Terry with coffee, and I eventually got him back to my condo, where he quickly passed out on the couch. Luckily Cheryl went to bed early and also left for work at the crack of dawn.

I spent the weekend trying to entertain Dad and avoid the bars. It was not an easy task because his happiness revolved around his ability to smoke and drink. On Saturday night, my friends and my boyfriend joined us at a local microbrewery. We tried to show him things that we enjoyed about living in California, but it didn't seem like he was having too much fun. He was a little hungover for sure, but he definitely didn't like the local brew and just wanted his favorite Busch beer. I tried my best to get through the weekend without another intoxicated nightmare.

On Sunday, I drove him up to the top of Mount Diablo to see the views. I showed him where I worked and took him to lunch at Chevy's. In general, I could tell he wasn't impressed with California, and he struggled with someone else controlling his social calendar. I felt like he wasn't enjoying himself and I had totally failed to show him a good time. But I wasn't willing to go sit in a bar all night and deal with the aftermath of his binge. I think being around me made him feel like he had to alter his lifestyle and act like a functioning adult. In other words, I rained on his parade.

Having him in my new domain reminded me of one of the reasons I had left my old world. I felt ashamed that I was looking forward to him leaving, but I was. My new life wasn't filled with any drama, and I didn't have to babysit adults. I drove him back to the airport and dropped him off at the curb outside the terminal. I knew not to stay.

A few months later I got a new job at a bank. To get my foot in the door, I started as an internal courier. I still did my catering and cleaning jobs, but I took a break from working in restaurants.

Terry was still in a relationship with his girlfriend, Michelle. They moved to Ohio and were living in an apartment located in Michelle's parents' basement. I think Dad was trying to get another semi-truck, and she was going to school.

My roommate Cheryl wanted to get back together with her husband, so I moved into a new apartment with a friend from high school named Julie. She wanted to escape Michigan, too, so she jumped at the opportunity. It was a small two-bedroom, one-bath efficiency apartment that was part of the landlord's home. We had a private entrance and shared the washer and dryer in the garage with the owner. It had a tiny "L-shaped" kitchen with a hot plate and a small refrigerator. The kitchen opened to a living room, which was just big enough to fit a couch, loveseat and a TV. It was perfect for us, and we felt safe.

In June of 1989, I came home from work and there was a message on our answering machine from Gram. She wanted me to call home right away. I called her back, but she didn't answer. It was not like her to call me; she hated talking into answering machines. So I called my mother's sister to see what was going on. I could tell she had been crying when she answered her phone.

"What is going on?"

"You need to get home now, because Ted's been in a bad accident. It doesn't look good. He probably won't make it," she said, obviously holding back tears.

The thought of my little brother dying made me instantly feel faint. I became frantic and wondered how I would get there because I knew last-minute tickets were super expensive.

"Okay, I'll get there as fast as I can, but I'm not sure I have enough money," I said.

"Your mother said she would cover your expenses and not to worry about it."

"Well, what if she doesn't? Then what?"

"Then I will pay for your ticket. Just get home."

I frantically called my boyfriend and asked him to come over. Ben called on airline tickets while Julie helped me pack. I had no idea what to take with me, and I still didn't own a suitcase. I had thrown Gram's gold one away. Julie lent me her bag, and she loaded it with a combination of my clothing and some of hers. I noticed she tossed in a black dress and black heels. We connected eyes, but we didn't say a word.

The time was flying by fast, and I had to catch a red-eye out of San Francisco. I used my credit card to purchase a one-way ticket. I didn't have enough credit limit for the price of the ticket, but somehow it went through. I didn't buy a round trip because I had no idea when I could return. I arranged for a friend in Michigan to pick me up at the airport in Detroit.

We all jumped in my car, and Ben drove us to the airport. I sat in the back seat, and Julie was in the front. On the way there, the traffic was horrendous, and there was road construction everywhere. Ben merged lanes, and some jerk rear-ended us. After some heated exchanges with the guy that hit us, I started screaming, "Just keep going, I don't have time for this shit! I can't miss my flight!" So Ben weaved in and out of lanes as fast as he could, and I made it to my seat about ten minutes before they closed the doors to the plane.

On the flight I thought about how sad I was that I hadn't seen or spoken to Ted in over five years. He had turned eighteen about a month before, and I had been excited that he was graduating from high school and would finally become a legal adult. I hoped we could have a relationship again without having to deal with my mother's rules. Our father had not seen Ted in over ten years. Neither of my brothers kept in contact with Terry, primarily because of the obvious divorce rules; a relationship with both of my parents wasn't allowed by either of them, so we had to pick a team.

I didn't sleep a wink on the plane because I knew I was about to walk into a big pile of emotional baggage. When I landed the next morning I was exhausted. I had to stay calm, so I did a lot of self-talk about staying conscious and being brave. My friend was right on time and took me straight to Ann Arbor.

I found my aunt and Gram in the hospital lobby and ran over and gave them both a huge hug and a kiss. They looked worried, stressed, and exhausted. Gram told me that my brother was on life support and had a really bad head injury. A few days after Ted graduated from high school, he was driving his truck and a few drunk kids, also in a truck, hit him head-on. I think that's what she said. I was still in shock from hearing the words, "he's on life support," so I couldn't really focus on the details. I still hadn't called Dad to tell him what was going on and decided I would wait until I could see Ted for myself.

Gram and I took the elevators to the critical care floor. I felt nauseous and shaky. As we approached the room I could hear my mother talking to her husband. When I walked in, I saw Ted lying in the hospital bed with tubes coming out of a hole in his head and all kinds of equipment attached to him. As I approached his bed, I could feel my stomach churning and the tears welling up in my eyes. I passed out and fell to the floor. The nurses sat me in a chair and gave me some orange juice. I looked around the room and realized I was there with Gram, my mother and her husband. I tried to ignore everyone and just focus on Ted.

"Give your mom a hug," Gram demanded.

I literally wanted to run. I hadn't spoken to her in over five years, but out of respect for Gram, I reluctantly complied. After I left the room, I did my best to avoid everyone except Gram. The hospital staff was limiting the number of people that could go into Ted's room. My mother and her husband were in his room constantly. It made it difficult to get any time alone with my brother, so I finally walked in and stood next to the bed. I reached out and held Ted's muscular forearm in my hand. My back was to Mother's husband who was sitting in the corner of the room, facing the bed.

"What exactly did your mother ever do to you anyway?"

"Could I just have a minute with my brother?" I snapped.

He got up from the chair and stood in the doorway facing out. I stared at my brother noting that he was all grown up; he'd lost all of the baby fat in his chiseled, dimpled face.

"I'm sorry Ted. I'm so sorry this happened to you. I really wanted us to get together again when you were free from Mom's rule of staying away from me. I love you, Ted," I said through choked-back tears.

I was exhausted and light-headed. I was about to pass out again, so I sat down in the chair and placed my head between my hands in my lap.

"Jesus, this sucks. When will this end? How long will he suffer?"

"Never say that shit in front of your mother," I heard from the doorway.

"What the hell are you talking about?" I asked.

"We're not pulling the plug," he said with a nasty tone.

"I never said that. I didn't say that!" emphatically denying his grotesque assumption, as I stormed out of the room.

I decided I had to call Terry. It just didn't seem right that he didn't know what was happening. If people expected me to have empathy for my mother after five years of her absence from my life, then it was only fair that my father have the same opportunity with Ted. Besides, it wasn't about my mother; it was about my brother.

I didn't tell anyone I planned on calling him. I just did it. At the time, I actually assumed that everyone expected it. I hadn't had much sleep and was feeling like a zombie at that point, so I don't remember the conversation with Dad. I do remember he met me at the hospital the next morning. I needed to be strong for Dad, so I didn't allow myself to cry. I calmly told him that Ted was still in a coma and that his head injury was being relieved with a tube. He was still on life support, and his feet were starting to show signs of "posturing." I explained to Dad that the doctors saw this as a neurological sign of a major head injury.

Neither one of us wanted to run into my mother, so we carefully maneuvered around the critical care floor looking for Ted's nurse. When I spotted her, I waved her down, and she took us into a private room away from the larger waiting room. I introduced her to Terry and explained the delicate situation with my parents. She suggested that Dad speak directly to the doctor and asked us to wait there. A few minutes later she led Terry to a desk near the nurse's station. I couldn't hear most of what he said, but I did hear him say, "Yes, I am his father."

After about ten minutes, I saw Dad place the phone down and slowly get up. We went back into the private room, where he told me that the doctor basically said that Ted will most likely not wake up. If he did, he would probably live the rest of his life in a vegetative state. I knew Terry wasn't hopeful when he got there, and it seemed the doctor had confirmed his fears.

"What did the doctor say should happen next? How long can we keep praying for a miracle?"

"There's not gonna to be a fuckin' miracle, honey. I asked him what he would do if Ted was his son, and he said he would remove the life support and let him go peacefully."

His words punched me in the gut. I felt a lump in my throat and a weakness in my legs. I grabbed Dad's hand and fought back the tears.

"I love you, Dad. I'm so sorry."

He reached for his cigarettes, and I said, "Come on, Daddy, you can smoke outside."

As we walked toward the exit, I noticed out of the corner of my eye my mother was standing at the nurse's station. I purposely didn't look in her direction and quickly pushed Dad into the elevator. My heart was pounding; now she knew Terry was there. After he had a couple of cigarettes, I asked him if he wanted to spend some time with me while I waited for an update on Ted. He agreed, and we found a waiting room far away from the rest of the family. I could feel the anxiety welling up inside of me. I could sense a confrontation was coming with my parents.

Dad and I sat together holding hands and catching up on our lives for a couple of hours. Things seemed quiet until I saw my mother and her husband walk into the room. My mother's eyes were bulging and piercing; she had a mean look on her red face. She started screaming at us, and all the other people in the room looked horrified.

"You are not his father. You are an asshole. You need to leave, now," she demanded.

"We're not bothering you. We're minding our own business," I shouted back.

"And you can get *your ass* back to California. You will *never* see Ted again. Do you hear me? Never!" she screeched as she approached me.

Dad and I stood up and tried to walk around them and out of the room. My mother stepped closer to me and poked me hard in the chest repeatedly with her long fingernail.

"And I will never speak to you again," she screamed.

I couldn't restrain the powerful hatred she brought out in me. I had vowed when I moved out of her house that she would never touch me again. When her finger jabbed me the third time, I lost my damn mind. I shoved her back out of my personal space.

"If you ever touch me again, I'll put you in the bed next to Ted, you fucking bitch!" feeling the veins in my neck popping out as I screamed.

I felt Dad's arm wrap around my neck and pull me next to him. He started chuckling and said, "Let's go, Honey Babe. That cunt's not worth your energy."

He knew that if he didn't get upset and he laughed at her, it would make her even angrier. He understood all of her buttons and pushed them with style. As the elevator doors were closing, my mother watched to be sure we left.

"I will get my ass back to California. And I never want to hear from you again. You're dead to me!" I screamed before the doors knocked together.

I felt bad for the other people at the hospital. They didn't deserve to hear all that. But I didn't regret what I'd said, because I knew she was right. I would never see Ted again. So I just unleashed my feelings and went for her jugular.

Dad and I headed to a bar nearby and ordered some nachos and beer. I sat quietly while he filled the dead air.

"Ya know, I've been eighty-sixed from a lot of places, but never a hospital," he joked trying to break the tension.

"Well, I guess you're still tough as nails, honey. But it's too bad you've had to be. You deserved a better mother. I'm sorry about that," Dad said apologetically.

"Well Dad, it's still just you and me. We still have each other."

"That's right Honey Babe. Now we gotta get you back to California."

"Yeah, except I've got a huge problem. I don't have any money."

My aunt had reneged on helping me and basically told me that what I did by bringing Terry to the hospital was disgusting. I called Gram, and she was pissed, too. She said that my mother had enough on her plate with Ted, and I had made it worse. She also told me that if my mother knew she was talking to me, she wouldn't be able to see Ted, either. It infuriated me that once again Ted was being used as a pawn.

"If you listen to her and decide not to speak to me, that will be your decision, and I won't talk to you either. You don't have to pick sides just because your daughter is a manipulating asshole!" I screamed into the phone.

That was the first and last time I would ever yell at Gram.

I explained to Terry that I had charged the first flight, about $850, on my credit card, and my mother was supposed to pay for it and for my return trip. He just laughed, and said, "Honey, you can never trust that pig. She would sell her soul for a buck." I felt like jumping out of my skin. All those emotions I had felt when I was a kid listening to my parents' fights, had returned. All those feelings of helplessness washed over me. I excused myself and went to the bathroom to get a break from the bullshit.

When I returned to the table, Dad said, "Honey, don't worry, I'll pay for your ticket back to California. I called a friend and got the money."

"Really? Are you serious?"

"Yep. You leave tomorrow night, it's all booked. Fuck that bitch. You don't need her, you never did," he said, with a look of pride on his face.

Terry was my hero.

Dad never did get to see Ted at the hospital. We talked about him at the bar that day and he said, "When your mother would get pissed at me, she used to say he wasn't mine. He probably isn't, but I always thought of him as my kid. Now he's basically dead. He'll never be the same."

When I arrived back in San Francisco, my boyfriend was waiting for me. We walked down to baggage claim to wait for my luggage. As we watched all the bags go around the carousel, I told him about everything that had happened, and he looked horrified. Even though he had also endured his parents' messy divorce, his family was a lot more civilized. Most people had a hard time understanding my situation. When asked about my parents, I eventually stopped telling the truth because the outright judgment got old.

When the conveyor belt stopped spinning and the light went off, I realized that my bag wasn't there. I spoke with customer service, and they told me it would probably show up on the next flight, and they would deliver it to my door later. Sadly, my bag never did show up. Not only did I miss a week of work, spend $850 on my credit card, now I had to buy Julie a new piece of luggage and replace the clothes she lent me. I felt like I was starting all over again, except this time I was in debt. The airline eventually sent me some money for the bag, but it barely covered the cost of what I owed my roommate.

I got back to work at the bank, and every day at lunch I called the hospital to check on my brother. Every day they told me: "nothing has changed." They wouldn't give me any other information, no matter who answered the phone. I called for weeks, and finally a nurse said, "Sweetie, you probably need to stop calling. Your mother has instructed us that we are only allowed to say 'nothing has changed.'"

Four months after I returned to California, Gram called me. I guess she decided to risk the possible backlash from my mother. She felt terrible that I was cut off from all information regarding Ted. She told me that he had woken up after being in a coma for three months. He couldn't eat, speak, or walk. He had a feeding tube and only had slight use of one arm. She was helping care for him at my mother's house. It broke her heart to see him like that. She always had a soft spot for kids; before she retired she drove a school bus that picked up mentally and physically challenged children. She treated them like every other typical kid. I remember she would decorate the bus on Halloween and wear a costume every year. They all loved her. I was happy that Ted would have Gram near him, but I felt so sad that he now had to live the rest of his life with my mother. That was the day I buried Ted. I realized that I would never have the opportunity to have my brother in my life. It was gone and so was he, for that matter. For my own mental health, I had to let him go.

Then I buried myself in work and slowly dug my finances back to black. I hated owing anyone anything. I continued to live paycheck to paycheck, but I had my freedom, and that was priceless.

The bank that I had been working for was purchased by another commercial bank. They asked me to take a customer service position in Oakland. I had to drive to the Concord BART station, take the train and then walk three blocks once I arrived. I hated the hour-long commute, and the culture there was cold and unwelcoming. So when the bank offered a small severance package of $2100 to anyone who wanted to leave, I took it. I knew I could get another job and that money would help me while I transitioned into another position and started school.

Later that fall, I was finally considered a resident of California. I enrolled in classes at the local community college because I couldn't afford the university yet. I decided to take some cheaper, transferrable classes until I could. My tuition wasn't expensive, but I still had to charge the classes to my credit card. By the time the next quarter came around, I had paid off the balance, so I could do it all over again. I didn't buy any of the required books because they often cost more money than the tuition. I only had time and money to take two night classes, but I figured time was going pass by anyway, so I might as well take some courses, even if it would take me forever to graduate.

I tried to stay in touch with Dad, but it was becoming more and more difficult. He continued to struggle financially and was still drinking heavily. Michelle was a typical enabler, and he took full advantage of her role. But I didn't feel sorry for her because I believed she had choices, too. After trying to reach Terry for several months, I finally heard his voice.

"Dad, it hurts my feelings that you never call me."

"Well, I can't afford to call you all the time."

"I'd just like to know you're still alive once in a while. I mean, you're all I have, Dad."

"Well, right now I'm just trying to get things set up to get another rig. So, it is, what it is."

Back then, phone companies charged a lot of money for long-distance calls and the minutes added up quickly. I also realized my request was too much pressure and made him feel inferior. It hurt me that he felt like he couldn't speak to me because of money.

"I just started working at a chiropractor's office. I don't have a lot of money right now either, but I do have a phone card that you can use to call me. If you want to talk to me, I'm happy to pay for your call."

He wrote down the number and the PIN and promised he would do a better job of staying in touch.

November seemed to jump out of nowhere as I grinded through work and school. My unopened mail was stacking up on the counter; I noticed my phone bill was balancing on the top like a bloated pig. I dropped my purse on the chair and ripped the thick stuffed envelope open. As I pulled apart the pages, I could see a line of calls on both the front and back of about twelve pages. Perhaps this was someone else's bill? I didn't even have that much time to talk on the phone; how could this be right? As I looked closer, numbers we're flagged as phone card calls. I quickly looked for the total: it was over $350.

As I read each line of every call, it became obvious what had happened. Some of the calls were hours long. Most of the calls were to Terry's brothers, with the longest to his twin brother, Tim. I could just imagine those two getting all sauced up and solving all the world's problems, night after night. He used my calling card not to call me, but to call *everyone else on God's green earth*. To add to my fury, Michelle probably used it too because there were lots of numbers I didn't recognize.

I immediately called Dad. He didn't answer so I called back again—no answer. Then I called a third time and Michelle answered. I could tell by her tone she was in a snotty mood. "Yes!" she answered, sounding exasperated.

"Where's my dad? I want to talk to him right now," I demanded.

"Well he's not here, can I leave him a message?"

"Yes Michelle. You can tell him I need him to pay my $350 phone bill."

She sat there silent for a few seconds and then she said, "Okay, I'll let him know."

"And tell him I want him to call me back, please."

I didn't sleep well that night; he didn't call. I had a sinking feeling Terry knew he had crossed the line, and he was too embarrassed to own up to it. It would be easier for him to get pissed off at me than to admit he was in the wrong. I was positive he was angry at me for being rude when I spoke to Michelle and that I didn't deserve a call back. I knew him well, but I also knew that that was just his excuse to avoid taking responsibility for his actions and to place the turd back on my plate.

Late the next night I called Dad again. Michelle answered and I asked if Dad was there. She was cold and said he wasn't home yet.

"I gave him your message last night, but Terrina we don't have $350," she whined.

"Michelle, I don't give a shit what you have to do. You guys better pay me for that bill," I demanded.

"Well, I'll tell him to call you when he gets home."

I slammed the phone down. I was so damn mad at that point, I didn't even care about upsetting my father. I certainly didn't care about Michelle's feelings; I took her as just another adult shitting on me.

Later that night, Terry finally called me back. He said, "Look, I was gonna call you back, but I've been busy."

"You know I hate being ignored. I don't understand why I got this huge phone bill. Are you going to be able to pay for it?!" I yelled, cutting him off.

"Don't ever call here and talk to Michelle and me with that tone," he barked back.

"Are you fucking kidding me right now? You have some big balls, Dad. I'm making eight bucks an hour and trying to go to school, and you charge hundreds of dollars in calls on my phone card. I gave you that to call me. Not all those assholes on my bill. There wasn't one single call to me. Not one! What the fuck is wrong with you?"

He could never take the truth coming at him that hard. It was easier for him to run away, just like he had done my whole life. Even before I heard the sound of his phone slamming down, and then the loud dial tone, I knew the call was over. I knew him like the back of my hand. By confronting him, I had become a mirror to his failures, and he resented me for it.

Sadly, he never paid my phone bill, and he never called me back. And when I say he never called me back, I mean, *never*. Honestly, after that confrontation, I felt my heart harden just a little more.

CHAPTER NINE

My Twenties

W hen I left Michigan in 1988, no one believed I'd be able to take care of myself. They were all certain I'd eventually have to return to Michigan and fall back into line, as if I were born into some sort of caste system.

I didn't stay in touch with Dad's side of the family. I felt like he was the conduit to them, and if he and I weren't speaking to each other, there was a good chance they wouldn't want to speak to me either. I had heard secondhand from some distant cousins that Terry had been saying negative things about me. He had supposedly said, "She's just like her mother." That was the worst insult he could possibly bestow upon me. Obviously, he needed to justify our lack of relationship and build a narrative that made me the villain.

My whole life I had witnessed, on both sides of my family, major grudges and nasty battles. It was hard to keep up with all the family fighting, and on-again-off-again relationships. If I didn't agree with carrying their grudges, my parents would get angry with me and treat me like a traitor. My uncle Joe used to say, "Well honey, we're not the Waltons." Or, "Who needs enemies? We have relations." It was just easier to shut everyone out of my life. Everyone, except Gram. We continued to stay in touch no matter what dysfunction was going on. She used to say in disgust, "This is one heck of a family."

I got on with my life in California and stuck with my plan. I was already a motivated person, but I also felt if I failed, it would bring too much joy to my judgmental family. There was no way I would give them that satisfaction.

Eventually I started bartending at fancy private parties and catered more events when I could. I worked my cleaning jobs and was also employed as a receptionist for a sports physician. I continued to work six or seven days a week for years and went to school at night. I also spent a lot of time working on my feelings and reading every self-help book that I could afford to buy. I cried a lot and did my best to process everything that had happened in my childhood. My education helped with that journey a little bit, but ultimately I learned through my life experiences to become truly independent, tenacious, and confident in myself. With each new achievement, I felt myself becoming unshakable.

On September 2, 1994, I graduated from California State University with a degree in sociology. I was two classes shy of a minor in psychology, but once I knew I could get that diploma, I was done. It took me nearly eight years to get a Bachelor of Arts degree, earned just one month shy of turning twenty-six. Frequently, I would get the question, "What the hell are you going to do with a sociology degree?" I always answered back, "I'm gonna make money. That's what I'm gonna do." All I wanted was the chance to compete, and I knew I needed that "piece of paper," if I ever wanted to break the cycle of living paycheck to paycheck. I didn't graduate in June when the university had its commencement ceremony, so there wasn't a big celebration when I finished after the summer quarter. I didn't care about walking down the aisle in a cap and gown. They were finally done pitchin', and I was finally done catchin'.

Eight days after I graduated, I got married to my boyfriend Ben, the same guy, and only guy I had dated since I had arrived in California. He had a liberal arts degree, but he decided to get a degree in engineering. His father and stepmother lived in Michigan, and he really wanted to be near them and attend the University of Michigan. Even though I wasn't thrilled about returning, I told him that if he was accepted, I would support him.

March of 1995, we left California and moved to Michigan. My husband was accepted at U of M, and I started my career working as a software trainer. I took a position with a temp agency that had a six-month pilot project with one of the automakers. They basically wanted someone college educated, willing to travel, and cheap. I was paid $400 a week and I flew out of Detroit every Monday and returned every Friday night. I never had a nonstop flight, and I absolutely hated to fly. But I loved the idea of facing my fears head-on. And as the new person on the team, I was assigned all the "awesome locations," like Tempe, Arizona, and Corpus Christi, Texas, in July, and Mobile, Alabama, during hurricane season.

My job entailed training auto dealerships and the credit branches on interactive financial software. I worked with the loan personnel on the credit side, the dealer's car salesmen, and the finance and insurance staff. This experience gave me a backroom glimpse into the sleazy sales mentality that Glee and I had dealt with back in 1988. I quickly learned that I didn't love living in hotels and airports, and I really didn't enjoy getting my ass slapped by the good ole boys. My initial plan was to make a good impression on the auto executives and get offered a permanent role. But as it turned out, I needed a Plan B.

Plan B entailed networking while traveling in hopes of making a professional connection. In the fall of 1995, on my very last trip at the end of the six-month grind, I met an executive named Dave. He worked for an electronic funds transfer (EFT) company, based in Dearborn, Michigan. Dave had the misfortune of sitting next to me on a very bumpy flight from St. Louis to Detroit. As fate would have it, his company was growing, and he was looking for someone who understood financial transactions, software, and hardware. When he asked me why I was traveling, I told him I was an EFT software trainer, and he started the job interview at thirty thousand feet, despite the nausea. Within a few weeks, I had implemented Plan B and launched my career in the financial services industry.

The decade from 1990 to 2000 consisted of some of the most transformational years of my life. I had graduated from college, gotten married, found my career, supported my husband through his college degree, gotten divorced, and bought my first house. Sadly, I did all of those things without ever speaking to either of my parents.

Dealing with any alcoholic is difficult enough, but having one as a father was very complicated. I had come to terms with who he was. Terry's heart was sensitive and sweet, but his head was controlled by his demons, and substances that he apparently could not overcome. I certainly considered him the smartest man I had ever known, but his Achilles' heel was powerful. His tortured soul overruled clear thinking and sabotaged his life. We all have choices, and we need to live with our decisions: this was a tenet he had taught me long ago.

With all the work that I had done processing the dysfunction of my past, I felt clear about my boundaries. I was not easily intimidated, and I felt there was nothing I couldn't figure out. And I had no doubt that I had *earned* every ounce of that strength and confidence. Ultimately, I was at peace with the possibility that I might never see my father again.

PART TWO

CHAPTER TEN

Joe Shit the Ragman

Starting a new decade and a new millennium, I just kept pushing ahead, dreaming bigger dreams, and making new plans.
But you know what they say, "Make a plan, God laughs."

In the spring of 2000, I started working at a new company head-
quartered in Dayton, Ohio. My position was in sales with a territory
of thirteen Midwest states and eastern Canada. I worked about seventy-five hours a week, and when I wasn't on the road, I operated
out of my home office in Birmingham, Michigan. Taking that job
was one of those pivotal decisions that moved my career forward,
exponentially.

When I traveled in the car for work, it was my time to catch up on
the phone with friends and family. That was back when cellphones
were giant gray flip-phones. I had mine mounted on a phone stand
in the car floor. I could operate it hands-free by using the stereo system to listen and speak to the person on the other end of the call. I
remember that before I had the floor cradle I had to hold that heavy
phone to my ear, and after about thirty minutes I had a cramp in my
hand, and my ear was on fire.

Occasionally, I would call my dad's mother to say hello. On several phone calls that summer, Margot kept mentioning that Terry
had a mechanic shop in Taylor, Michigan. According to her, he repaired semi-trucks and was doing really well. I never knew if she

was telling me the truth, or if she was just trying to appear proud. She liked to brag about her kids, grandkids, and extended family—nothing pleased her more than knowing her relatives were working hard. Margot was known for being a little pushy sometimes, and on one of our calls she mentioned my father's business again. With a determination in her voice she said, "Well Dolly, just pull over and let me give you his address." I really wasn't interested, but I guess I didn't want to upset her, so I obliged. I tossed the small notepad in my glove box.

About a month later, I was driving back to Birmingham from Ohio when I noticed the gas gauge was low. My Jeep Grand Cherokee was a gas hog, and I still had about forty-five minutes to go. So I pulled off the interstate into a large gas station. As I pumped the gas, I grabbed my map out of the glove box to see exactly where I was, and I noticed Terry's contact information. After reviewing the map, I realized I wasn't very far from his shop. Feeling curious, I decided to drive by and check things out. It was about seven o'clock at night, so I figured he probably wouldn't be there. Dusk was settling in as I pulled behind some industrial buildings. I navigated a dozen deep potholes and cautiously proceeded because the area looked a little rough. There were a few businesses on each side of the driveway and a couple of cars parked at each. I drove deeper into the complex and saw the address my grandmother had given me. I turned left and pulled up to the large garage doors and parked. A giant motion-detection light turned on, illuminating everything in the parking area. I didn't see any cars there, so I decided to be nosey and look in the windows. Unfortunately, even in my high heels, I was too short to see in the garage, so I walked back toward my SUV. Out of the corner of my eye, I saw someone coming toward me from around the back of the building. My heart jumped in my chest, and I steadied myself for a confrontation. I stopped and turned around to deal with the situation, and saw a tall, thin man. He stopped walking about ten feet away from me, stood there and stared at me; wearing dirty old Levi's and a greasy T-shirt with a pocket on the chest. He was a stranger, but he was also my dad.

He hadn't changed much, still handsome with a little more gray in his hair and slightly older looking in the face; he was still sporting Popeye forearms from all the years of wrenching on engines. His large hands rubbed his eyes in disbelief.

"Hi Dad," I softly forced out of my mouth.

He smiled and quickly walked over to me, "Oh my. Honey Babe. I can't believe it's you."

He wrapped his arms around me, hugged me as tight as he could, and started sobbing. I'd never seen my father cry let alone sob. He placed his hands on my shoulders, leaned back and, speaking through his tears, said, "Is it really you? Look at you. You're gorgeous!"

"Yep, it's really me," I stated emotionless.

I didn't cry. I just stood there feeling numb and acutely aware of everything happening. I had cried so much over that last decade, I literally didn't have any more tears left. While he held me, I took in the familiar smell of diesel fuel, cigarettes, and beer. But I could tell he wasn't drunk but just looked like he had finished a long workday.

As he wiped his face off with the bottom of his shirt, he said, "You look so pretty in your suit, and I look like Joe Shit the Ragman."

"I'm so glad you stopped by. Do you want to come in?" he said, hugging me tight again.

"No, I can't stay. I've been on the road all day. I've gotta get home and let the dog out, and I have an early meeting tomorrow morning," I said without hesitation.

He looked disappointed and a little rejected, but it didn't bother me. I had my walls up, and I wasn't expecting to see him that night. I needed to think about how I was feeling.

He asked me where I lived, we engaged in some small talk, and we exchanged phone numbers. He grabbed me again and hugged me so tight I thought he might break my neck. Still sniffling he said, "I'm so happy you came by. Drive safe honey, and let's talk on the phone next week."

I didn't answer him. Seeing him brought back a lot of painful memories, but not anger. I had worked through all my feelings long before that day, but that didn't mean I had forgotten everything that had happened. He opened the door to my Jeep, and I jumped in, shut the door, and rolled down the window. He stood there leaning on the driver's-side window opening with his large hand rested on my left forearm, obviously trying to stall my departure.

"Okay Dad, I'll talk to you next week."

"Good. I love you, baby girl," he replied with a wink and look of satisfaction.

And as I put the Jeep in reverse, I said, "I love you, too."

I think we both knew he had missed the window of opportunity to be my father. I was all grown up, independent, and I didn't need him anymore. He had never been comfortable with that role anyway. And now I wasn't comfortable being a daughter. Neither one of us had had much practice with these roles, but perhaps we could be friends.

CHAPTER ELEVEN

Friendship

For several weeks, Terry and I spoke on the phone catching up on each other's lives. He told me that his driver's license had been revoked; I guess those DUI tickets finally caught up with him. I didn't ask about any details, and he didn't offer any. He still drove, just not legally (and according to him, much more carefully). Not having a license made it difficult for him to continue being in the transport business; so that's when he decided to open up his mechanic shop. He knew a lot of truckers, so it made sense for him to focus on semi-truck repair. He was one of those rare drivers who could fix his own truck, so he wasn't intimidated to start that type of business. He had an office in the front of his building that had a bathroom and a cot, so most of the time he slept at the shop. He and Michelle were still together; she lived in Ohio in a trailer on her parents' property. When he wasn't busy in Taylor, he traveled south to see her.

Eventually, I felt comfortable with inviting him to my home. Since it was my first house, I had a lot to learn. I had started renovating and had several projects that still needed to get done. Having lots of questions about construction was a great way for Dad and me to connect again.

The first time Terry came to my house I had given him very detailed directions. He knew how to get to Birmingham, but he wasn't familiar with the specific city block that I lived on. I told him to look for a small, yellow cottage on Bowers Street, just two houses off Eton Street. I remember telling him that he would see my purple Jeep in the driveway. I also told him I would leave the door unlocked and he could just come on in, in case I was in the backyard.

I was in the kitchen when I heard the door open. I walked around the corner into the living room to make sure it was Dad. While he slipped off his boots, I noticed he was red in the face, and he was giggling under his breath.

"Well honey, I'm not sure I made a very good first impression on your neighbor."

"Which neighbor?"

"Well, when I came around the corner from Eton, I saw a purple jeep in the second house's driveway. I parked behind it, walked in the front door and yelled, 'Hey baby girl, it's Daddy!' and out came a tall, blond lady with big tits, and she didn't look too happy to see me."

"Oh my God, Dad. I told you my house was yellow, not gray."

It never occurred to me to warn him that my neighbor who lived directly across the street, had the exact same Jeep.

"What did she do when she saw you?"

"Well, let's just say it was a short chat. I asked her if Terrina was there, and she just pointed to your house. I apologized to her and slowly walked backward out the door before she could kill me," he explained with a big belly laugh.

I shook my head, rolled my eyes, and said, "I thought you were good with directions."

"You know, she was kind of built like Peggy," he explained further.

"Oh shut up, and let me give you a tour."

That day I introduced him to my crazy wheaten terrier, Braddy. We both loved dogs, and he got a kick out of how much personality Braddy had. He was a headstrong, defiant, spoiled brat; that's how he got his name. But he was my baby, and I couldn't have loved him more.

During the tour, I showed him all the projects that I had already completed. He seemed impressed and told me how proud he was that I was creating such a great home. He didn't stay too long that day, but it was a nice visit, and I enjoyed his company.

A couple weeks later Braddy was out in the backyard playing. I looked out the window to check on him and noticed he was limping. He used to run up and down the fence chasing all the dogs on all three sides of "his" yard. There were paths worn into the grass along all the fences, and an "x" pattern in the middle going from corner to corner. With all of his activity, I thought maybe he had sprained his front leg and with a little rest he might be okay. Terry called me, and I told him what was going on. He insisted on driving up to see if he could help.

When Dad arrived about forty minutes later, he held Braddy while I ran my hand up and down his leg. I noticed something hard as I pulled his hair back.

"Oh no! He's got some sort of sliver deep in his leg."

"Dad, hold him still and I'll pull it out."

"Well, do it fast, because you only get one kick at the cat," he groaned as he struggled to control the dog's strength.

I grabbed the top of the hard, woody end and yanked it out as fast as I could. When I pulled it out and held it up, Dad and I looked at each other wide-eyed.

"What the hell is that?" I asked.

It was a thick, two-inch-long spike that had somehow stayed intact. Terry let go of Braddy, stood up, and walked to the kitchen window overlooking the backyard.

"Well, that fuckin' Hawthorne tree's gotta come down."

In the middle of the yard, there was an old, ugly tree that Braddy used to run around and chase squirrels up. Sometimes he was so determined to get the critter, he would jump halfway up the tree.

"Just soak his paw in some peroxide and he'll be fine. I think you got all of it out."

So that's what I did, and Braddy was back to terrorizing all the vermin the next day.

A couple of days later, Dad called to check on the dog.

"Well, I bet that tree is already gone, right?" he asked with a chuckle.

"Yes, I had it cut down yesterday."

"Well, it didn't have a chance after it hurt Braddy Boy."

"Did they leave the stump?"

"Unfortunately, they didn't have a stump grinder with them, and because I wanted it done quickly, I just had them leave it."

"That's no big deal. I'll just bring up some wood and build a box around it. You can plant some flowers in it."

"Oh, that would be nice Dad, but you don't have to do that."

A few days later I found Terry in my backyard with a stack of 4x4 lumber, and some long metal dowels. He had drilled holes in the ends of each piece of wood and then stacked six of them on each side in the shape of a box. I watched him use a sledgehammer to pound the stakes in each corner of the box, all the way through and into the ground. I had the sturdiest flower box in town, and I teased him that I could build a guesthouse on top of it.

"Well Honey Babe, if it's worth doing, it's worth doing right," he explained.

"I noticed you made some flowerbeds around the front deck. What are ya gonna use for a border?" he asked when he was done pounding the stakes.

"I'd really like some field stones, but I can't find any around here."

"Yeah, that would look nice."

About a week later, there was a big pile of rocks in my front yard. I called Dad and asked him if he'd been by my house lately. He laughed and said, "What gave it away?" He'd been up north doing something for a client and visiting Uncle Joe. He asked his brother if I could have some of the field stones he had lying around at some of the farms he owned. My uncle also had an excavating business, so he had lots of equipment at his disposal. According to Dad, his brother fired up a tractor with a bucket, drove to one of his properties, and scooped up a bunch of rocks. He filled up a large rusty oil barrel with the perfect stones and placed it in Terry's pickup truck bed. Dad made the four-hour trip south to my house and dumped them next to my driveway. I used the rocks to make a border around all my flower beds, and it made me happy every time I looked at them. I liked the aesthetic, but it really wasn't about the rocks.

I continued to improve my house and desperately needed a new washer and dryer. I asked Dad if he thought I should get an electric or a gas dryer. I told him the one I was getting rid of was electric, but my home had both outlets. His advice was to get a gas dryer, so that's what I ordered.

The appliance delivery man told me that I had the gas outlet, but I didn't have any of the connecting tubes or pieces needed to actually hook up the dryer. Terry was in the middle of ripping apart a diesel engine and couldn't come over to help when I called.

"Dad, I'm headed out of town Monday morning, and I need to get all my laundry done, should I call a plumber, or can a handyman do this?"

"Oh fuck no. You don't need to spend your money on those crooks. They'll fuck ya like a house cat. Just go down to the hardware store and find one of them old guys. They'll tell you what you need, and you can do it yourself. But make sure you ask somebody with some gray in their hair; those young assholes don't know shit."

Luckily, there was a great hardware store a couple of blocks away. It was the kind where there were lots of friendly people willing to help, and they had several cats around. (Maybe it's a Midwest thing, but it's not a real hardware store if they don't have cats.) I took Terry's advice and found a really old hunchbacked guy wearing a vest with his name on it.

"How can I help you little lady?" he asked.

"I need to hook up my gas dryer and I'm hoping you can sell me the parts I need."

He gave me a funny look and he said, "Well, I probably shouldn't tell you how to do this, but come with me."

He took me to the aisle with all the copper tubing and connector pieces. He handed me everything I would need and then gave me a tool to bend the copper without pinching it.

"Thank you so much, sir. You've been so helpful. My dad was right, you guys are smart."

"Well, I don't know about that. But make sure you're careful sweetie, this is dangerous stuff," he said with an apprehensive gaze.

"Um, okay. Have a great day," I said, feeling confused.

When I got home, I pulled out all the parts and just took it one step at a time. I connected the nut and tubing to the gas outlet and shaped the copper in a coil without pinching it. Then I connected it to the dryer and turned on the valve at the wall. That was it? It seemed way too easy, but I didn't have time to dilly-dally. After doing my first load, I went to check on the dryer. I immediately noticed a strong gas odor in the kitchen next to the utility room. I called Dad in a panic, "Dad, my whole house smells like gas. I think something's wrong." He asked me what I did, and I explained I followed the older gentleman's advice to a T.

"Oh, you're fine. Don't even worry about it. Just open up some windows and doors, and finish your laundry. I'll come check it next week when you get back to town."

The following week, Terry went into my utility room and reached over and touched the gas outlet connection. He started quietly snickering and said, "Honey, when you installed this nut at the wall, did you use a tool to tighten it?"

"No, I just used my hand. The guy didn't tell me I needed a tool."

"Well, this son-of-bitch's so loose, you're lucky you didn't blow up your house."

"Dad! Are you kidding me?"

"I've got a wrench in my truck; I'll tighten it up and you'll be good to go."

"Well, next time, you old guys gotta be more specific. I mean, what the hell do I know about this shit?"

"Well, you know a lot more about it now, don't ya?" he said with a smile.

I don't know why I was surprised that he was so nonchalant. This was the same man who let me drive a car with a hole in the gas tank. He was right about one thing; life required lots of tools.

Later that summer, I had to fly out of town for a business convention. I tried to get Braddy into the kennel where I usually took him, but it was full. I would drive an hour out of my way to take him there, just to make sure my dog was safe. I was lamenting to Terry that I needed to find a better resource.

"Oh honey, just bring Braddy Boy down to stay with me."

I was so shocked he'd offered that I didn't know what to say. I stammered, "That's so nice of you Dad, but I'm sure he would just be a distraction from your work."

"Oh that's bullshit! You'll be driving right by me when you go to the airport, so just drop him off on your way."

A couple of days later, I packed Braddy's suitcase with all of his bedding, toys, leashes, dog food, and favorite snacks. When I arrived at Terry's shop, he was standing in his large garage with the door open. I jumped out of the SUV and said, "Hi Dad! I've just got a few things I need to give you. I've got the instructions all written out. It explains how much to feed him and when he can have snacks. Here's his suitcase. Let me grab his other stuff."

"Jesus Christ Honey Babe, does he come with an armed guard, too?" he said through laughter.

"No, Dad. But if you hurt him, you'll wish you had an armed guard," I said with a straight face.

"Yes, dear." he said playfully.

"Okay, here's a couple of baby gates. You'll need several because he's smarter than we are. And I don't want him outside without a leash because if he gets loose, you will never catch him. Okay?"

"Yes, dear."

"I'm not kidding, Dad," I said laughing. "He's not some country dog that will just come wandering back. Trust me, you'll be glad when I come back and get him."

He smiled, looked at the dog, and said, "Oh, we'll get along just fine, won't we Braddy Boy?"

"Okay, I've gotta get to the airport. I'll call you when I land to see how you two bad boys are doing."

He smiled, gave me a big hug and kiss, and said, "Okay honey, I love you. Be safe and give 'em hell."

"I sure will— Love you, Dad."

As I drove off, I said a little prayer that Braddy would be safe and that I wouldn't regret this decision. I called Terry to check in as soon as I landed in Boston. Everything sounded fine and things were calm, so I went about my week at the conference and checked in with Dad every couple of days. The more time that went by the less I worried; Dad seemed happy, enjoying the company.

When I returned to Detroit, Terry was waiting outside for me. I said, "Hi, Dad. How did it go?"

"Well, we had a lot of fun." Then he paused before he went on to say, "We did have one little issue, but it's all good now."

"What do you mean, issue? Where's Braddy?"

"He's inside. He's fine."

"What happened?" I snapped.

"Well, you weren't kidding when you said not to let him outside without a leash."

"Oh my God, Dad. How did that happen?" I asked with a gasp.

"Well, I had the back door to the shop open and he slipped past me. So I hustled out there to get him, but before I could grab him, he spotted a rabbit."

"Oh no! How did you catch him?"

"Well, luckily he caught the rabbit, so he stopped, and I grabbed him by the neck."

"Caught the rabbit. What the hell?"

"Oh, he was just having fun. But he had me scared for a minute because I knew if I didn't catch him, I was gonna have to leave the country," he said, chuckling.

"Well, you're right about that. Is there anything else I should know?"

He was quiet for a second and then said, "I don't think so."

"Okay, well let me see my boy, I missed him."

We walked inside to his office, and I heard Braddy barking, but I didn't see him.

"Where is he?" I asked.

"Oh, I just let him have the run of the place. He's probably in the back hanging out with my customer."

"Are you kidding me? You let him run around your shop?"

"Oh yeah, he had a blast."

I walked around the corner, deeper into the garage and Braddy came running over to me and gave me his typical wheaten-greetin'. He was jumping all over me, bouncing up and down like a maniac.

"What the fuck happened to my white dog, Dad? He's black," I asked in disbelief.

"Well, he did help me wash the underbellies of some of the semis while I worked on 'em," he stated with his usual smirk.

"Are you kidding me? You let him run through oil?"

"Like I said, I let him do whatever he wanted."

"Oh my God, how am I going to get him clean?"

"Well, I wouldn't use that frou-frou soap. I'd try a little Dawn dish detergent. It's great for handling grease."

"Thanks for the soap commercial, Dad. Where's his food? Did you have any trouble getting him to eat?" I said after rolling my eyes.

"Oh, hell no. I just dumped it all out in a big tub, and he ate whenever he wanted."

I must have looked horrified, because Terry took a step back like he thought I might slug him and said, "He's a smart dog. He didn't pig out. When he was done he just walked away. I don't like it when dogs don't have all the food they want. I mean, it's not like they can go to the fridge when they get hungry."

"Well, I'm so glad I gave you all those instructions. They were obviously a big help."

We both laughed and I continued, "I'm thrilled you two had fun. Now I've gotta go home and wash him a thousand times."

In some ways that dog was Dad's kindred spirit—always up for a good time and not fond of rules or authority.

By the fall of that year, the company I was working for had attempted to go public but failed. The sales manager gave me a heads up and told me to get another job before they sold out to a large manufacturer.

I started work a few weeks later at a local ATM sales and service company based in Farmington Hills, Michigan. My new territory was much smaller, but I had a lot more accounts. Once again, this was a financial step up, and because I traveled mostly by car, they gave me a company vehicle.

I still had my Ford Festiva and my Jeep. I didn't need three vehicles, so I decided to sell my personal cars. One day Terry came for a visit and asked me what I was going to do with my cars. I told him I was going to sell them and that I already had a buyer for my SUV.

"What do you want for the Ford?" he asked.

"Well, it's in perfect shape and only has about 80,000 miles on it. Why? Do you need a car?"

"You're right about the shape. You babied that thing so much it looks brand new. I've got this kid that works at my shop that needs a car. I was thinking about buying it for him."

"Well, he must be a good kid if you want to help him out. I'll sell it for $500."

"Well, it's worth a lot more than that," he said looking surprised.

"If it helps you and he can get to work easier, I'm fine with that price."

I was feeling financially secure and wasn't really worried about the value of the car. I knew he wouldn't have taken it if I had just given it to him for free. So charging a small amount seemed like the best way to avoid hurting his feelings.

"I don't have the money with me today, can I give it to you later?"

"Sure, Dad. I'm not worried about it."

For the first time in our relationship, I seriously didn't care about his promise. I had plenty, and it made me happy to help someone else who really needed a vehicle. I remembered that terrible feeling like it was yesterday.

CHAPTER TWELVE

Hat Bar

Dad and I continued to work a lot, but having cellphones made it much easier to stay in touch. I always called him whenever I was close to his shop. I also made an effort to see his mother whenever I planned a business trip to northern Michigan. A couple of times I spent the night at the farm with Grandma Margot and took her to dinner for her birthday. Most of these trips were uneventful, but there was one time I will never forget.

In March of 2001, I had mentioned to Terry that I was going to Alpena for some business meetings with the local bankers and staying at Margot's house for a night. He told me that he had some business there too and asked if he could follow me. I thought that would be nice, so I asked if he could join me, Margot and her second husband for her birthday celebration. He didn't seem too thrilled but agreed to do it.

The morning we left, Terry was right on time, and we headed up the road on our four-hour journey. I always loved the drive north, as it reminded me of my childhood trips. Most people probably take I-75 as far north as possible before heading east toward Alpena, but not us. We always exited at US-23 and drove the two-lane road through all the small towns along Lake Huron. When I was a child, I memorized all the town names and announced them to Dad as we passed the time. I always knew that when we hit Oscoda, we didn't have far to go. And then when we drove through Harrisville, it was the last stop before Uncle Joe's house in Spruce. Dad would drive like a bat out of hell through the Black River Hills, and I would scream, "Faster Daddy! Faster!" If driven fast enough, you'd get that funny feeling in your tummy when hitting all the dips, and I loved it. When I saw the giant Paul Bunyan statue up on the hill, I knew we were really close to the farm in Ossineke.

We weren't far from our destination when Dad called from his truck in front of me and said,

"Hey honey, wanna grab some lunch?"

"Sure Dad, where do you wanna to stop?"

"Well, the ole Mountain Inn is just up on the right; they have some decent food."

I remembered the bar well because it was a frequent pit stop of Terry's and his trucker friends. I always called it "The Hat Bar." It was a small, roadside building with very few windows. Inside it was dark, with a small stage area in the corner for live music. Cork and Styrofoam brim hats were stapled everywhere on the walls and ceiling. The bar sold the hats to patrons, and they would write stuff on them like, "1982—Dick and Carol were here." Then the staff would staple them to whatever surface they could find.

That day, we were the only people there, so we pulled up a stool at the bar and ordered a couple of beers and some chili.

"Why do you like stopping here?" I asked.

"Well, honey it's the last bar ya can hit before Uncle Joe's house," he said in a serious tone.

"Did you used to stop here when I was a little kid? Did you drive a van with teardrop windows on the sides?" I asked while searching my memory bank.

"Oh, probably. Why?"

"I remember sleeping alone in the van in the parking lot."

"I can't believe you remember that," he said with a look of astonishment.

"Yeah, I guess stopping here triggered that memory; like a flash-back."

After lunch, Terry decided he would go directly to see his brother Joe and get settled in, while I went to his mother's farmhouse. He never called him "Joe," because his nickname, for as long as I can remember, was Par. When Joe was young he had a go-cart that he always drove as fast as he could. The most famous racecar driver at the time was Parnelli Jones, so his brothers called him Par. One of the properties Par owned had a farmhouse on it that he used as sort of a guesthouse, and everyone called it "The Price Farm." Dad loved the peacefulness and stayed there whenever he visited his family.

I drove north a few minutes on US-23 into Ossineke. I took a left onto the two-lane road with the old Wagon Wheel Bar on the corner. Seeing everything in its place made me feel that time passed slower there; it made me wonder if perhaps change wasn't inevitable.

As I reached the top of the hill, I could start to see the farm down on the right. There was a big red barn behind two small homes near the paved road. Everything looked exactly the same, including the Catholic Madonna statue in front of Margot's in-laws' house. I pulled into the circular drive that went behind the homes and in front of the barn. I parked in the back next to the gas pump and the chicken coop near the house on the left, where Margot lived with her hus-band. It was cold so I rushed into the mudroom and yelled, "I'm here Grandma!" Nobody ever knocked at her house, and the door was never locked. She greeted me with her bright lipstick smile and her twinkling Irish eyes, "Well, hello Dolly. Glad you made it." After big hugs and kisses, I dragged my suitcase to the guest room and settled in for some catching up.

Later we met Terry and had some dinner at a local restaurant. Dad was quiet and let me drive the conversation. I could tell he really didn't want to be there, but I just figured it was because he'd rather be hanging out with Par. After our meal, I took my grandparents back to the farm. Dad and I decided we would spend some time together at a bar in Alpena. He came by his mother's so I could follow him north. I didn't want to ride with him in case our dinner triggered him. And I wasn't in the mood to get into a fight about "handing over the keys."

I said goodbye to Margot and told her I wouldn't be out late because I had an early morning meeting with my client in town. She seemed annoyed that I was going out, but I ignored it and walked out the door.

I followed Dad north for about fifteen minutes where we reached a small bar on the west side of US-23. There were lots of cars in the parking lot, and inside it was full of people. It had a large U-shaped counter in the middle, and we found two open stools on the end. Sometimes when we drank together, I'd also smoke some of his cigarettes. I smoked for a few years when I lived in California, but I had quit before I moved back to Michigan, years earlier. But I could enjoy a few smokes now and again, and it wouldn't develop into a habit. Terry had smoked since he was about fourteen, maybe even before that. While we were waiting for our beer, I asked him why he was so quiet at dinner.

"I was just trying to be on my best behavior so I didn't embarrass you."

"Why would you embarrass me?"

"Because my mother's married to that no-good motherfucker. I wouldn't piss on him if his guts were on fire. But I was a good boy and bit my tongue."

"Okay. So what you're saying is he's your best friend," I said sarcastically.

"Ha! Let's just say, I sucked it up for you and Mother. Otherwise, I would never have had dinner with that fat fuck."

"I get it, Dad. I wasn't aware of how you felt. I will never ask you to do that again. Life is way too short for that shit. I don't believe in doing things out of obligation. It's just not a healthy thing."

"Well, you are much wiser than me. I let that Catholic guilt bullshit get to me sometimes."

"Well, old dogs can learn new tricks, Dad. If you don't want to do it, just don't."

We sat quiet for a minute and I waited to see what he would say. What I heard next would make me see my father in a totally different light. I never in a million years expected him to get so serious.

After a few minutes of sipping our beer and dragging on our cigarettes, he looked at me and said, "Ya know, I feel really bad that I wasn't the father I should have been. I did a lot of things wrong, and you really deserved better."

I was taken aback by what I had just heard, but I didn't let him know that. I responded quickly, "Well, ya know what Dad? You don't need to carry that bullshit around with you anymore. You can just let that go. Because if you weren't who you are, than I wouldn't be who I am today, and I have worked hard to become the person I am. I'm proud of who I am. I don't think about any of that shit anymore. So you don't need to either."

His arms rested on the bar, hands wrapped around his beer bottle, he lowered his head and started to cry.

A few seconds later, without lifting up his head he responded through his tears.

"Really?"

"Yeah, Dad. It's over. It will never be like that again."

"What did I do to deserve such a great kid?"

"Nothing. Now please light me another cigarette," I joked, breaking the tension.

As we laughed, he wiped his eyes and gave me a tight hug. While he was holding on to me for dear life, he said, "You are just the greatest person I have ever met."

I had come to the conclusion in my twenties that my parents' decisions and behavior had nothing to do with me and everything to do with their own issues. I refused to take their parental failures personally. It was a night I would never forget because Terry wasn't known for apologizing; that was an enormous admission. It did make me happy that he was acting more like the person I knew when I was a little girl, the one that believed in me, and told me I should never take a backseat to anyone. As our friendship progressed, I would see glimpses of the man I knew he wanted to be. And when I did, I always made a point of telling him that I was proud of him. Sometimes I felt like I was the parent, and he was the child. But it didn't matter to me, because I was beyond needing parenting and was very grateful for his friendship.

That night when I returned to the farm, I walked into the family room where Margot and her husband were sitting in their recliners watching the ten o'clock news. I said, "Hi Grandma, I'm back." She stared straight ahead and didn't say a word. It felt so cold and strange; I was confused. I went straight to my room and went to bed. The next morning I loaded up my car and returned to find Margot in the kitchen making breakfast.

"Well, did you have fun with your dad last night?"

"I did. We had a nice chat."

She pursed her lips together and continued frying the eggs in bacon grease.

"Well, breakfast is almost ready."

"No Grandma, I'm sorry but unfortunately I don't have time. Remember I told you I had to be on the road by 7:30 for my meeting?"

"Well, the bank president won't mind if you're late. You just tell him you were here with me. He knows who I am—I've been banking there for years."

"I'm sure you're right about that, but I hate being late, so I've gotta go. Thanks so much for letting me stay here, I really appreciate it. I hope you enjoyed your birthday dinner."

She looked very disappointed and a bit perturbed, but I didn't care. There was no way I was risking being late after how uncomfortable she made me feel the night before. I was ready to get out of there. I never knew which grandma I was going to get. The warm "Hello Dolly" grandma, or the one that wouldn't say "I love you" back to me. That day, as I stood in her mudroom by the back door, I gave her a hug and told her I loved her. She sent me off with, "Goodbye dear. Take care."

I called Dad and described his mother's bizarre behavior. He wasn't very happy with someone treating me that way, and he snapped, "She's a bitch. The only crime you committed was spending time with me at the bar. Christ, it's not like you came back drunk. Just blow her off."

After that visit, I got a glimpse into their relationship, and I learned I didn't enjoy being in the middle. Terry had never made any derogatory comments to me about Margot before, so I was a little surprised. He didn't offer more information, and I didn't ask. That was the last time I suggested a dinner with the two of them.

CHAPTER THIRTEEN

Eastern Market

L ife seemed like it was moving at a faster pace in the early
2000s. Technology was changing and affecting just about
everything. For people who struggled to adapt, it was easy to
become overwhelmed with basic things like using a credit card at the
gas pump, or buying an airline ticket online.

I remember Terry asked me what Craigslist was. I told him how
it was first started and explained that they occasionally had some
problems and that it could be used for nefarious deeds.

"Like what?" Dad curiously asked.

"Oh you know, like hookers and drugs."

After a brief pause, he responded, "Well, maybe I should get a
computer."

At fifty-three years old, Dad was starting to slow down, and I
could see he didn't have the ambition he once had. He wasn't interested in learning how to fix the new, fancier, high-tech big rigs. With
just about everything being built with a computer in it, he knew his
"old-school" ways were numbered.

Sometime in 2001, Dad said that his shop building was going to
be torn down because Walmart wanted the land. He had to make a
decision to move his business or just close the doors. He was physically and emotionally tired of the hassles of running the business,
and it was difficult to get good help because young people didn't want

to learn the trades anymore. And sometimes his clients would take advantage of him by not paying his invoices on time. Having been a trucker, he would sympathize with them because he understood that if their truck was broken down, they weren't making any money. But when they took several months to pay, or in some cases never paid him at all, it brought his operation to a screeching halt.

One night at a bar in Taylor, he met a guy that sold freight trailers for a living. He sparked up a conversation with him and asked him if he had any decent old trailers for sale. The guy mentioned he had a forty-four-foot box with no title he could sell him. Terry bought the old Fruehauf double-axle freight trailer and loaded it up with all his tools and equipment. He closed his shop and dragged the trailer down to Ohio and parked it on Michelle's parents' property near her single-wide trailer.

Dad's youngest brother Ty, was an executive in the food service industry; he knew a lot of people in supply chain businesses. He introduced Terry to a guy who needed a mechanic at his produce packing plant in the Eastern Market in Detroit. Dad didn't know much about the packing business, but his brother was confident he'd figure it out.

It seemed tomatoes were his future—he was hired. He worked all the time and started sleeping at the plant on a cot in the office area. It took him less than a week to figure out how all the equipment functioned. Every time something would break, he would fix it and speak to the owner about how he could reengineer it so it would operate more efficiently. He quickly learned all about conveyor belts, tomato loss, production volumes, and distribution schedules. He really acted more as an efficiency manager than a mechanic. He lacked patience for people who couldn't see ways to do things better. He hated people who were "book smart" but couldn't find their ass with both hands. He just chalked it up to laziness and stupidity. He'd tell me stories about how the line workers would piss him off when he had to stop his important work to fish their pagers out of clogged toilets. Toilet repairs were not his favorite; it was a surefire way to land on his shit-list.

The only time he left the plant was to eat some dinner and have a few beers in the evenings. He was never a big eater, and his whole life he usually only ate one meal a day. When he was really busy, he'd live on coffee, cigarettes, and beer. Sometimes I would drive to the Eastern Market and meet him for dinner when I was passing through Detroit for work. The first time I told him I wanted to come by, he gave me very specific directions to get there.

"Honey, I want you to use my directions. Don't use that MapQuest shit."

"You got it, Daddy."

"When you're on St. Aubin, don't bother stopping at any of the stop signs. Just blow right through 'em."

"What? Why?"

"Cuz there's a bunch of crack houses and dumbasses hanging around there. Don't even stop for the cops."

"Jesus, Dad. This place sounds terrible."

"You'll be fine once you get inside the parking lot on Wilkins Street."

I knew better than to question his directions, so I followed them to a T. He was right about the drug scene. I gladly blew the stop sign, hung a left on Wilkins and found the plant on the right side. It was surrounded by chain-link fencing and barbed wire coiled across the top. The entrance was marked by a large metal gate that I pulled up to. In the middle of the parking lot there was a small guard shack, and as soon as I stopped, a thin, black woman in a security uniform ran over to the gate and hastily opened it up.

I rolled down my window and said, "Hi there. I'm here to see Terry."

"I know girl. Hurry up an' git in here," she said as she pointed to the parking lot.

"Hi Honey Babe. Did you have any trouble with my directions?" he said, greeting me at my car.

"Nope. Your directions are always the best. Thanks for the heads up about the crack dealers hanging around. I was gettin' low on my stash."

As Dad chuckled at my smartass comment, he put his arm around my neck and walked me into the plant for a tour. Being with him on his turf and learning about all the ins and outs of his new adventure, reminded me of how much I loved going to the gravel pits as a teenager. He walked around like he was the owner, showing me the sorting room and how much work he had done to get the conveyor belts working properly. I noticed that it was a large building and all that walking was wearing on him. He looked tired and hobbled with a slight limp; he never wanted to talk about his health. He believed avoiding doctors was the key to staying healthy.

After the tour, we jumped into Terry's pickup truck to go grab some beer and dinner. He told me to ride with him and leave my car at the plant, where it would be safe. He drove us to a bar that he frequented a couple of blocks away, where he enjoyed the Polish barmaid's off-colored jokes. The Eastern Market was diverse, and people were proud of their heritage. The Italians and Polish owned many of the businesses there, and it wasn't offensive to them when people described them by their ethnicity. The bar was a small, local joint that had a counter with stools and a few tables. He assured me that even though it wasn't fancy, the food was decent. I could tell he was a frequent guest, because the lady at the bar brought over a can of Busch beer as soon as we sat down at one of the tables. He introduced me to the barmaid, and she told us some risqué jokes. He laughed so hard he had to take off his glasses and wipe his eyes. She was a character and definitely not politically correct, so I understood his attraction to the establishment.

I noticed a sign at the front door that read, **WEDNESDAY NIGHT IS LINGERIE NIGHT! LIVE MODELS!** I was grateful it was Thursday night. I had my back to the door, but I could tell the bar was getting busier as the tables around us became full. Dad scoped out the room and gave me the lowdown on the people that walked in. He could gossip better than any little old lady I'd ever met. We were enjoying our beers, getting caught up and waiting for our food, when a guy walked up to our table. I remember my dad saying hello to him, but I don't remember his name. He asked who I was, and I reached my hand out to shake his, and said, "Hi. I'm Terrina, Terry's daughter."

I noticed he held one arm behind his back, which struck me as odd. "Well, you don't need to hang out with your ole man when you can come join me at the bar," he proclaimed as he shook my hand with a creepy stare.

I yanked my hand away, and I looked at Dad as he took a long drag on his cigarette with a smirk on his face.

"Well, thanks for the offer, but I don't get to spend that much time with my dad, so I'll pass."

Out of the corner of my eye, I saw Dad put his cigarette down in the ashtray and lean back in his seat. He placed his hands on his knees; steadying himself to stand up quickly. I knew this was not going to end well if I didn't get rid of this loser.

Unfortunately, the man persisted and said, "You're too pretty to waste your night with this asshole. Come on, let me buy you a drink."

"No thanks. I can buy my own drink," I raised my voice and snapped.

Then from behind his back he pulled out a tacky red lacy piece of lingerie on a small plastic hanger. He held it up and said, "How 'bout you take this into the bathroom and try it on for me?"

I looked at Dad. He had a big smile on his face but not the kind of smile like he thought it was funny. He knew that I had reached my limit with the bullshit. I leaned back in my chair, crossed my legs, and grabbed my beer. I pointed at Terry with the beer bottle and said, "You've got a better chance of gettin' him to put that on, than me. Listen, you're obviously a slow learner so let me save ya some time. Get the fuck away from me with that nasty, piece of shit. I'm not your type. Got it?"

The guy looked at Dad and said, "Well, I guess the apple doesn't fall too far from the tree, eh?"

Before Terry could respond, I said, "And the next time you call my dad an asshole, you better hope I'm here to save you."

He finally got the hint and turned and walked out of the bar.

"I was ready to jump in if I needed to, but I was pretty confident you'd run that fucker off," Dad said proudly with a chuckle.

"I thought I was being pretty nice."

We both started laughing and he said, "You're way outta that cock-sucker's league, honey. He had no idea who he was messin' with."

"Well Dad, one of things you taught me a long time ago is to make sure ya always speak their language. If I need to talk at their level for them to get it, then that's what I'll do."

"Yeah, Honey Babe, unfortunately assholes are always gonna un-derestimate ya. Never compromise your principles, you don't need to take anyone's shit. You're a Troy."

"Who was that guy anyway?"

"Oh, just a local undercover cop. That cocksucker's about as crooked as they come."

After we finished our meals, Terry called the barmaid over to the table and asked her to make another meal to go. I didn't ask him why he needed it, but I knew it wasn't for him. A few minutes later, he grabbed the take-out bag, dropped some cash on the table and we headed to the parking lot. He walked around his truck and looked at all the tires before he opened the passenger's door for me.

"Dad, whatcha looking for?"

"Oh nothin'. I'm just making sure that prick didn't puncture my tires after our little chat."

"Seriously? People do that shit?"

"Oh honey, you'd be surprised at what I see down here in the ghetto. It's not your little Birmingham-bubble, baby."

While headed back to the plant I realized he was comfortable there. It took a special kind of skillset to navigate the rules of the streets. I felt grateful that I could straddle our very different worlds, and I learned a lot about staying alert and reading people. As we entered the plant, the guard greeted us at the gate. Dad handed her the takeout meal he'd purchased at the bar, and then drove up next to my car.

As we were saying goodbye, I said, "That was nice of you to buy her dinner, Dad."

"Well, she's a nice lady and a single mother. She has a couple of kids by some dickhead that didn't stick around. I make sure she gets a good meal every night, and she's sweet enough to keep an eye out for me."

I met my father several more times in the Eastern Market. Usually it was just the two of us, but occasionally he'd invite one of his friends to join us. We had several great meals at the famous Italian restaurant on Riopelle Street, called Roma Café. It had been in business well over a hundred years. He told me stories about how Jimmy Hoffa used to eat there, and mob members still pulled up in their limos with their fancy-dressed girls on their arms. It's the kind of place where you could smell the garlic out in the parking lot. I loved how original it was with the dark, carved wood bar, red vinyl tablecloths, and tin ceiling tiles.

One of Dad's friends was a guy named Eddie. He was a heavy-set, rough-looking character with shoulder-length hair, a full beard, and lots of big moles all over his face. He reminded me of Jerry Garcia from the Grateful Dead, only much more tough-looking. I'm sure most people found him intimidating, but I knew he was a pleasant guy with a big heart. Dad had gotten him a job as a truck driver at the tomato plant. Whenever Eddie was in town dropping off his final tomato load for the night, he'd join Terry for some drinks and dinner. Several times I met up with both of them and enjoyed some fun evenings hanging out at Roma's. Eddie was a loyal friend to Dad and, because I was family, that loyalty was extended to me as well. He used to say, "Sweetie, if anyone ever fucks with you, you just let Ole Uncle Eddie know, and I'll kill 'em." Terry and I would just laugh and thank him, but we also knew he was serious.

I was dating a guy named John, who was much older than me. In fact, he was two years older than Terry. I told Dad about him, and he said, "Why don't you invite him to join us for dinner? Eddie will be in town, too. The four of us can go to Roma's."

"Well, that sounds like fun, Dad, but I'm not sure if John will be comfortable going down to Detroit. I'll ask him."

John was not from the same scene as my father. He was educated, white collar, and raised in country clubs. Oddly, he was also fascinated with Terry's world, so he agreed to dinner.

I drove us to the Eastern Market and told John what to expect. I went on and on, about how sweet Eddie was and also warned John that Dad would probably bust his balls a little bit, but I assured him he'd survive. John's eyes became very alert when we drove through the streets of boarded-up buildings. As I was laughing and blowing through the stop signs, John said, "Who are you?"

I remember getting to the parking lot, having the sweet guard wave us in, and introducing John to Terry. While we waited for Eddie to show up, Dad gave John the plant tour, and they were hitting it off great. Afterward, we were standing in the fenced-in parking lot when we saw a large semi-truck come around the corner from St. Aubin Street. There was a car on Wilkins Street that had pulled too far through the stop sign and slightly into the intersection. It was preventing the truck from making a wide turn with his long trailer, which narrowly avoided smacking the car's front bumper. We heard the trucker slam on his brakes, then he opened his truck door, leaned halfway out, and with the deepest, scariest voice I'd ever heard, screamed, "Back the fuck up, you stupid motherfucker. Now! Before I kill you!" The sound of his voice was reverberating off the industrial buildings. I guess the guy in the car got the message because he quickly backed up, and then the truck pulled into the tomato plant parking lot. I looked at John and said, "Well, Eddie's here." As John's eyes became the size of saucers, he replied, "That's sweet Eddie?" Dad burst out laughing and said, "Yep, he's a real teddy bear."

We had a great time at dinner that night with Eddie and Terry. The food was amazing, and their stories were always entertaining. When I said goodbye to Dad that night I remember telling him that I didn't care what people thought about me dating someone a lot older. We talked about it for a few minutes, and he said, "Honey, you can't date anyone your age. They could never handle you. You intimidate ninety-nine percent of the men you meet. If John treats you well, fuck what anyone else thinks!"

"I know Dad, Fuck 'em all but six."

I was happy that he genuinely liked John. Knowing he was older, as a joke John called him "Pops," and in kind, Dad referred to John as, "Sonny boy."

Unfortunately, not all of my memories of the Eastern Market are good ones. I'll never forget the night Dad called late from a bar. He was angrier than I'd ever heard him. He'd driven his truck to the bar after work. It was a red 1999 Chevy with a cap on the back. Under the bed cap he had a box of paperwork with his taxes, bills, and other important documents. His tools, clothes, cash, and gun were stowed behind the front seat. He had parked in front and when he finished, he walked outside to find his truck was gone.

"Oh no. Do you want me to come pick you up? I'll be right there."

"No. I'm at the bar waiting for a friend to come get me and he's bringing me a gun. And when I find that fuckin' nigger, I'm gonna kill him!"

"Dad. Stop. Please don't do that. And how do you know who stole your truck?"

"Because I called my phone and that no-good motherfucker had the balls to answer it," he growled.

"What? Oh my God. What did he say?"

"You ain't ever gettin' your truck back, cracker."

"Oh shit. I'm so sorry Dad. Did you call the police?"

"They don't give a fuck about a white guy losing his truck. Half these asshole cops are in on this shit. They don't even bother looking."

"Please Daddy, let me come get you. This scumbag is not worth going to prison over."

"I've gotta go, my ride is here," he said, slamming the phone down.

About a week later Dad called and said he'd been busy finding another vehicle, a cellphone, and getting back to work. He never told me which friend picked him up, but I assumed it was Eddie. He said that they had driven around all night in the worst parts of Detroit, looking for chop-shops, or any sign of his truck. He never found it, and thankfully, he didn't find the criminal that had stolen it either.

I felt terrible knowing he'd lost everything that night, including several thousand dollars in cash. He still wasn't a fan of financial institutions, and he always cashed his checks and kept the money in a bank envelope, either in his coat pocket or in his truck. I worried he'd get robbed, or murdered; too many people knew he paid for everything with cash.

This type of situation led to perhaps one of the greatest lessons I ever learned from Dad. It's critical to decipher the difference between someone's words and someone's actions. Too many people take words at face value, especially when they are hearing what they want to hear. People's *behavior* was a much truer indicator of who they really are. The story of the stolen vehicle, and Terry's abhorrent language, was an example of how I learned to discern situations carefully.

I never heard him speak like that when I was a child, but when I was an adult, he spent more time working in the inner cities. Many occasions my father was called a "cracker," a derogatory racial slur used toward white people. I observed many times when he was discriminated against for being blue collar or daring to work in the slums. It seemed the streets were saying "his kind" was unwelcome and deserved to be preyed upon. I never liked hearing "street" language, but it seemed there are places and people that communicate in ways that *require* English to be twisted.

This is probably a good time to share something from Dad's past that might complicate your opinion of Terry.

In the 1960s, my parents were teenagers living in Howell, Michigan. The town was all white, with the exception of one black family. Howell's reputation for being home to the Ku Klux Klan was because of an infamous resident named Robert Miles. He was a Grand Dragon of the Michigan Ku Klux Klan and founder of a white supremacist church. In 1963, my mother was sixteen years old when she became pregnant by a man related to the local black family. She instantly became a pariah when she gave birth to my older brother in March of 1964.

The amount of racial tension during this time was high throughout America, and especially in nearby Detroit. In 1966, when Terry had just turned eighteen years old, he married my mother and adopted Tony. In 1968, my mother was three months pregnant with me when Martin Luther King Jr. was murdered, and riots broke out in Detroit. Many people disapproved of my father's marriage and his adopting Tony. Some were just bigots, while others feared for our family's safety. But Terry didn't care what anyone else wanted him to do, and he didn't live in fear; he only needed six.

I don't think my parents set out to change the way people thought about race in our small town. Actually, I never heard them discuss race. I didn't even realize my older brother was different until I was ten years old when he told me his father was black. Over the years,

Terry's bold actions taught me that he wasn't a racist, but I still didn't condone his language.

The next time I went to the Eastern Market it was St. Patrick's Day. Dad was 100 percent Irish, so I knew he'd enjoy me joining him for a few drinks after work. He asked me to hop in his old beat-up van that he bought to replace his stolen truck. He drove us to the Polish side of town, where we ended up at some dive bar that only the locals knew about. His barmaid friend told him it was her cousin's place, so he wanted to check it out. It was freezing outside and super dark. We rushed down the block, where we entered through a dilapidated old door that led into a basement. I'd seen some seedy places, but this was a little sketchy, even by Terry's standards. After we downed a few beers, smoked some cigarettes and had some good laughs, he suggested we give his aunt a call. Aunt Bun was his mother's older sister, Bernadine. She was about three years older than Margot and lived in South Bend, Indiana.

"We probably should have done that earlier, Dad. It's almost midnight now."

"Nah, she's up having a nip, too. I call her late at night all the time," he said with confidence.

We walked back toward the bathrooms where he used the payphone to dial her number. She picked up the call right away, and after a few minutes of small talk, Dad handed the phone to me and said, "Say hello to Aunt Bun."

"Hi Aunt Bun! Happy St. Paddy's Day! How are you?"

"Hello dear, it's just so nice of you to call me. Are you enjoying your evening with your dad?" she asked in a proper kind of tone.

"Oh, we're solving all the world's problems and having a great night. I was a little worried about calling you so late, so I hope we didn't wake you."

"Oh no dear, I'm just so happy to hear your voice, and I always love hearing from your dad."

After our call was over, we went back to our table and Terry seemed a little melancholy, so I sat there quietly. He took a drag on his cigarette and said, "Aunt Bun's gettin' up there in age now. She'll be eighty-one next month, on the fourteenth. She's a great lady. I try to call her a lot. I feel closer to her than my own mother."

"Well, I'm glad we called her. She sure was warm and friendly."

"Yeah, I know she loved talking to you; family is really important to her. It's too bad you haven't seen her since you were a kid. We'll have to change that."

Later that summer, Dad called me and said he was in Ohio. I asked, "Are you spending some time with Michelle?"

"Yeah, I had a little problem at work, so I'm down here trying to figure out my next move."

"What happened?"

I remember him saying something about pulling an all-nighter at the plant and then oversleeping the next morning. The exact explanation was fuzzy, but the net result was that the plant owner fired him. I was surprised because I knew how hard he had worked there. But I also knew Terry had trouble working for other people.

"We weren't makin' cookies, honey. He's a fuckin' crook. And you know what else? I always give myself away too cheap. Never let someone undervalue you like I have. We can run circles around most of these assholes we work for."

"I'm sorry you got fired, Dad. Giving too much to them and then becoming resentful when these dicks take advantage of you isn't healthy. Maybe now you can do something where you can work for a better person."

I had met the owner of the plant a couple of times. He reminded me of the used car salesman that had screwed me over when I bought my Ford. Terry had mentioned that he thought the owner was playing around with the books. Dad had seen some things in the office and overheard some conversations that led him to believe the real business was underground. I thought Dad was just bitter about being fired, but years later Terry called me and told me the plant owner was in legal trouble.

"Honey, nothing good ever comes from ill-gotten gains, and that cocksucker finally got what he deserved. He lost it all."

"Well Dad, if that's true, Karma's a bitch."

"Yep. Liars figure, and figures lie. He was busted for laundering money."

"Ya don't say. I guess you got the last laugh, Dad."

"Honey, never forget the best revenge is to live a good life. People like that are just miserable assholes, and they can't stand to see other people happy."

After my father was fired, Eddie quit working there, too. Even though that was the best-paying job Eddie ever had, his loyalty to Terry mattered more. He was a Vietnam War veteran, and like many from that war, he was suffering the effects of Agent Orange poisoning. That Christmas, I sent Eddie some money and a letter thanking him for his service in the military. Dad told me Eddie was so touched that I would think of him, he got choked up. I was so glad that I'd taken the time to acknowledge him when I did, because a few years later at age sixty-one, Eddie passed away from multiple cancers. He never complained, and most people didn't even know he was sick. It saddened me that so many of our soldiers came back, and had, in some cases, even longer and harder battles to fight. With a low, sad tone Dad said, "It sucks, Honey Babe. I've lost a lot of good friends, but only the good die young."

I will always remember how safe I felt knowing Eddie was in the world. He would've done anything for my father and me. The world could use more loyal friends and characters like Eddie.

CHAPTER FOURTEEN

Big Changes

D ad and I didn't see each other much after he moved to Ohio, but we did talk on the phone several times a week. He managed to get his driver's license reinstated after at least a decade without it. Uncle Joe helped him get back on his feet by giving him a blue Peterbilt semi-truck and a trailer. Terry's girlfriend Michelle had become a truck driver earlier that year and worked as an employee for a trucking company in Ohio. She helped introduce Terry to her bosses, and they eventually hired him as a contractor to haul logs and other timber products.

My career was as busy as ever; I was working constantly. My employer decided to discontinue their company car program and offered a car allowance instead. I had been hearing rumors about this for a couple of years, so I planned on getting my own vehicle. I'd been saving my money so I could get a car I really wanted. John had been encouraging me to test drive all kinds of luxury cars. When I drove a 2001 BMW 530i, I fell in love; it was super smooth and full of kick. But I wasn't sure if I should spend that much on a car, so I asked Terry what he thought.

"Honey, you've worked your ass off your whole life, and you deserve to get whatever you want. If you can afford a BMW, go for it. Just walk in there and tell those pricks exactly what you want and don't settle for anything less."

"Thanks, Dad. I really appreciate the encouragement. I know I'll get judged, and some people will be jealous, but I can't worry about that. That's their problem."

"Fuck those jealous assholes. If they'd get off their lazy asses they could have what you have, too. And as far as spending the money, you can't take it with you baby girl, so get the car you want. Don't give it a second thought. You deserve it."

On my thirty-third birthday, I walked into the BMW dealership and ordered the exact car I wanted and wrote them a check for the full amount. I am not sharing this story to be a braggart. My point is that at a time when my father had far less than I did, he was one of the few people in my life that didn't act jealous or petty about my accomplishment. I felt proud of Dad for supporting me; sometimes it felt like he was living vicariously through me. It made him happy to see me loosen up a little bit and enjoy my success.

A couple months later on Christmas Eve, John asked me to marry him, and I said, "Yes." After some hard conversations, we agreed we wanted a fresh start. We decided Arizona or bust.

On March 6, 2002, Dad called to report that Aunt Bun had passed away. A few days later, John and I drove down to South Bend, Indiana, to attend her funeral. She had been a prominent person within the University of Notre Dame community. Her husband was the dean of business for many years there before he passed in 1994. Due to her commitment to the school and the Catholic Church, her funeral was held at the beautiful Basilica of the Sacred Heart. Terry was one of the pallbearers. I remember Dad looked so handsome wearing a black suit and white gloves while carrying her casket. But I'd never seen him look so sad and serious before; it broke my heart watching him carry out his duties.

I'd also never seen that many Irish family members and friends in one place either. I noticed that everyone was friendly, calm, and quiet, but I didn't see anyone crying, not even my Grandma Margot, who considered Bernadine her best friend. I guess the Irish are tough and stoic, definitely proud. While we were outside waiting to toss roses on Aunt Bun's casket, Dad wrapped his arm around my neck, pulled me close to him, and said with a tone of disbelief, "What a great lady. I sure will miss her." Even though he was holding back his pain, I knew he needed me, and being there meant a lot to him.

A few months later Dad and Michelle offered to help us move to Arizona. On the morning of June 8 we all met at my house. I told Michelle ahead of time that I wanted her to drive the truck, and only her name would be on the rental agreement. We both knew why that was best.

We had hired movers to pack the moving truck the night before, so we started our caravan west that morning. John drove his gold Chrysler 300 and was the lead car. I followed him in my car with Braddy riding in the back. Michelle was behind me in the moving truck, and Terry drove his small pickup truck and followed the Penske. He insisted on driving his own vehicle because he hated flying, and he wanted to go camping and enjoy a little vacation on their return trip back to Ohio. We all had walkie-talkies so we could communicate along the way. We put in a really long day and only stopped a few times. The first night we pulled into a motel not too far off the highway, somewhere in southern Illinois.

"Hey Dad, while I'm getting us a couple of rooms, do you want to go get us some take-out from that Mexican restaurant we just passed?" I asked while jumping out of the car to stretch.

"Where? What place?" he said with confusion.

Before I could answer him, Michelle spoke up and said, "I'll go. I know where to go."

I went inside to rent the rooms while John walked Braddy around the parking lot. When they returned with the food, Michelle waved me over to her.

"Where's Dad?"

"Terrina, he's drunk. He didn't understand what restaurant you were talking about because he's been drinking the entire way here."

"Who does that?" I asked rhetorically.

Usually when John was around, Terry would be on his best behavior. He would drink, but he didn't get drunk. I handed Michelle some cash and said, "Well, thanks for getting dinner. Here's your room key. Let's just meet up in the morning. He can sleep it off."

The next day everybody was up and ready to go, including Dad. Our plan was to make it to Albuquerque, New Mexico, and then complete the trip the following day. It was a very long day of driving, but we were right on schedule. Terry had been drinking, but he wasn't drunk this time.

The following afternoon we made our way to Scottsdale and arrived at our new home around three o'clock. I was so relieved that we had actually made it there, I fell into John's arms and cried like a baby. It had been a long time since I had relied on Dad, and we didn't have a good history when came to moving. I'd never been more grateful for Michelle in my life.

Terry loved our new home and spent most of his time sitting on the patio watching the golfers and smoking cigarettes. He commented several times that "John and I were living in a dream world." I remember him saying that he was happy for us, but he was sad that we would be so far apart now. I had spent most of my life away from him, so it didn't seem that different to me. He and Michelle stayed for a few days and then headed off to their first stop at the Grand Canyon.

On June 22, John and I got married in the living room of our new home, with our realtors as our witnesses. It was small, quick and intimate. We joined the country club that was affiliated with our neighborhood and spent the next three months playing golf and telling people we were still on our honeymoon. We didn't know what we were going to do for work, but we decided we'd worry about that in the fall.

In August, I spoke with Terry and said, "Dad, all of my old clients keep calling me and asking for advice about all the new ATM regulations. I keep telling them I'm on my honeymoon and I'm not working right now."

"Well, Honey that sounds like an opportunity to me. Why don't you just work for yourself and help 'em out?"

"I can't do that, can I? I've never had my own business before."

"Well of course you can run your own company, honey. If those dumbshits you worked for in Michigan can figure it out, you sure as hell can."

With the encouragement of John and Terry, I started researching how to piece together a business plan. Twelve months later, I had sold over a million dollars in ATM equipment, working from my desk squeezed into my walk-in closet. Dad used to say, "Service is dead. If you can offer great service, you'll have loyal customers and more business than you'll know what to do with."

In July of 2003, I got a call from an old credit union client. The CFO told me that she was desperate for some help. She had called her two ATM service providers and they basically told her they weren't in the business of buying ATMs; they only sold and serviced them. I listened to her issue, and I was up for the challenge. In a nutshell, the credit union had ATMs spread all over the Midwest and needed all of them removed within a few weeks. It was a huge coordination nightmare with cash removal, a tight timeframe, and no budget to spend on it. I told the CFO that I would mull it over and get back to her in a couple of days. I called Terry and told him that I thought I had most of the details worked out. I had brokered a deal with a manufacturer to purchase the ATMs for their refurbishment program. I had created a route for my two rigger contacts, but I still needed to find one more person to go pick up all of the Chicago-area ATMs. Dad immediately offered to be the third rigger. Because I didn't have any other ideas, I agreed to hire him and hoped for the best. He didn't know anything about moving ATMs, but I knew he could figure it out.

I jumped on a plane to Michigan, explained the plan to the credit union, and had them sign a contract. I agreed to uninstall all seventy-five ATMs within a five-day period, drop them off at a freight hauler, get them delivered to the manufacturer, and send the credit union a check—after taking my cut, of course. I was going to do all the work for them, meet their deadline, and pay them. They were thrilled. But I was scared to death.

When the project began, I was working from my Arizona home office. I checked the traffic and booked hotels for Dad and Michelle as they made their way around the route. After the first couple of ATMs, Terry had worked out the kinks and started making better time. He was using a pallet jack, but some of these machines weighed sixteen hundred pounds and were difficult to handle. I was grateful Michelle could help him with the driving. I was relieved when he checked in with me each night and reported he'd made that day's pickup. He maintained the schedule pretty well, only falling behind a couple of times when the traffic in Chicago didn't cooperate.

The last machine he needed to pick up was located in the Water Tower building on Michigan Avenue. It wasn't the easiest place to park a large Penske truck, but I knew if anyone could do it, it was Dad. He found a space to park and was told he needed to use the freight elevator because the ATM was on the top floor. Terry waited for his turn to use the service elevator, but every time he tried to move the ATM onto it, they would yell at him, "No. Not you, cracker."

After about four hours of watching others use the elevator, Terry said, "What's it gonna fuckin' take for you cocksuckers to let me get this loaded?" One of the workers said, "Figure it out, asshole." Dad reached into his pocket, grabbed a hundred dollar bill, and tossed it at one of the men. About five o'clock that afternoon he called and explained what had happened.

"I'm sorry I'm late, honey. If I wasn't doing this job for you, I would have killed those lazy motherfuckers. But I wasn't going to jeopardize your deal. They were pitchin' and I was catchin'." If he had been working for himself, there's no doubt that day would have turned out differently. Perhaps, he would have revisited his old friends at the Cook County Jail—not for a social visit.

After Terry was home for a few days, the manufacturer called me and said that they never received four of the ATMs from the Chicagoland freight company.

"Dad, please tell me you have proof that you dropped off all the machines?" I asked, calling in a panic.

"Hell yeah I do. I have the bill of lading right here in front of me. I was just getting ready to mail it to you."

I thanked him profusely and couldn't have been more proud of the job he did. He was always great at paperwork. I look back on that time now and am so grateful that I pushed through my fear and tackled a project that nobody else was willing to do. Not only was it lucrative, but it was a rare moment where both mine and my father's skillsets worked in harmony to accomplish something neither one of us had ever done before. I also think it was a boost to Dad's self-esteem that he had made more money in one week, doing something new, than he had made in a long time.

CHAPTER FIFTEEN

Black River Hills

L iving in Scottsdale, Arizona, there was never a shortage of visitors, especially in the winter. Our guest room felt like it had a revolving door for a long time. In October of 2003, even Gram came for a long weekend. She wasn't fond of not sleeping in her own bed, unless it was at the Imperial Palace in Las Vegas.

November 24, Terry and Michelle arrived for Thanksgiving. We arranged for their tickets and a car service so I could avoid an airport scene. I was pleasantly surprised that Dad was in pretty good shape when he arrived. I could tell he had been drinking, but he wasn't falling-down drunk. After he and Michelle got settled in the guest room, Terry took to the sofa and asked me if I had any chocolate bars. I thought it was an odd request because he never really had much of a sweet tooth. I offered to run up to the store and get him whatever he wanted. He specifically asked for some Hershey chocolate bars and some pop.

When he woke up from his nap, he consumed most of the chocolate and quickly started on the can of soda. He devoured more chocolate and lots of desserts that weekend. I was confused by this behavior, but by the end of the visit I realized he was craving sugar because he wasn't drinking as much alcohol as he normally did. Over the years, "the chocolate request" became a tell-tale sign of where he was in his binge-drinking episodes.

We had a really nice visit with both Dad and Michelle. We took them out to eat, which I knew was a treat for them. I arranged a pedicure for Michelle and even talked Terry into letting me take him shopping for a new wardrobe. I loved buying him clothes because it made him feel good, and everything always looked great on his twenty-nine-inch waist. Throughout the trip my father would frequently say, "This place is nothin' short of Hollywood, Honey Babe, and we can't thank you and John enough for treating us like royalty."

We wanted to start a tradition of having Terry and Michelle out for Thanksgiving each year, but the following year my cousin's wedding was in Alpena, Michigan. Uncle Joe's youngest son, Brian, was getting married on November 23. Dad was especially close with Brian, and whenever he went to Alpena, he primarily spent time with Par and Brian. I hadn't seen my cousin in years, but I really wanted to support Dad and reconnect with his family.

Uncle Joe and his wife Kathy had three children. But tragically, on July 15, 2000, they lost their middle child and only daughter, Tracy, in a freak accident. She was only twenty-five years old. Dad used to say, "There aren't enough years left for Par to get over the loss of Tracy," and he would follow it up with, "If something happened to you Honey Babe, it would be over for me. I'd just blow my head off."

Perhaps the horrific loss of Tracy made Brian's wedding even more important. It gave the family something positive to think about and a fun excuse to all come together.

John and I flew into Detroit and rented a car. I was excited to travel all the familiar roads I used to take with Dad when I was a child. As we traveled north, I shared with John all of the milestones along the way, and he was kind enough to indulge me. I told him all about the silly traditions we had, like announcing the small towns before we arrived along US 23. He even drove super-fast over the Black River Hills, so my stomach would feel funny from the dips in the road. There's something really special about "going up north" that can only be understood if you grew up a Michigander.

On November 22, we met Terry and Michelle at the Holiday Inn in Alpena. It was conveniently located right next door to the wedding reception hall. Later that night we all drove to the Price Farm where Uncle Joe and Aunt Kathy were having a pre-wedding get-together. They had tons of food, beer and a bonfire burning. At one point we were all gathered inside trying to stay warm, sitting around a long table. Since we were the out-of-towners, people started asking a lot of questions about our lives, and specifically directed several at John. For a moment they became the conversational equivalent of a firing squad. I looked over at Dad, and he had that famous smirk on his face, like he was about to put a stop to the inquisition. Just then, one of my uncles said, "So John, what do you do?" And with a quick-witted response, John replied, "Me? What do I do? I play golf."

Dad almost spit out his beer and started howling. He said, "Good for you Sonny boy. Best answer you could've given." Later he told me privately, "I was so proud of John for saying he played golf. That shut them right-up. Nosey bastards."

The day of the wedding we all went to the church in the morning for the ceremony. It was a traditional format, so there was a long break in the afternoon before the reception started that evening. Grandma Margot insisted that Terry, Michelle, John, and I meet at her house and spend time with her and her husband.

We were all gathered in the farmhouse kitchen pretending the energy wasn't tense and awkward. Margot said to me, "Well, Dolly, how about we all go down to the Wagon Wheel and have a drink and a snack before we head to town?"

"That's a great idea. I've been wanting to show John one of the local pubs," I said as I jumped to my feet.

A few minutes later, all of our vehicles had converged in the parking lot of the bar. As we walked inside, Margot's husband announced,

"Well, Mag hasn't been in here in a long time. The last time my wife was in here, she found a curly in her beer." With his face packed with chewing tobacco, he flashed a big smile, leaned up on one hip and let out a series of loud farts. My grandmother displayed her usual reaction by rolling her eyes, raising one eyebrow, pursing her lips tight, and trying not to smile. Dad just ignored him; his material was old. John and Michelle could not hold back from laughing out loud. Like Terry, I was unfazed, as I had seen this show before. When I was a little kid he used to ask me to pull his finger, and then he would let out a huge fart. I whispered to John, "I warned you that you would hear and see things you've never experienced before." Then Dad leaned over to me and whispered in my ear, "That lazy fat fuck is killing himself with a knife and fork." After a few beers and some small talk, Terry looked at his watch and announced it was time to head north to the real party.

I was on high alert at the reception, but everybody seemed to be keeping it together. There was a giant Kamikaze ice luge with a constant line, and enough alcohol to supply the entire county. I didn't see any fistfights or food plates flying, so by those standards the night was a giant success. Dad didn't get drunk. I'm confident it was because John was there, and he didn't want to embarrass me, which I was grateful for. Otherwise, I think it could have turned into a shit-show pretty quickly with that many Troys under the same roof.

When we were leaving the reception to walk back to the hotel, Uncle Joe came outside, gave me a hug and said, "Thanks for coming honey, I really loved seeing you." Dad always said, "Family is really important to Par. He has a big heart."

That's exactly how my uncle had made me feel. I attended the wedding to support him, but he ended up making me feel good. That was him in a nutshell—sweet and kind.

CHAPTER SIXTEEN

Double Vision

I n the summer of 2005, Terry and Michelle rented a mobile home on a wooded piece of property in Ohio. Dad was thrilled to gain some privacy from Michelle's parents. I was still selling ATMs in Michigan and living on East Coast time. The upside to working in that time zone was that it made it easier to stay in touch with Dad, so we spoke at least once or twice a week. But I felt like I was burning the candle at both ends and caught between two worlds with a crazy schedule.

In October, John had a golf weekend planned with a bunch of guys from our country club. It just so happened to fall on my birthday, so Glee came to keep me company. On October 19, John wished me a happy thirty-seventh birthday, loaded up his golf clubs, and headed to the Seven Canyons course in Sedona. One of the many courses he would, no doubt, dominate over the next few days.

Later that day, I took Braddy to the dog groomer so he was fluffy and handsome for Glee's arrival. As I started to drive off, he climbed in between the front seats with his front paws on the middle console. He loved to look out the windshield and lean into my right shoulder. As we drove off, I looked over at him and noticed his eyes looked funny. I couldn't quite pinpoint what it was. I grabbed him under his chin and said, "Are you okay buddy?" He jerked his head away and went back to looking out the window. When I picked him up a few hours later, the groomer handed me his leash and assured me that he was totally normal; she didn't notice anything odd.

Before I left for the airport, I fed Braddy dinner. Fifteen minutes later he vomited it all back up. I poured him a few more kibbles, and he quickly ate it, like he was trying to please me and prove that he was okay. I could tell by the expression on his face, and the way he held his head, that he thought he was in trouble. I said, "Its okay Braddy. Take your time sweetie, you didn't do anything wrong." I was really worried, but grateful he managed to keep the smaller meal down.

The next morning, Glee and I were catching up in the kitchen while I fed Braddy breakfast. Unfortunately, the exact scenario that happened the previous night happened again. I immediately called the vet and was told to bring him to the clinic right away. After the doctor took a quick look at him, she said, "I'd like you to leave him here for the day so we can do some bloodwork and take some x-rays."

A few hours later, the vet called and told me that Braddy's liver enzymes were elevated, and his white blood cell count was also high. He was very jaundiced, and his ears, eyes, gums, and nails were all yellow. What she was describing was terrifying.

"How did this happen? Why is he having liver problems? What can we do?" I asked.

"We don't know why he is sick, we started him on some IV fluids and antibiotics. I'm hoping he will show some positive response. I need your permission to do an ultrasound, it's our next step."

"Of course. Yes. Do whatever you need to do."

Later that evening, John called me from Prescott, and I filled him in on what had happened with Braddy.

"Well, I'll just pack up my stuff and get a ride home so I can be there with you."

"No, no, I'm okay. Glee is with me, and we'll keep you up to date on what's going on. Besides, tomorrow is Saturday, and you need to kick some ass so you're leading on Sunday. Just try to enjoy yourself. There's nothing to do but wait, anyways."

On Saturday afternoon, the vet called and said that Braddy had had a difficult night. He was still vomiting and couldn't even keep water down. She had performed two ultrasounds and determined that his liver was extremely small and appeared to have been damaged by something.

I choked back the tears and said, "Damaged by what? What happened to him?"

"We don't know. Did he get into anything in the yard? Or in the house? Something toxic like a dead animal or prescription medication?"

"Absolutely not. We are so careful to keep everything off the floor. He never has full run of the house when we are gone, and he's never outside without one of us with him."

"Well, I'd like to give him some barium and take some more x-rays just to see if there is some sort of blockage we missed."

"Fine," I said.

"And I'd like to do a liver biopsy. But because we will be closed and no one will be here overnight tonight, I don't want to do it until Monday, when I know we can monitor him better after the procedure."

As I hung up the phone I started to freak out. Her words were repeating in my head.

"Do you want to move him to a twenty-four-hour facility?" Glee asked.

"I don't know what to do. I'm inclined to leave him there because she has all of his records, and she's already done so many tests. I'm conflicted."

Late Sunday morning, just before I was getting ready to take Glee to the airport, the vet called and explained that she'd stopped into the clinic and decided to give Braddy barium and take the x-rays.

"Unfortunately, Braddy has vomited up the barium, and that's a very bad sign. The x-rays didn't reveal any blockages."

"He's only seven years old. I can't believe this is happening," I cried out.

"We have his biopsy scheduled for one o'clock on Monday. You can come see him after the procedure. It's best to keep him calm for now."

I took Glee to the airport, but I don't remember doing it. Braddy was my security blanket; I was frantic. I was questioning every decision I had made and researching everything I could on the internet.

Late Sunday night, John returned from his trip. Neither one of us slept much, but we were up early Monday morning. About two o'clock the vet called and said that Braddy had made it through the biopsy. We raced over to the clinic where we spent the day lying on the tile floor rubbing his body and kissing his fluffy ears. At closing they asked us to leave. Our goodbye was heart wrenching. His eyes looked cloudy and distant.

When they brought Braddy in to see us the next morning, he looked thin, his belly bloated and shaved. His eyes looked cloudier; he acted confused and his legs were unstable. After spending several hours lying on the hard floor, I asked to take him outside so he could smell the fresh air. John had to go to a meeting, so I spent some time alone with him. I sat outside with Braddy for about an hour. He wanted to walk, so that's what we did. I returned to the clinic and John rejoined us. A vet tech brought a bowl of ice chips that I had requested and placed it on the floor, Braddy ate them as fast as he could.

As our baby lay on the floor with an IV bag dripping into him, he needed to go potty, but he couldn't get up. Orange urine was pouring out from under him because he could no longer stand. Then he had diarrhea, and his breathing became labored. It sounded like his lungs had fluid in them. I was trying to grab anything I could to mop it up as it spread toward his belly and our shoes. He had never had an accident before, and he looked humiliated.

"It's okay Braddy, nobody's mad. It's not your fault sweetheart," I assured him.

"Where the fuck are the lab results? And what are we doing? It's obvious he is dying!" I yelled out loud.

I flagged down a tech and said, "What is taking so long? Can you ask the doctor to come into our room?" About ten minutes later the vet came in and said that she had called the lab repeatedly, but they still didn't have the results.

"It doesn't matter anymore. He's suffering and this is ridiculous," I said, pissed off.

"Well, let me evaluate him real quick," she said, acting surprised at my statement.

She leaned down on one knee and lifted Braddy's hind end up, and he quickly fell back down. "Well, I think it's okay to wait a little longer to get the results back."

"Hell no! I'm done with this shit. It's time to help him. Now!"

"Do you agree?" she asked John.

"Yes, my wife is right, he's suffered enough," he answered, fighting back tears.

"Okay, I'll go get the paperwork," she responded, sounding annoyed.

I lay back on the floor cuddling Braddy the best I could. My whole body hurt from spending days lying on the tile. But with everything that Braddy had been through, there was no way I would complain. John was trying to clean up more of the mess on the floor and then the door opened. A male doctor leaned in and said, "Don't worry about that, we'll clean that up." And after a short pause he said, "I know this is hard, but cirrhosis of the liver is a terminal situation. Something ate up his liver and it became very hard and small. You're doing the right thing." And then he closed the door.

I looked at John and said, "Why didn't she tell us that? What the fuck have we been doing here? The lab results are not relevant." Braddy had lost his neurological function. His last meal had been a bowl of ice chips, and he had been poked and prodded over and over for days.

When the vet returned, she told us the results are still not in, and she handed us the paperwork to sign for euthanasia. It took every ounce of my being not to call her an incompetent idiot. But I knew I had to switch my attention back to the few moments I had left with our baby. Braddy lay on the cold hard floor with an IV in his frail little arm, covered in piss and shit, his head resting on his toy, and our arms wrapped around him.

The vet injected him with the first shot to help him sleep, and he immediately jumped up and then fell back down to the floor. I let out a scream, "Oh my God!" And then as she gave him the lethal dose, John and I were repeating, "We love you, Braddy. We love you, Braddy." Within ten seconds our baby's heart stopped and his body was still, but his eyes stayed open like he fought it all the way to the end. John said through his tears, "Go to the clouds buddy. Chase all the bunnies you want. Run. Be free. No more pain little man."

I immediately felt regret. I was screaming inside, but nothing came out. I wanted him back. I wanted to wake up and have this all be over. But as I stared into his still, empty eyes, I knew this was real. More real than anything I'd ever experienced before. On Tuesday, October 25, at 2:42 in the afternoon, we kissed Braddy's head one last time and covered him in an old towel.

When we got into our car, I pounded on the steering wheel and hysterically screamed, "This is fucking bullshit!" John tried to reach over and hold me, but I pushed him away. I only wanted Braddy back.

The next morning when I woke up and realized Braddy was still gone, I started crying all over again. I could not stop reliving that horrible experience over and over in my head. I was angry at my-self because I felt like I had failed my sweet, little angel. Why did I trust that doctor? Why didn't I take control sooner? I had never been through anything like that before. How could I have known? But I was too pissed off to cut myself any slack. I vowed that I would never let anyone I loved go through that again.

I was having a hard time trying to come up with the words to say to Dad. I went into our master bedroom closet, shut the door, and started wailing. I couldn't hold it back no matter how hard I tried. I slumped to the floor, reached for my cellphone, and dialed Dad's number. I heard him pick up the call and say, "Hell-o!" in his deep warm voice. I couldn't get the words out.

He repeated, "Hell-o? Are you there?"

"I'm here Daddy. I'm here." I muttered.

"Honey Babe is that you?"

"Yes, it's me," I said crying.

I could hear a bunch of noise in the background. It sounded like he was driving his semi-truck.

"Can you hear me? What the hell is going on?" he asked frantically.

"Yes, Dad, I can hear you. I need to talk to you."

"What's wrong honey?"

"Daddy, Braddy died," I sobbed.

There was a short pause and then I heard him yell, "Hold on hon-ey, I need to pull over so I can talk to you. I need to get this asshole to move over so I can get off the fucking turnpike. Hold on hon-ey!" And then I heard him drop the phone and start yelling, "Move the fuck over you cocksucker! I've had my blinker on for a mile you dickhead. Oh yeah, you wanna meet me on the side of the road—you pussy?"

As I sat on my closet floor with my eyes closed, crying, listen-ing to the familiar sounds of my father's voice desperately trying to get to the shoulder, I felt Braddy's paws wrap around my neck and his tongue lick my tears. I jerked my eyes open to see him. I looked around wanting it to be true—I know I felt him.

Dad picked the phone back up and said, "I'm sorry about that honey I had to pull over so I could hear you. What did you say?" I said through more tears, "Daddy, Braddy died."

"Oh Honey Babe. I'm so sorry. What happened?"

After I told him everything that happened, I was pissed off and crying even harder.

"Please don't cry. Please. Please stop crying honey, I hate it when you cry," he pleaded. "We all loved Braddy. He was a special dog, and he sure was a good friend to you. He was loyal; he's gonna be missed, that's for sure."

"Dad, I loved that dog more than most of the people I'm related to," I muttered.

"Well, I sure can understand that. He never let you down."

"I don't mean to be rude, but that's just the truth." I insisted.

"Ya know my dad died of cirrhosis of the liver. It was totally unnecessary. I told him to lay off the hard liquor, but he just wouldn't listen. I told him he didn't have to stop drinking, he just had to stop all the hard shit. He died on September 20, 1975, one day before he turned fifty-four."

I knew what my grandfather had died from, but I'd never heard Terry talk about his death before. Dad was only twenty-six years old. In that moment, I felt the pain that he must have endured all those years before. So young. Just like Braddy—way too young.

"Well, Honey Babe I hate to cut you short, but I have to get this load over to an asshole in PA. Oh, and before I forget, thanks again for that plaid shirt you sent me a while ago. I'm wearing it right now and it sure is a nice one."

"Which plaid shirt?"

"You know that tan, long sleeve one." I let out a belly laugh, "Oh, that Burberry shirt? I'm glad you like it, Dad."

"Call me anytime baby doll. Hang in there, I love you."

Terry Troy was probably the only trucker on the planet wearing a $300 shirt to haul lumber, and that was alright with me. When I told John he laughed and said, "Well that shirt my sister sent didn't fit me, so I'm glad he's getting some good use out of it." Then he hesitated and said, "I've gotta tell you something now that your Dad has you all settled down."

"I'm not sure how much more I can handle at this point. What now?" I asked.

John proceeded to share that after I told him Braddy was gravely ill, he was really stressed out about not being with me. Standing on the third green of the Seven Canyons golf course, he looked down to putt for a birdie, and he saw two balls.

"What are you talking about? Were you drinking?"

"No, I had double vision," he said with a laugh.

I sat there stunned for a second, and then he said, "And my eyelid is starting to droop, and the vision issues come and go."

CHAPTER SEVENTEEN

Greasewood Flat

A few weeks after Braddy passed away, John and I discussed getting another dog. I wasn't ready, but John instinctively knew that the only thing that would mend my broken heart was the sweet smell of puppy breath. He convinced me that getting two puppies was just as easy as one. I called the same breeder I had gotten Braddy from and asked her if cancer or any other health issues had shown up in her breeding program. She assured me that she did not have any major health problems that ran in her wheaten terrier lines. She just happened to have two six-week-old male littermates. After more convincing from John, we had both of them flown to Arizona from Georgia a couple of weeks later. We decided on their names before they arrived and agreed that the first puppy to walk out of the crate would be named after Braddy. And since soft-coated wheaten terriers are an Irish breed, and we loved golf, his name would be Mulligan Bradford. And his brother was assigned Bailey Flanagan. Their nicknames were Mully and Bails O'Hay (or B.O.H. for short).

I called Dad and told him about the two bundles of energy that were now ruling my life. He was happy for us and said, "Well honey, you always loved animals. I remember when you were a little girl I used to take you to the pound and let you pick out new kittens. For some reason, you always picked the ones that were deaf or blind. I tried to convince you to choose something different, but nope, you were pretty hard to convince once you got your heart set on one."

"Yeah, I remember we always had dogs and cats. It seemed I had a run of bad luck with some of those kittens. One got run over by a motorcycle and those German shepherd-husky mixes weren't real fond of cats. I'll never forget the day my kitten got out on the screened-in porch and our dog attacked it and killed it right in front of my eyes."

"Well, those dogs would have laid down their lives to protect you kids, but they sure were a pain in my ass. Every Friday when I'd get my paycheck, I'd stop by the neighbor's house and pay the farmer for the chickens our dogs killed that week. I never questioned his number, I just paid him and apologized," Dad lamented.

I spent most of November training Mully and Bails, sleeping on the floor with them, and downing a lot of caffeinated drinks. In retrospect, John was right, I needed something to pour my attention into with everything that was going on with his health and the loss of Braddy.

Terry and Michelle decided not to come to Arizona for Thanksgiving that year. I understood, but I was a little disappointed because I hadn't seen my father in a year—not since my cousin's wedding—and I really missed him.

After taking John to multiple doctors and undergoing many tests, on November 29, he was finally diagnosed with Ocular Myasthenia Gravis. The first thing the ocular specialist said was, "Don't read about this disease on the internet, it'll scare you to death." So, of course, we immediately started researching it online, and she was right.

The following months became very difficult for John. With his droopy eyelid and double vision, he could no longer play golf, drive a car, read a book, or watch TV. Everything was frustrating, and the drugs weren't working. Eventually, John started taking Prednisone in large doses, and his vision returned to normal. We were grateful, but he was far from cured, and later he began having issues with swallowing and speaking. Then he was diagnosed with generalized MG and would experience systemic weakness. We kept telling ourselves that we were lucky that the situation wasn't worse. We had a young friend who was dying from Lou Gehrig's disease and another from breast cancer, so how dare we complain?

On March 8, 2006, my father's eighty-three-year-old mother had heart surgery in Traverse City, Michigan. Terry traveled eight hours and drove over five hundred miles just to be there when she woke up. Later that night, I called him and asked how she was doing.

"Well, I figured she was getting up there in age, so I'd better go," he explained.

"Were you able to speak with her?"

"Oh, yeah. She told me I shouldn't have come because the drive was too long. I told her, 'Well Ma, I didn't pack my black suit, so you better get your ass outta here,'" he answered with a giggle.

Luckily, a few days later, she did just that.

Later that summer, I called Michelle and told her that I had an upcoming Michigan business trip, and I'd like to come down to Ohio to surprise Dad. She agreed to keep it a secret and gave me directions to their trailer in the woods.

On August 2, after my last client appointment, I drove my rental car south. I was so excited, because I hadn't seen them in over a year and a half. When I pulled into their dirt driveway, I could see the front of their trailer and a wood deck off the left side, in front of the entrance door. The lot was about two acres and full of trees around the perimeter of their property. I knocked on the door and it popped open. I called out, "Anybody home?" The silence was unnerving, but I walked inside. "Hel-lo, I'm here."

I called Michelle's cellphone. "Hey, where are you? I'm at your house."

"Well, I've been trying to get your dad out of the bar all day but he won't budge."

"Oh great. Well, tell him you have a surprise for him at home and you have to leave now."

"I've been trying. I'll get him out of here as soon as I can."

I sat outside on the deck steps watching kittens scamper around the grass. I recalled the time I waited for Dad back in California when I surprised him with the limo. After about an hour, I called Michelle back and she told me they were finally on their way, and she had done her best to deal with the situation. I asked her to put Terry on the phone and the minute he said hello I could tell he wasn't just a *little* tipsy.

"Hi Dad, how are you?"

"Oh, I'm doin' good honey. I'm just headed home," he said, slurring words.

"Well, I miss you Dad. I sure wish I could see you."

"Yeah, me too. It's been too long Honey Babe."

As I watched them about to turn into the driveway, I said, "Dad, you're breakin' up." I hung up the phone and stood there waiting for him to realize it was me on his porch. He got out of the car, pulled up his jeans that were falling below his skinny waist, and shouted, "Well, son of bitch! Is that you honey?" he asked, stumbling over and giving me a hug and a kiss.

"You look so pretty baby girl. What are you doing here?"

"I hadn't seen my daddy in so long I thought I'd spend the weekend with him."

"Wow, that's great, come in and let me get you a beer," he slurred.

I locked eyes with Michelle as we entered the trailer. No words were needed.

A few hours later Terry's buzz was wearing off a little. He asked me if I was hungry, and I explained that I had skipped lunch. He wanted to take us out to dinner, so I drove us to Pondi's Restaurant and Bar. Dad became quieter as the night went on; occasionally trying to act happy.

As he tried to eat and talk without sounding drunk, he gave Michelle a dirty look and said to me, "Well, I wished I knew you were coming honey, I wouldn't have gotten so shitfaced."

"I'm sorry Dad, I shouldn't have surprised you, that wasn't fair."

"It's good to see ya. When are you leaving?" he asked in a low, solemn tone.

I told him I'd planned on staying three nights, then I'd head back to Detroit to catch my flight to Arizona. He stared at his meal in silence, like he was calculating in his head how long he would need to behave.

The next day Terry asked me to go with him to drop off a truck radiator to a mechanic in New Castle, Pennsylvania. He always took the country roads. He'd probably had his fill of traffic after all those years of driving on turnpikes. I kept commenting on how green everything was; a nice departure from the desert. He'd drive slower by the farms so I could watch the animals.

Later that day I took Dad and Michelle to lunch at Lone Star Steakhouse. While there, they told me that we were meeting Michelle's family later at a park to celebrate her grandson's birthday. Terry was still quiet and distant. Luckily, Michelle could talk nonstop so we avoided dead air.

That evening we drove to a country park in the woods where Michelle's daughter Jamie, her two children, and other family members had gathered to celebrate. I had met Michelle's daughter and children years earlier before moving to Arizona. Jamie was twenty-nine years old and was working her way through college, delayed by bad decisions made when she was younger. We had a great time chatting, and I told her I was really proud of her for choosing a better future. I also promised her that when she was done with school, I would send her some of my business suits for her interviews. I couldn't imagine the stresses of going to school while being a single mother.

The next day Terry and I drove out to Austintown, Ohio, to get his pickup truck. I noticed that Dad seemed weary and reserved. I wondered if he was truly happy. On one hand his life seemed complete, filled with Michelle and her family. They appeared to have accepted him, and he thought of Jamie as a daughter; her kids called him Grandpa. But there was something about his eyes. Perhaps it was just my poor timing.

The next morning I felt I had overstayed my welcome. I quickly left for Detroit, and Dad followed me. We stopped just shy of the airport to say goodbye. He said he needed to take a truck part to Uncle Joe in Alpena, so it was a good excuse for him to make sure I got to the airport safely.

After that trip to Michigan I started to acknowledge that I was unhappy with the ATM business. I had done it so long that it wasn't challenging anymore, and the travel was a real drag. I still hated to fly despite it being easier with frequency. I just wasn't fulfilled; I felt like I had proven myself in that industry. I was annoyed by 4:30 a.m. East Coast conference calls, and I wanted to live like an Arizonan. I was thirty-eight years old with a solid career in financial services. Could I walk away? Start anew? I had some soul-searching to do.

In November, Terry and Michelle came for Thanksgiving. When they arrived at our home I could immediately tell the chemistry between them was different; their negative energy was palpable. On Michelle's birthday I took her to the nail salon where she mentioned she was having "trouble" with Terry. She said his drinking was out of control, and they'd been fighting like cats and dogs. They had been doing the same dance since 1988. I noticed that every night Michelle would take a long walk in the dark around the golf course with her mobile phone. I cautioned her about the wildlife outside: javelina, coyotes, bobcats, rattlesnakes, and mountain lions. In the past, that information had freaked her out, but oddly, she proceeded.

Before they departed for Ohio, I spoke with Dad about my desire to change careers. He encouraged me to make the leap. He said,

"Honey, it doesn't matter what you do. You'll figure it out, you always do."

John and I had many long talks about closing the ATM company. Around that same time, the economy was struggling, and Michigan was hit hard. The banks had deficient budgets; ATM orders were scarce. It was a sign from the universe, so I put together a plan for a home-staging business.

December of 2006, I started networking with local builders and realtors that I'd met at our country club and through our remodel projects. After our renovations were finished, one of them had asked me to work as his designer.

"I'm not a designer, I sell stuff to banks."

"The hell you're not. I know a designer when I see one. You designed everything at your house, right?" he snapped.

But I declined the offer. I was too insecure about my lack of formal education.

I continued to run the ATM business while I started designing small projects for friends and neighbors. I offered my services and design plans for free and volunteered at the country club redesigning their entrance and parking lot landscaping. As I gained more confidence and grew my portfolio, I felt ready to start charging for my time.

In February of 2007, Dad called and told me that Michelle had moved out. She had found a new boyfriend and moved in with him. I remember having a brief conversation with Michelle after they split up. She said, "I knew I was going to leave him back when you flew us out for Thanksgiving, but I didn't want to ruin anyone's holiday. I just couldn't keep living like that, Terrina." I wished her well. I knew my gut was correct when I felt something was off, and those walks late at night on the golf course gave her the perfect opportunity to call her new man. I wasn't angry; this is how all of Terry's relationships ended. I wondered what would happen to Dad now. He'd been able to rely on Michelle as a safety net for nineteen years.

In March, I was offered an opportunity to take on a larger design project. A young general contractor was building his first custom home for a client in an upscale neighborhood called The Boulders. He needed someone who could not only create custom designs but also perform some project and vendor management. This was a big breakthrough moment for me when I realized that all my skillsets could be utilized, including giving a presentation to the new home-owners. I had never dreamed that I could leap from running an ATM business to designing a two-million-dollar property, but somehow I'd convinced myself to take the opportunity.

I didn't see Dad the entire year of 2007. I was running two ventures on two different time zones and trying to take on as much business as possible. Terry was struggling with working as an independent truck driver, so when he was offered an employee position with a lumber company, he took it.

On January 16, 2008, John had his thymus gland removed. We were told that the procedure could allow his autoimmune disease to go into remission. They used a robot to cut into his chest and neck, deflate one of his lungs, and remove the thymus gland from his heart and neck region. Thankfully, the cardiologist was a patient and talented man. He told me after the surgery was over that John's gland was much larger than most, making it a complicated procedure.

On June 3, I received a call from Dad. He was in the hospital; alert and furious. He said he hauled a load of heavy, large logs to a client. At offload, the straps weren't coming off, so he reached up with his knife and cut them, causing the cargo to shift. He backed up as fast as he could, but he was unable to outrun the logs; they crushed his right ankle and foot. He had five major fractures, and the bones in his foot were mush.

Terry was fifty-nine years old, weighed 160 pounds, had never had surgery, and wasn't taking any prescription medication; he had been perfectly healthy. His entire life changed in that split second. He took complete responsibility for the mistake.

"I should have respected the damn load more," he snarled.

"Dad, I'm so sorry. What can I do? Do you want me to come?"

"No. Don't come. I'll be fine," he snapped.

"Dad, this is a big deal. It's going to be really difficult for you to do certain things."

"I said don't come. You have your hands full there. I'll be staying at Barney's house for a couple of weeks. They said I have to wait for the swelling to go down before they can fix the fuckin' thing anyways."

Barney was my dad's drinking buddy and Michelle's biological father. He was diagnosed with Mesothelioma and didn't have long to live. But he loved Terry and allowed him to sleep on his couch while he waited to see the surgeon.

Coincidentally, John was flying to Michigan to visit his son around the same time that Dad had his surgery scheduled. On June 17, he drove to Toledo and surprised Pops on the morning of his surgery. John and Barney paced the waiting room together until Terry was out and assured Sonny Boy he was fine.

I had assumed that after Dad was released he would go back to Barney's house, but my stubborn father had other plans. He went to his trailer by himself. I was reminded of the time he had a colonoscopy; they wouldn't let him drive himself home. He thought it was a stupid rule, but as he said, "They're pitchin' and I'm catchin'." He parked his vehicle a couple of blocks from the hospital and had a taxicab take him to his truck. He drove an hour and half home, post-procedure.

I offered to come get him and bring him to Arizona, but he said, "Absolutely not. You have too much on your plate right now, and besides I'm fine here."

"Dad, how did you get up those steps on your deck with your crutches?"

"Well, it took a few tries, but eventually I got up 'em. I mean, getting up 'em wasn't that hard. It was balancing the case of beer while I got up 'em that was the real son of a bitch."

That was Dad in a nutshell. No challenge too big. So I stopped offering to help him and let Terry work his plan.

A few months later in September, I had finished designing the custom home. It was terrifying and fun all at the same time. I was hooked on the building process and soaked up as much as I could. Ultimately, that experience gave me the confidence to finally shut the ATM business. The following month I would turn forty. I told John that I felt a little burned out and was desperately in need of a vacation. On October 17, we left on a road trip that would end up in Jackson Hole, Wyoming.

Our first night, we stayed in a hotel near Bryce Canyon. I could not believe how beautiful Zion National Park was. My father called us late that evening. Sort of odd to call on our vacation, but I welcomed the chat. The next day, we drove through Salt Lake City and northeast to Idaho Falls. I saw a large group of sheep being herded along the freeway by some authentic-looking cowboys. I could have watched them all day. The next morning I woke up to my phone ringing.

"Hel-lo?" I mumbled.

"Happy birthday, Honey Babe. Have you had your iced tea yet?" Dad said with a chuckle.

"Well not yet Daddy, but that's okay," I responded, laughing.

"How far did you make it yesterday?"

"Idaho Falls. We'll be in Jackson later today."

"Sounds like you're making good time. Will you call me when you get there?"

"Sure Dad. Is everything okay?"

He stammered a little and then said, "Well, I'll just be glad when you get there safe."

Later that day, we checked into the Four Seasons Hotel in Teton Village. Some friends had connections and surprised us with a major upgraded room, a nice bottle of wine and tray of chocolate-dipped strawberries. Once we were settled in, I called Terry and told him about the famous Teton Mountains, the view from our hotel room, and the amazing field across the street full of elk. I thought it was unusual that he continued to call us every other day until we arrived back home to Arizona.

Since Terry was turning sixty, ten days later, we flew him out to Arizona for his birthday gift. When he got to our home, he gave me that biggest, longest hug he had ever given me. I wasn't sure why he missed me so much. I thought maybe the time off with his accident had made him feel lonely.

For his birthday celebration we decided to take him to Greasewood Flat, which was near Pinnacle Peak Mountain in north Scottsdale. Greasewood was a famous old outdoor western bar that had been there since 1975 and would draw clientele from all walks of life. It was located across the street from the Troon Four Seasons Hotel, on a well-traveled biker's route. It wasn't uncommon to see a limousine parked next to a bunch of Harley Davidson motorcycles. People rode their horses and tied them to the hitching post behind the bar. Centered on a raised stage was a cement dance floor. Picnic tables and fire pits with roasted peanut shells scattered on the ground. They offered a limited menu of burgers, hot dogs, and beer. At the time, the owner was a ninety-two-year-old man named, Doc. You could always count on him to be there to greet everyone. I used to tell him how much I loved his place, and he would always say, "This is a family place, dear. I like seeing the families." To add to the charm, for years patrons had been writing their names on dollar bills, and Doc would staple them behind the bar, on the ceiling, and all over the walls. It started when he told people that when times were good, leave a dollar. And when times were bad, you'd have a dollar waiting for you to buy a drink. There were thousands of dollar bills stapled everywhere. It reminded me of the old "Hat Bar."

Terry had a great time and said, "This place is just perfect. I could sit here and people watch all day." After a couple of beers, even though his foot was killing him, he asked one of our cute friends to dance. It made me happy that he was comfortable with us in Scottsdale.

On November 3, it was time for Dad to go back to Ohio. We were sitting on the back patio watching the golfers tee-off on the sixth tee box. Terry was smoking a cigarette and staring off into the distance. I was absorbing my black tea.

"Daddy, would you like to stay longer? Are you sad to go home?"

"Well, I sure do love Arizona honey, and being with you and Sonny Boy has been great, but I need to get back. I've got some doctor appointments coming up for this damn foot," he stated while blowing the familiar smoke out of his nose.

"I need to tell you something sad, honey. Jamie died," he calmly stated while staring straight ahead.

"Did you say Jamie died?" I asked in shock.

"Yeah, she died in a car wreck on October 15. I didn't want to tell you because you guys had that road trip coming up for your birthday," he slowly answered, then continued. "She was leaving early in the morning to go to work, and a kid was texting while driving and crossed the centerline. She was all the way over as far as she could go. She didn't have a chance. She died at the hospital in Michelle's arms. And that cocksucker that killed her, survived."

"Oh my God, this is horrible, Dad. I'm so sorry. Is that why you were calling me so much when I was on vacation?" I asked, holding back my tears.

"Yes. I just couldn't bear the thought of something like that happening to you. Such a damn waste."

"I get it, Dad. I'm so sorry. How is Michelle?"

"Well, Jamie was her best friend, so it's been pretty devastating.

And I thought of her as a daughter, too."

"Of course you did. I know how much she loved you."

"If something ever happened to you, I would just shoot myself in the head."

"Dad, don't say that. That's a lot of pressure for someone to carry around."

"Well, without you baby girl, there's no reason to stick around."

"Daddy, remember you said your ticket is punched the day you are born? You don't get to choose."

"Yes, but you're all I got Honey Babe."

"You also said we're not promised tomorrow, so we need to enjoy every day the best we can. I know it's hard after such a big loss, but I think Jamie is in heaven looking down on us, wanting us to live happy," I said, trying to change the energy.

"That's all bullshit. When you're dead, you're dead. It's all over. I don't believe in that shit. Especially after dealing with all the Catholic bullshit I'd been fed."

The emotional roller coaster of a year had taken a toll on everyone. The financial crisis of 2008 was affecting the entire country. I was trying to pivot into a new direction at a time when housing values were plummeting. I couldn't have picked a worse career path. And Dad, for the first time in his life, was not able to take care of himself financially. He wasn't much of a complainer, especially when it came to pain, but I'll never forget him saying, "If I had known how bad this was going to be, I would've told them to amputate it."

CHAPTER EIGHTEEN

Plowing Through Life

With the economy continuing to tank, we made the decision to sell our home before the housing market hit bottom. We'd also purchased another house down the street with a partner, as a flip project. At the same time we were selling two homes, I went to real estate school and shuttled John to never-ending doctor's appointments. Watching his debilitating lower back pain from stenosis was heartbreaking. Unfortunately, he required lower back surgery. The medication that was saving his life and suppressing the symptoms of MG, was also wreaking havoc on his entire body—a seemingly unavoidable double-edged sword.

Dad was trying every pain remedy he could, including weed and barbiturates, chased by liquor. Balancing everything on my plate was becoming more challenging, so I asked Terry if he would consider moving to Arizona. We offered to get him an apartment so he could maintain his privacy and I could preserve the remaining scraps of my sanity. But Terry declined our solution with a constant barrage of lame excuses. I resolved to respect his wishes, and released the anxiety about my inability to support him more. He had choices, and my hands were tied two thousand miles away.

On March 20, 2009, my Grandma Margot passed away, one week after her eighty-sixth birthday. She had been having strokes and generally declining for a few years. Dad told me not to come to Michigan because they couldn't have a funeral for her until the permafrost melted in Alpena.

A few months later in May, Terry called and said, "Well, that asshole picked the date for my mother's funeral. He didn't even care that it was on Tracy's birthday. I feel so bad for Par and Kathy." The shocking loss of my cousin was still a sensitive situation. But I was not surprised to hear that my grandmother's husband didn't care that he had chosen a day that would be extra difficult for my father's side of the family. They didn't exactly respect each other, and weddings and funerals highlighted this kind of dysfunction.

By the time Dad told me about the date for Margot's funeral, it was too late for me to make arrangements to get there. I felt awful that I wasn't going to be there for Dad, but he was keeping it real when he said, "There's no need for you to spend a bunch of money to come back here. She's been dead for months, and I'm fine. She lived a long life. We should all be so lucky to live to eighty-six."

On August 11, John had lower back surgery to remove the pressure on his spinal cord. A month later we sold our home and the flip house in the same week. I spent my forty-first birthday nursing John, packing and moving us into a rental property less than a mile away.

That same month, one day after Terry turned sixty-one, his longtime friend Barney died. Dad was devastated and refused to discuss it. With Barney's passing, I worried that he didn't have much of a support system there. I asked him one more time if he would like to come to Arizona. He snapped, "No. I don't want to leave Frank." His friend Frank was his new focus for avoiding my pleas. I quit asking.

Terry was becoming more negative; frustrated with his foot. Desperate, he underwent surgery for a spinal cord stimulator in March of 2010. He claimed it didn't help him at all, and carped that his back hurt where they had implanted it. His discomfort broke my heart; I could hear his hopelessness.

"Daddy, I'll do some research, to see if there is anything else you can try," I expressed on one of our calls.

"Thanks honey, but I've come to the conclusion it's probably as good as it's gonna get. It is, what it is."

"Don't say that. We'll figure something out," I insisted.

"I'll never be half the man I used to be," he said with shame, driving a stake through my heart.

I gave him some space and then called to check in. He sounded miserable.

"Daddy, you sound so grumpy. Is your foot really hurting today?" I asked empathetically.

"No. It's my fucking teeth," he growled.

"Oh no, what's wrong with your teeth?"

"Well, they just hurt like hell. I think I need to get some pulled, but I'm not spending money on that right now."

"If you need to see a dentist, we'd be happy to pay for that. You can't go around with pain or an infection in your mouth."

"I don't have time for that. I'll take care of it myself."

Confused, I was silent for a second, and then he snapped, "I gotta go honey. I'll talk to you later."

The next day I called him. "Dad, do you feel any better? Would you consider going to the dentist?"

"Well honey, I don't need to go to the dentist anymore. I took care of it."

"What the hell does that mean?" I asked, frightened of the answer.

"Well the truth is, I got really drunk last night and used some pliers to pull out three of my bottom front teeth," he proudly stated with a lisp.

I covered my mouth as I cringed. I screamed, "Oh, hell no!"

He started to laugh and said, "That ain't no big deal honey. They sure as fuck feel better now."

I fought to suppress the images I conjured up of the scene; it gave me the heebie-jeebies. I questioned my surprise. He was a problem solver.

About a year previous to this heinous event, he'd already had all of his top teeth pulled by a dentist and was using an upper denture plate. He was dog sitting his friend Frank's Labrador, Tank; he left his denture plate on the coffee table while he took a nap on the couch. Apparently, Tank thought it was a snack and chewed it in half.

I couldn't contain how grossed out I was when I squealed, "Oh my God. That is so disgusting, Dad. You got a new plate, right?"

"Oh fuck no. I just super-glued it back together and used it to eat my dinner," he laughed, feeling satisfied I was appalled.

"Daddy stop it. It's probably not a good idea to have super glue in your mouth. Doesn't it taste terrible?"

"Nope. It's no big deal," he asserted with confidence.

Life became a blur between the years 2010 and 2012. John and I had purchased a new home down the street from our rental and took it to the studs. While managing that project, I started working with a brokerage firm selling real estate. I also designed and renovated a friend's kitchen, simultaneously gutting and remodeling our new home in the mountains—our "happy place" and escape from the summer heat.

Terry tried several more epidural-type treatments, all of which failed to help. He was beginning to give up hope of ever getting relief. His personality began to change as he struggled to find his sense of humor. He had been on workman's comp for about four years and his finances were strained.

In April of 2012, his disability checks came to a halt; they claimed he had reached "maximum medical improvement." I advised him that he needed to sign up for Social Security disability insurance as soon as possible, but he wanted to wait until the attorney he hired was able to file a complaint against workman's comp. I cautioned of the likely long, drawn-out process ad nauseam, but he brushed off my forewarnings. He chose to succumb to his old pal: procrastination. Unable to convince him, I felt defeated and annoyed, forced to accept that this was *his* journey.

That summer John's right Achilles' heel snapped in half. It literally fell apart. The doctor said the long-term Prednisone use was the probable culprit. He required immediate surgery and wasn't allowed to put any pressure on his right foot for about three months. He had to use a knee scooter to get around and couldn't drive a vehicle until the doctor released him. John felt frustrated and helpless, and I was failing as a cheerleader.

In late September, our dog Bailey became sick. I had felt for about a year that B.O.H. had not been acting normal. I had taken him to the vet at least six times. The doctor probably thought I had Munchausen Syndrome by Proxy disorder. But I wasn't looking for attention, I just knew my dogs, so I persisted. We were finally told that Bailey had a positive Valley Fever test and that we needed to put him on an antifungal medication, which we did immediately.

About a week later, John and I took Mulligan and Bailey to the cabin for a long weekend. Late on Sunday night, I noticed Bailey's urine was dark orange. I called the animal clinic, and they told me to bring him in first thing in the morning. I wanted to leave right away, but John reminded me that it was rutting season for the elk, and we should wait until the sun came up. I stayed up all night shutting down the cabin, packing our car, and getting ready to hit the road. As soon as the sun came up, I loaded up John, his knee scooter, and the dogs and raced down the mountain. We were at the clinic for several hours with John and Mulligan sitting in the car, me in the waiting room, when the female vet sat next to me on the bench.

"The good news is that Bailey's Valley Fever test came back negative. Perhaps the other test was a false positive. But unfortunately, we have found a mass on Bailey's chest x-ray," said the doctor, straining not to look me in the eye.

"He's only seven. What could it be?" I questioned choking back tears.

"Well we're not one hundred percent sure, so let me keep him overnight, do some more blood work, and a needle biopsy of the mass. I'll call you when I know more."

"What do you suspect this is, Doc?"

"Well, it could be a Hemangiosarcoma, but we want to do some more tests."

The next day, the animal clinic called and told me I could come pick up Bailey. The biopsy was inconclusive, so he needed an ultrasound of his abdomen. But unfortunately the only doctor that could perform that test was, ironically, the boy's regular vet, but he was out of town for a week.

As the days ticked on, I felt helpless. Each night I would sit on the couch while John watched TV, and Bailey would crawl onto my lap and let me hold him like a baby. As he lay on his back looking into my eyes, I would rub his chest and tell him what a good boy he was. I tried to stay as calm and present as I could, consciously soaking in every second with him.

On the night before his ultrasound appointment, I was holding Bails on the sofa. He jumped down and grabbed a toy away from Mulligan. They started to play tug-o-war and make all the crazy, grizzly bear noises they used to make when they were puppies. I looked at John and said, "Look at them. Maybe he's feeling better?" And John just smiled at me and didn't say a word. He didn't have to. He would always say, "When people are dying from cancer, they always rally for a day or two just before they die."

I went to bed that night praying that John was wrong. The boys were sleeping with me, and John was staying in the guest bedroom. The bed was lower to the ground, which made it easier for him, with the cast on his leg.

I woke up to Mully licking my face and the sun peering through the drapes. He wanted to go outside, so I let him out the back door. I said, "Come on Bails, let's go." Bailey was lying on the bed panting, and staring off into the distance. I ran over to the bed and said, "Are you okay buddy? Come on, let's go potty outside." But he wouldn't budge. I carefully scooped him up and took him to the grass; his legs immediately collapsed underneath him. I struggled to lift his forty-five-pound body and carried him back to the bed. I sequestered Mully in the master bathroom and ran to the guest bedroom. I screamed, "John, get up! Get up! We have to take Bails to the vet now."

John gathered himself, while I found my clothes and shoes. I yelled, "Go to the garage and I'll load Bailey, and your scooter!" I grabbed my purse, threw it in the car, loaded John into the passenger seat, threw his knee scooter into the car's hatchback, and ran back inside. Mulligan was crying and pacing because he couldn't get to his brother. I was holding back my tears as I grabbed Bailey and carried him to the car.

I peeled out of our driveway and got to the vet's office in twenty minutes. I jumped out and unloaded John's scooter for him, grabbed Bailey from the backseat, and rushed into the lobby. I placed Bails down on the cushioned bench, collapsed onto my knees, buried my face into his furry neck, and started crying. Our doctor's vet tech, Nancy, wrapped her arms around my shoulders and said, "It's okay sweetie, let me take it from here. You guys come, too." As we walked back to the exam room, his doctor was coming in the back door. He quickly popped his head into our room and said, "Let's take Bails into the back, where we can get that ultrasound done." We all walked back to a dark room where they had placed Bailey on his back. Both John and I were allowed to stay with them as the tech and the two vets were performing the ultrasound. Bails was being stoic and just lying there quietly, staring at me. I stood next to the table and held one of his front paws while telling him he was being such a good boy.

Fighting back tears, Nancy commented on how he looked like a cute, fuzzy, white teddy bear.

Our vet was teaching his protégé how to do the ultrasound, so we heard all of their findings in real time. The boy's doctor had known them since they were eight weeks old. He also lived in our neighborhood and belonged to our country club, so he saw them frequently. When he golfed, he used to look over our fence on the sixth tee-box, where Bailey and Mulligan would give their "wheaten-greetin" to all the golfers. They always made him smile whenever he saw them, but not that day. His face was sad, and his voice was soft. When he completed the test, he looked at us and confirmed that Bailey had a Hemangiosarcoma. It had started in his liver, and the fluid in his chest was coming from his abdomen. He thought he might live a few more days but probably not any longer. And then he asked us what we wanted to do.

My heart was racing, and my eyes were filling with tears. I took a deep breath, gathered my strength, and said, "I want him to be made as comfortable as possible. Please give him something to make him sleepy so he can relax first. I know we need to let him go; he has suffered way too much already."

As I held our Bails O'Hay, and John held me, the doctor administered the medication. On October 3, 2012, as his eyes slowly closed, John and I cried and told him, "You are the best little man, Bailey. Braddy will be waiting for you. We love you. We love you, Bails. We love you. We love you." And then the vet said, "He's gone."

I tried to be brave, but inside I was screaming. His doctor gave me a hug and said he was sorry. I turned to Nancy who was also crying and said, "I can't leave him alone." She said, "I've got him. I promise to take good care of him." As we walked toward the back door, I heard our favorite office worker, Patti, say, "Terrina, wait." When I turned around several of the staff were crying. She walked over to me, held me and said, "We all loved Bailey. I am so sorry, sweetie.

Love you." I will never, ever, forget her kindness in one of the worst moments of my life.

We sat in the car contemplating how we lost another dog at the age of seven. I had been a better advocate for Bailey, but he still suffered too much. I scolded myself because I should have done better. I vowed once again, that in the future, I would get it right.

When I called Terry, I fought back the tears and tried to be calm.

"Dad, Bails got sick, and we had to put him down."

"Well, that's a damn shame. You sure haven't had good luck with these dogs, have you?"

I didn't answer. Then he realized he was harsh.

"I'm sorry honey. I know you were his favorite person. He was a great dog."

"Yeah, thanks Dad." I said, without trying to hide my irritation. He snapped, "This is exactly why I will never have another dog. This fuckin' bullshit sucks."

It was a short chat.

The next day, Terry called to see how I was doing. I'm sure he felt guilty for being a dick. I told him not to worry about me and that I would get through it.

"What's going on with you, Dad?" I asked, changing the subject.

"Well, I'm pretty stressed out because I still haven't heard from Social Security. Things are wearing a little thin here."

"How much do you need?" I asked, getting straight to the point.

"Never mind, I'm fine," he snapped, sounding pissed off.

I was in a lousy mood that day, so my curt answer was, "Okay, Dad. Well, maybe you can find a cheaper place to live. Let me know how I can help."

It was another short chat.

My frustration probably got the best of me, but Terry had to deal with the results of his decisions. I would have sent him some money if he'd told me what he needed, but I was in no mood to play games.

Later that month, for his sixty-fourth birthday, John and I sent him $500. When he called to thank us, he said he had found a new place to live that would be cheaper than the trailer. He used our birthday gift for his moving costs and rental deposit.

On November 1, Dad moved into a small apartment in Salem, Ohio. He shared that he was happy about not having to spend another winter paying the high fuel oil costs at that old trailer. His new place had a small kitchen, bedroom, bathroom, and a living room. It wasn't much bigger than a hotel suite, but it was perfect for him.

On November 15, Terry called me and sounded distraught.

"Dad, what's wrong?"

"Well, things have gotten pretty bad here. I got my first Social Security check, but in the meantime, I had to file for food stamps. I've never been more embarrassed in my life."

I know that must have been difficult, and I sincerely felt sad about his situation, but I also needed him to hit rock bottom, which I'd hoped was nearby. John and I sent him some more money for Christmas, and that winter Uncle Joe gave him a couple of snowplows and another pickup truck to make some extra money.

He managed to get several snowplowing jobs with some of the local businesses in the area. His friend Frank owned a fabrication shop, and from time to time he would help him out with odd jobs, too. Even though his foot never stopped hurting he plowed forward and found a way to make ends meet.

CHAPTER NINETEEN

Cleveland

In June of 2013, I had to fly to Detroit to handle some personal business. I asked Dad if he could drive up from Ohio and spend a few days with me. Terry didn't want to travel on a plane anymore, and I rarely left Arizona, so this was a good opportunity to see him. I realized when I booked the trip that it had been almost five years.

After landing in Detroit, I rented a car and Dad followed me north to a hotel, where I had reserved two rooms. He knew of a good Mexican restaurant close by, so after we checked in we revived our tradition of eating some nachos and beer. After dinner, he asked me to take him back to the hotel so he could rest while I ran some errands.

When I returned, Dad was sitting outside on a bench smoking a cigarette. He was talking to a tall, thin, black woman wearing army fatigues, also smoking.

"Hi Dad, I thought you were resting."

"Well, the fuckin' hotel is non-smoking, so I decided to move the party outside."

"I see that. Why is your garbage can out here?"

"That's not a garbage can. You better get your eyes checked, honey. That's a cooler," he said with a smirk.

Sure enough, he had filled the hotel room garbage can with ice and a twelve-pack of Busch beer. Problem solved.

"Of course it is. I'm going to get my room settled and I'll be back in a bit."

When I returned thirty minutes later, the same woman was standing next to Terry drinking one of his beers and taking something from his hand. As I walked closer, I could see Dad's money clip; he was pulling out a few bills. He handed them to the lady, and she slipped them into her pants pocket.

"Hi, I'm Terrina, Terry's daughter," I said, as I approached his new friend.

"Oh I know. He's told me about you," she said with a laugh.

When she walked away, I asked Dad why he was giving a strange woman his money. He explained that she was getting ready to return to Afghanistan, and the most needed item during deployment was socks. He said, "I gave her some money to buy some nice socks for her unit."

I spent two days with Dad, and I could see he was slowing down. His foot was hurting, and he had a hard time climbing stairs and carrying heavy things. I wrapped up my business on the second day in the early afternoon. I asked Terry if he wanted to hang out another day or two and go visit Gram with me. Sitting on his pickup's tailgate, he looked at me and said, "Oh Honey Babe, your ole man is tired. I think I'll just head back home."

"Okay, Dad, I understand. I really appreciate you coming up to help me with this grunt work on such short notice."

"Well, it was my pleasure, and it was great to see you. It's been too long. I love you, honey."

I handed him some gas money and hugged and kissed him goodbye. I told him I loved him and watched him drive away. I felt sad that he had declined an opportunity to spend time with me, but as I drove to the airport, I felt grateful for the time I did have.

On September 7, Mulligan turned eight years old. I cried like a baby because I finally had a dog survive past seven. But after Bailey died, Mulligan wasn't himself. He and Bails were littermates, and they had never spent a day apart. So even though I wasn't ready for a new dog, I knew Mulligan was, so John and I began our search for his new companion.

On October 27, I was in Napa, California, visiting my friend Jill and celebrating my belated forty-fifth birthday. Terry had driven to Alpena to celebrate his sixty-fifth birthday with his family. Jill had stopped at a gas station when I received a text message from Uncle Joe. When I opened it, there was a picture of Dad standing next to my Uncle Joe's granddaughter. I vividly remember gasping and just staring at it.

"What? What's wrong?" Jill asked.

"It's a picture of Terry. He looks so bad," I slowly answered.

I turned the phone to show her what I was looking at and she said, "Oh no. I'm so sorry."

His skin was a grayish color, his eyes sunken into his head, and he looked even thinner than normal. I had just been with him a few months earlier in June. He had been tired and in pain, but he didn't look like death warmed over.

On October 29, I called to wish him a happy birthday and make sure he had received the box of steaks I'd sent for his party. I noticed he sounded like his head was stuffed up. I asked him if he was feeling okay, and he brushed me off. Uncle Joe was throwing a barbeque birthday party for Dad and his twin, so I kept the call short.

A few days later Dad returned to Ohio and called me.

"Oh, I must have caught a damn cold when I was up north. I seem to catch one every year."

"I'm sorry Daddy, I wish I was there to make you some chicken noodle soup. Will you go see a doctor?"

"I don't need no fuckin' doctor, it's just a cold."

A few days later I called and asked Terry how he was feeling.

"Like shit. I'm still out plowing snow, but it's kickin' my ass."

"It's time to go see a doctor, Dad. They can give you some meds to make you feel better. Stop fucking around."

The following week, Terry made an appointment with a local female MD. She ordered some lung x-rays, and ultimately told him he had pneumonia. I asked him to get a second opinion, but he said he really liked the doctor and that he was comfortable with her assessment. I felt in my gut that something more serious was going on, but he was calling the shots.

On November 13, John and I picked up the new addition to our family, Payson Brie. She was the cutest little girl Coton de Tulear puppy you've ever seen. A five-pound fluff ball, full of life. Earlier in the day, Mulligan had been put under general anesthesia to have a cyst removed, so when we brought the puppy home, he was still pretty groggy. He climbed up on the couch with a blow-up tube around his neck, which prevented him from chewing his stitches out. We carefully lifted Payson up to the sofa so she could meet her new big brother. Mully slowly lifted his head, looked at her, looked at us, and then dropped his head back down. Payson immediately wiggled out of my hands, walked right up to Mulligan, and snuggled in next to his head. It was love at first sight, and they became inseparable. She wasn't his littermate brother, but he took her in with an open heart, and she quickly brought Mully back to his playful, happy self.

On February 20, 2014, Dad's twin brother was found dead in his home. It was Uncle Joe's birthday, and unfortunately, he was the one to find him. Terry called me and said matter-of-factly,

"He drank and smoked himself to death. It was his own damn fault. Just like our dad, Tim wouldn't slow it down."

"Well, that's a shame. I'm so sorry Daddy."

"We hadn't been talking much lately. I got sick of him calling me all hours of the night, drunk," he snapped.

There were times when it seemed the twins were in a race to see who could be more reckless. Some days Terry was winning, others

Tim. With this new loss I knew Dad was thinking more and more about his own mortality.

Later that winter, Terry continued to struggle with being sick. He would get bouts of what he called the "stomach flu" and lots of colds. He went back to the same doctor, and she again diagnosed him with pneumonia. I pleaded with him to get a second opinion, but he overruled me, again. After several months of him continuing to fight the pneumonia, his doctor finally ordered a CT scan of his lungs. She called him and told him there was a mass in his right lung, and she wanted him to get a biopsy.

On May 22, Terry drove himself to the local hospital where they performed a biopsy under general anesthesia. When he went to check out, they told him he had to have a driver. So he called a cab, had the driver drop him off at his truck two blocks away, and drove himself back home.

"Dad. Are you crazy? You could have killed someone."

"Oh, bullshit. I was fine. Fuck all that bureaucratic shit," he snarled.

After a couple of weeks of asking Dad about his biopsy results, I was getting annoyed that he still hadn't heard from his doctor. I was starting to wonder if he had the answer, and he was avoiding me. After thirty days, he still had not heard anything.

"This is total bullshit, Dad. It doesn't take a month for a damn biopsy report. You need to call that asshole and light him up, or I will."

Twenty minutes later Dad called and said they had made a clerical error, and the doctor was very sorry. Then he said, "I have lung cancer."

"I'm so sorry Dad. I want to see the report, and I want you to get a second opinion at the Cleveland Clinic, okay?"

"Well, he wants to schedule me for surgery to remove most of my lung."

"Dad, this idiot couldn't even tell you your results in a reasonable amount of time. I don't want him touching you. I'm begging you.

Please make an appointment with the Cleveland Clinic. I will get you the phone number right now."

For once, Terry listened and after a consultation, the team at Cleveland Clinic decided they wanted to do their own biopsy and several other tests. The lead pulmonary surgeon told him that he'd never seen a patient with a plum-sized tumor in the lung who didn't also have cancer somewhere else. So they set up appointments for a PET scan, bloodwork, and an EKG. They never found any other cancer in his body, even after repeating several PET scans. His blood work was perfect, with all of his labs in normal range. The doctors were stumped, so they decided to perform a second biopsy, which was set for July 22.

On July 5, Dad drove to Toledo to see Uncle Joe, Uncle Ty, and his son, Travis. They had lunch at the famous Tony Packo's Café. Uncle Joe sent me a text with a picture of all of them standing together with their arms draped over each other's shoulders. Once again, I gasped at how sick Terry looked. He was terribly thin, his skin was very pale, and it looked like his lips were almost blue. I called Uncle Joe later and asked him how Dad was doing. My uncle was always a positive person, and I knew he didn't want to upset me. He said, "I think he looked fine. He's gonna get this surgery and he'll be fine. I told him it's just a bump in the road, and Cleveland Clinic is one of the best, so I'm not worried."

On Friday July 17, I received a phone call from Dad's friend, Frank. He had never called me before, so I figured it wasn't going to be a social chat.

"Honey, you better get to Ohio. It's bad. He won't go to the local hospitals, because he says they're all quacks. He can't walk or stand up at all. I'm afraid he will die in the car so I wouldn't drive him to Cleveland."

I called Terry immediately, and luckily he answered his phone.

"What the hell is going on? Frank called me. Are you okay?"

"I'm fine now, honey. I'm doing much better now that I'm home."

"No, Dad. You're not going to give me that horseshit. I will pay for a private car service for you, a private ambulance, or a helicopter. I'll get whatever the hell you need, but you cannot stay at home. You need a doctor. You have twenty minutes to get a ride to the Cleveland Clinic or I will call 911."

"No, I don't want to go to the local hospital; they're a bunch of no-good, backwoods motherfuckers."

Then he acquiesced and said, "Okay. Okay. I'll call my friend Sarah and call you back."

"I'm not fucking around, Dad, if you can't get a ride in twenty minutes, I am calling 911."

He called me back five minutes later and said, "Okay honey, if you think I need to go, Sarah will take me."

"Thank you, Dad. Please call me when you get there. If I don't hear from you in two and a half hours, I'm calling the police."

"Oh Jesus Christ, don't do that. I promise she is taking me, and I will call you when I get there."

He called me right on time about two hours later and said they were going to do a work up on him. I called the hospital and told them he lived alone, and asked if they could hold him until I could fly in from Arizona on Sunday. They agreed, and I booked a red-eye flight for the next night.

Before my flight was leaving Phoenix, I called Terry. He answered the phone screaming, "Just a second, honey. Shut the fuck up. You need to shut up, you prick. You've been screaming all day and I've had enough of your bullshit!"

"Dad, who the hell are you talking to?"

"My roommate is a prick. He shouts a bunch of bullshit all day, and I can't sleep a fuckin' wink."

"Well, please calm down, I'm on my way. I'll be there in the morning to break you out."

"Let me give you directions from the car rental place because they're having the Republican Convention in Cleveland, and all the roads are fucked up."

As I arrived in Cleveland early Sunday morning, I had no idea what to expect. I didn't even know what was wrong with my dad at this point, other than knowing he had cancer, of course. I felt a little nervous because the last time I was in Cleveland, I was about ten years old, and Dad and his girlfriend Carol were taking me to Sea World in Aurora, Ohio. Somehow he'd made a wrong turn, and we ended up in some really scary part of town at some dumpy hotel. Dad told me he stayed up all night looking out the window and making sure we didn't get murdered.

Luckily, his directions were perfect, and I found the hospital without any issues. When I got off the elevator at the Oncology floor, I didn't need to ask which room Terry was in; the loud obscenities made it obvious. I stopped to speak with his nurse, and she explained that he had arrived extremely dehydrated but was doing better and ready to leave. She also explained that, unfortunately, he was the only one on that floor who could put up with his roommate, so he couldn't be moved. I wondered how it was possible to have a worse patient than Dad.

I walked into his room past his roommate and found Terry sitting up in his bed, wide awake and agitated.

"Hi, Dad." I said, as I hugged and kissed him.

"Hi honey. You look pretty. When can we go?"

His roommate was screaming nonsense, clearly experiencing some confusion. And Dad just wanted a cigarette and was so restless he was about to jump out of his skin.

"They told me that I was dehydrated, that's all. But I don't think it was fair that they said because I live alone, I had to stay another day."

I wasn't about to risk my life and admit that that was at my request. I replied, "Well, Daddy, it's probably a good thing that they made sure you are back to a hundred percent, so you don't have another episode."

Two doctors came in shortly after I arrived—one older, and the other appeared to be a resident learning the ropes. Then the nurse joined us and was giving the doctors a summary report.

"Lung cancer patient, waiting a biopsy, fifty-plus-year smoker..." Then the older doctor cut her off and said sternly to the nurse, "We don't judge." Then he turned to me and said, "Are you taking him home? Are you his daughter?"

"Yes sir, that is correct."

"We're sending you home this morning, Mr. Troy. We just need to get your discharge papers, okay?" the older doctor calmly stated.

"I wanted to get the fuck out of here yesterday," Dad announced.

The doctor just smiled at me as he walked out of the room, and said, "Take care of yourself, Mr. Troy. Perhaps try some nicotine patches if you can."

Once he was released, I pushed Terry outside in a wheelchair while I waited for the valet to fetch my car. As soon as I brought his chair to a stop, Dad stood up and lit a cigarette. He knew he couldn't smoke in my rental car, so he chain-smoked two cigarettes as quickly as he could.

Arriving at Terry's apartment I noticed his kitchen was a mess and laundry baskets overflowing. He explained that he hadn't had the energy to do his chores and asked me if I would help him with his laundry. I loaded up his dirty clothes in my car, and after five loads we were ready to go to the laundromat.

He commented several times that he just didn't have the strength to carry things to the car anymore. I said, "It's okay Dad, we'll get this done and you'll be in good shape."

When we returned to his apartment, he sat down on the couch, and I carried the laundry baskets to his bedroom in the back. As I walked past the kitchen, I tripped over something hard, it hit my shin and then bounced off the refrigerator making a loud crash noise. After I caught my footing and managed not to drop the basket, I looked down and saw a large shotgun, lying on the floor.

"Jesus, Dad. I almost killed myself on your gun. That's not loaded is it?"

"Well, it wouldn't be much good if it wasn't," he said, snickering.

"Is that where you usually keep it? In the kitchen?"

"No, I usually keep it under the couch, where I sleep."

Dad always slept on the couch, and he used the coffee table as his nightstand. It was his central command station with his cigarettes, ashtray, wallet, phone, eyeglasses, and other paperwork neatly organized next to him. Everything he needed, including his gun.

"One night I had some drug-head, asshole knock on my door. I grabbed my gun, walked to the door, and held it by my side, pointed at the floor. I asked him what the hell he wanted, and he mumbled something about a winning lottery ticket he could give me if I gave him some cash. I knew it was bullshit. So I just raised my gun, pointed it up at the ceiling so he could get a good look at it, and he took off running."

"Wow, Dad. You should sign up to be on the Welcoming Committee," I said, laughing.

Terry wasn't feeling strong like the old days, but his street skills were sharp. And apparently charm school was still paying off.

The next day, I went to Walmart and bought him a window fan. He didn't have any air conditioning, and Ohio was in the middle of a heatwave. I got him a bunch of electrolyte and protein drinks, and easy-to-make food that he could quickly microwave or grab a quick snack. I also purchased several months' worth of nicotine patches. I wasn't confident he would use them, but I was hoping he would at least try. Then I ordered him a pushcart that he could use to haul things from the parking lot to his apartment.

"You didn't need to do all that."

"Dad, I'd really appreciate it if you would try the patches, because over the years I've developed some asthma, and I can't sit in here while you're smoking."

"Okay," he said and quickly asked, "When are you going home?"

"What?"

"I know you have a lot going on in Arizona; when is your flight?"

"I don't have a return flight yet, I can stay as long as you need me."

"Honey, why don't you drive Frank's SUV to the biopsy tomorrow instead of the rental car?"

"No thanks, Dad, I don't need Frank's car. I would feel terrible if I damaged it. My rental car is fine."

On July 22, I met Dad at his apartment, and we drove to Cleveland for his biopsy. Terry wasn't allowed any food or drink before his procedure, so he wasn't in the best of moods without coffee. I stayed with him in the pre-op room until they took him back. They explained that he would be doing a lot of coughing when he was out of surgery and some hot coffee would help with that. As soon as I got word that he was out, I bought him some fresh, hot java and found him in post-op, sat by his side, waiting for him to come to. As soon as he woke up, he was coughing his head off. I noted that I'd seen that same expression on his face my whole life when he sipped coffee that was too hot to swallow. He squinted his eyes and curled his lips as he sucked some liquid in.

"Is it good, Daddy?" hoping I'd made him happy.

"Yeah," he said, still groggy.

As we waited for the doctors to come tell us their findings, he became more impatient and agitated. I knew he was having nicotine withdrawals, but we had to wait longer. I didn't leave his side because I was afraid I would miss the doctor's report.

After about two hours, a tall Indian woman in a lab coat approached us. She was a very pleasant and kind person; her name tag said she was an MD. She began explaining what they'd done and then what they had found. Dad interrupted her over and over asking short questions, "So it's the same as the other biopsy, right?" Then he said, "I can go now, right?" He didn't mask being annoyed and his behavior lacked basic manners.

The doctor patiently finished her conversation with us, and we were dismissed. I helped him get dressed while we waited for a wheelchair. I started wheeling him out of the post-op room and he snapped, "Hurry up!"

"Okay. Calm down," I pleaded.

"I'm going to use the restroom."

"Why didn't you go before?" he asked annoyed.

"I've been holding it so I could be with you this whole time. Just wait a minute, I'll be quick."

When I returned to push him down to the main floor, he was sitting quiet with an angry look on his face. As I approached the valet desk to get my ticket validated, the woman behind the counter took one look at me, practically rolled her eyes, and resumed talking to her friend. Under his breath Dad was muttering some of his favorite vocabulary words, finally ending with: "lazy bitch."

"Shhhh!" I snapped, with a dirty look.

As soon as I was able to get my ticket punched, I pushed him outside to the valet. There must have been thirty cars trying to navigate the circle entrance. Dad was still sitting in his wheelchair ranting, "These dumb fucks don't know what they're doing. Give me a fuckin' break. How hard is it to get your damn car?"

"Just get your ass out of the chair and go over there away from everyone and smoke a fucking cigarette!" I barked.

A few minutes later, he walked up behind me when the car arrived. All chipper as he pointed at my car, and said, "Well there it is."

"Just get in," I ordered.

As I pulled out of the parking lot, I slammed on the brakes, snapped my head toward him and yelled, "That was embarrassing.

You cannot speak to a doctor like that. She was being kind and patient, and you were so rude. And you didn't need to be such an asshole to me either. If you want them to take care of you, you better get it together, Dad!"

"I don't know how to do this, Terrina. I've never had to deal with hospitals and doctors before!" he yelled, with his face beet red.

"You know how to be nice to people. You better figure it out, because that shit-show was ridiculous," I said, punching the gas.

We stopped at Bob Evans and barely spoke. Then rush-hour traffic turned our two-hour trip into four hours. He continued to punish all the drivers around us for his lack of nicotine. When we finally arrived back at his apartment, he sat down on his couch, grabbed his cigarette pack and shook out a cigarette. Then he snatched the end with his lips, pulled it out, tossed the pack on the table, lit his cigarette, and stared at the TV as he filled the room with smoke. He blew more smoke from his nose and he said, "Did you schedule your flight yet?"

"No Dad. And it hurts my feelings that you keep asking. I don't feel very welcome."

"That's not it. I just know you have a lot going on back in Arizona, and I feel bad that I'm keeping you from it," he assured me, as he filled the small living room with more smoke.

"Okay, Dad. I'm going back to the hotel. I'll see you later," I said as I coughed and flashed him a pissed-off look.

"I forgot. I'll put it out," he said, raising his voice and still holding the cigarette.

I walked out the door, jumped into my car, and slammed it in reverse. When I backed up into the middle of the parking lot, I threw it into drive and hit the gas. It wouldn't move forward. I tried putting it into park and then drive again. The engine was revving, but without forward motion. Begrudgingly, I called Terry and was surprised he answered.

"Dad, my car won't go forward, I don't know what to do," I said in a panic.

He was there in split-second, messed with the gearshift over and over, and managed to get the car parked. When he got out of the car, he threw me the keys, marched back to his apartment, and snapped, "Call those assholes and tell 'em you need a new car, your driveshaft is dead."

Standing in the 95-degree heat, I was informed I wouldn't be getting a replacement until the next day. I emptied my belongings into a small roller bag and started walking. There was nothing but wooded lots between the apartment complex and the hotel. About two minutes into the walk, something felt creepy. I looked around and I couldn't see anyone in sight, and I had an uneasy feeling come over me. I made a snap decision that I didn't want to end up dead in the woods, so I turned around.

On one of the hottest, most humid days of the year, I ran as fast as I could, pulling my bag back to the main road, through several parking lots, down another four-lane road, through a major intersection, and back to the hotel. When I got inside, I was drenched in sweat, exhausted, and beyond over it. I called John and said, "Please book me on the first flight out of here."

The next morning, Terry gave me a ride to my new rental car, and I told him I was leaving.

"Pittsburgh's a tricky airport to get to. I want you to follow me."

"That's very nice of you, Dad, but I'm sure I'll figure it out."

"Look. You've been getting your way this whole time. I'm not going to take no for an answer, damn it. I will drive in front of you, so I know you get there okay."

"Okay, let's go," I said, feeling exhausted by the drama.

Part of me was happy to follow him. It was a long drive on numerous small country roads, and after what happened to my first rental car, I didn't have a lot of confidence in my second. The drive was enjoyable, green and lush, and I loved all the cool old bridges.

It had been a long time since I had been angry with my father, and it felt awful. We got out of our cars, Dad lit a cigarette, and asked, "How'd you like that drive?"

"It was great, Dad. I really didn't know how beautiful it was going to be."

"I love you Honey Babe, thanks for coming," he said, as he hugged and kissed me.

"Yep, I love you too Dad."

I turned around pulling my bags into the terminal, and I never stopped to look back. Not once.

CHAPTER TWENTY

Stress Tests

erry felt badly about how things had gone when I was in Ohio. He called me several times a week to keep me abreast of the oncology process. We never discussed what happened, but apparently he took my words to heart, because he made a point of telling me how polite and respectful he'd been when dealing with everyone within the hospital system.

After Dad's second biopsy, the surgeons agreed to perform the partial lung removal surgery, but not until he was able to pass a stress test. He admitted he was nervous about the test, given he was feeling weak and winded with even the smallest amount of exertion. Most of his life he had physically demanding jobs; he'd never been on a treadmill.

"You got this, Dad. Remember, its mind over matter. Just keep telling yourself that it will be over soon, and just keep going."

"I just gotta do it. I just gotta get through it. I want this damn tumor out of me," he said with trepidation.

The morning of his test, I called him to give him one last pep talk. He was at the gas station he always stopped at on his trips to Cleveland.

"Morning, Honey Babe. I'm just grabbing some gas, coffee, and my favorite donut."

"Wow, Dad. Breakfast of champions. If that doesn't kill you, this damn stress test sure won't," I said with a giggle.

"I'll get'er done. Don't you worry honey."

Later that day Terry called me when he arrived home. He sounded exhausted.

"It was really hard, but I did it," he reported.

"You did?" I snapped.

"Yep. Now we just wait for the report and hope they agree to cut me open."

Sometime in August, Dad said he'd passed the stress test, but the team of doctors that reviewed his case wanted him to have another PET scan and another biopsy.

"Gosh, Dad, this seems like a damn hamster wheel," I said with a sigh.

"Well honey, their pitchin' and I'm catchin'. I'll do whatever I have to do to beat this fuckin' cancer. If they think they're going to run me off, they've got another thing comin'."

On August 31, my father drove himself to Cleveland, parked his car at a hotel near the hospital, and took a cab. They performed another biopsy and ran a litany of tests. He drove himself home the next day and called to let me know he was safe. I was relieved he was being more responsible.

About a week later, Cleveland Clinic agreed to give him a surgery date. He called and said, "Well, baby girl, I'm finally done jumping through all the hoops. They're gonna remove eighty-five percent of my right lung on September 14."

Finally, after more than six months of tests and three biopsies, he was getting his wish. Even while Dad felt exhausted and sick, he was a tenacious fighter. I always knew that about him, but watching it at this level was eye-opening, even for me.

As the date was quickly approaching, I started researching everything I could about the surgery. Since Dad didn't have a computer, he allowed me access to his health records through the hospital's portal. I knew that this was a very serious surgery, but I felt grateful that he was in one of the best places in the world. I called Uncle Joe and was relieved that he planned on driving down to take Terry for his surgery. Every time I spoke with Dad about coming, he would tell me to stay in Arizona. He said I would just get bored sitting around doing nothing.

I remember telling my uncle that I was worried that Terry wouldn't quit smoking after they removed his lung. Uncle Joe responded, "What? I've never heard of that. That's crazy."

In a conversation with my father about a week before his surgery, he was lamenting that Par wanted to drive eight hours to take him to the hospital.

"I told him not to come. I'll be fine," Dad said.

"Dammit, Dad. Sweet Uncle Joe wants to be there with you. Just let him be there. This surgery is no fucking joke, and I want someone there with you. Plus, he'll be able to call me and let me know how you're doing and handle any issues that you might need help with. Will you please stop asking him not to come before you piss him off?" I pleaded.

He took a long drag on his cigarette, I could hear him slowly exhale in a way that sounded like he was too tired to fight me.

"Fine, honey. I will let him come. You're right, it'll make life easier to have a ride and someone there to call you. But I am going to be fine, and you need to stop worrying."

On September 14, Uncle Joe called and said that Dad was in surgery. He explained, "Well, honey, they took him back, and he's in great hands. One of the nurses told me that the surgery survival rates at Cleveland Clinic are really good because they just won't do surgery on people that they think won't make it. So I feel pretty good that everything will work out just fine."

"Thank you so much Uncle Joe. I am so grateful that you're there. Little bastard refused to let me come. How was he feeling before he went back?"

"Good. He was good."

I figured with his brother there, he would be stoic. Maybe that's exactly what he needed. While I had my uncle on the phone, I asked him how his stay with Terry went. He laughed and said, "Well, his neighbors are pretty interesting. I think they're all single old ladies. They saw me drive up in my Hummer, and one of them said to your dad, 'Terry, if I knew your rich, handsome brother was coming, I would've put my teeth in.'" Then he broke out in his famous belly laugh that sounded like he was running out of air. I knew the scene there—he was telling the truth.

My father came through the surgery, and Uncle Joe stayed until he could see Terry back in his room. I could finally exhale. I spoke to Dad later that night and he sounded tired but cognizant enough to take my call. He complained that his rib cage hurt quite a bit, and I convinced him to call for a nurse and ask for more meds. I encouraged him not to be shy about asking for stronger pain relief. No need to suffer.

"Oh, fuck no. I ain't gonna be shy about nothin'. This shit hurts. But I'll get through it."

His friend Sarah gave him a ride home five days after his surgery. I tried to convince him to let me hire someone to help him, but he refused. Some of his friends and his neighbor Ella checked on him from time to time, but he basically recovered alone.

Five weeks after Terry's surgery he turned sixty-seven years old. I was thankful to have him in my life another year, especially after what he'd been through. On November 2, he had his first chemotherapy treatment. I had asked him if I could come stay a few days after his appointment, but once again I was prohibited. I tried to explain that the treatments he was about to undergo would probably be debilitating, but he insisted that I stay with John and handle my own issues. I respected his decision and tried my best to support him from afar.

He drove himself to and from the first treatment. I called him every day for a week afterward. He told me that the first few days were tough, but after day five he started to feel much better.

His second chemo appointment was on November 25. That seemed kind of quick to me, but they wanted him to do four treatments, one month apart. Unfortunately, because of the timing, he said, "I can't make it to Uncle Joe's for Thanksgiving this year, which sucks. But it is, what it is. And I'm not too happy that all my damn hair is falling out, either," he lamented.

The side effects of the second infusion we're the same as the first; he bounced back within a few days.

His third chemo treatment was on December 15. He drove himself again, and then called me, just like he always did. I wasn't able to take his call, so he left me a voicemail message.

"I'm back home safe honey. But they must have done something different this time, because I really feel like shit. I'm going to bed. I'll call you tomorrow. I love you."

I called him the next day, but he didn't answer. So I called his neighbor Ella and asked her to check on him for me. She said he was spending a lot of time in the bathroom and didn't want to see anyone. She was very concerned that he would become dehydrated again, so she encouraged him to drink fluids. She also informed me that he was still smoking, which was no big surprise to me. There was no point in discussing it; he was going to do what he was going to do.

I called him the next day and he finally answered. He said with a raised voice,

"I hate that cocksucker, chemo doctor. I will never get another chemo treatment as long as I live. This is the worst experience I have ever had. My shit smells so bad, I vomit. I vomit so much I think my other lung is going to come out. My whole fucking body hurts. Fuck that asshole if he thinks I will be back for my fourth treatment."

I didn't know what to say. What he was describing, and the tone he was using, was frightening. I felt helpless and angry that he was hurting.

"Daddy, I am so sorry this is happening to you. What can I do?"

"Nothing. I gotta go, I can't keep my happy face on when I feel like this, and you don't need to hear about my problems."

"Dad, please stop. I just want to make sure you have everything you need to feel better. Should I call your doctor?"

"Fuck no. I'm never going back to him!" he shouted.

Once Terry started to feel better, he resumed treatment at the hospital, but not chemotherapy. He did a few radiation treatments, and then he was done. During that time, he learned to have faith in his radiologist. So much so, that he would only take advice from that one doctor. At his six-month checkup in March, the doctor told him he was cancer free. We were all thrilled and shocked that he had pulled through this horrific experience. He would need to continue to see the radiologist every six months, for the foreseeable future, but Terry felt relieved that he had beat cancer.

In April of 2016, Uncle Joe bought Dad a black GMC pickup truck. He texted me a picture of Terry standing next to it with a big smile on his face. Terry loved that truck, but he loved his brother even more. He used to tell me, "Honey Babe, you can always trust Par. He is one of the few people on this planet that will never let you down. If I'm not here anymore, and you need something, call your Uncle Joe."

In July, Dad made the seven-hour drive in his new truck to Alpena to see his family. He stayed at the Price Farm and spent the Fourth of July with Uncle Joe and his son Brian. They loved to shoot the shit, grill up a bunch of barbeque, and just be together. I was comforted that he felt well enough to make the long journey.

That October Terry turned sixty-eight years old. He struggled with feeling weak and fatigued, but he still managed to help his friend Frank at his shop with the occasional delivery or small project. We were all grateful that one year after having his lung surgery, his doctor told him he was still cancer free. It felt like things were getting back to normal.

CHAPTER TWENTY-ONE

Get Back on the Horse

Around the time that Dad had his lung removal surgery, I met a new neighbor who lived across the street from us. She was an older lady who lived alone and rarely had visitors. John and I believed that she had studied our routine because she would frequently greet us in our driveway when we returned home. She would talk her head off, annoying John, but I tried to be nice. It happened so often that he nicknamed her "Ambush."

She kept nagging me to meet her horse that she boarded at a fancy show barn a few miles away. I felt sorry for her because she seemed lonely and was socially awkward. I avoided her request because at the time I had a genuine fear of horses. On those childhood trips to visit my grandparents' farm, Grandma Margot's husband would tell me to stay away from the horses or they'd kill me. He made it especially clear that I should never walk behind a horse, or they'd kick me to the moon. He was probably smart to keep me away from them, given my track record of getting hurt on the farm while on his watch. After all, I was just a tiny, wild toddler, and they were eighteen-hundred-pound work horses. But it really bothered me that I loved animals so much, and yet I had this fear of equines.

I'd made a small attempt to rectify this issue back in September of 2013. My friend Jill and I took a girls' trip to Tucson and stayed at the Miraval Resort and Spa. It was made famous when Oprah

Winfrey went there and produced a show about challenging yourself and reconnecting with your soul's purpose. To be clear, we really just wanted great massages, facials, and some downtime. However, one of the "experiences" they offered was the Wyatt Webb's Equine Experience. It turned out Jill and I both had the same fear of horses, so we decided to sign up for the day class. The excursion was described as a powerful way to connect with an animal that will reflect your feelings and emotions and create more awareness about your personal paradigms. If the horse didn't think you were being genuine, it would not perform the task. In turn, one would benefit from self-reflection, pushing emotional boundaries and limitations—or something like that.

Jill and I rode in a small bus with about ten other women to a nearby ranch where the horses were boarded. The person in charge that day wasn't the famous Wyatt Webb; it was a female protégé leading us through the agenda. She had us pair off and then explained that we would be expected to find a horse in the pen that was tied up to the rail and wait for further instructions. We slowly followed the group toward the pen to pick out our poor victim. My heart was pounding, but I kept a cool demeanor, as we cracked some wise-ass remarks in an attempt to help each other feel comfortable. One by one, all the horses were chosen until it was our turn. The remaining soul was a large, mostly white gelding with a few chocolate-colored spots on his neck, head, belly, and back. As soon as the horse selection was over, I could feel the energy rise around me. The guests were animated, emotional, and speaking quickly. Jill walked up to our horse, wrapped her arms around his neck, and started crying. I said, "Oh my God! What?" As she sobbed, she said, "He reminds me of Belle." She had recently lost her giant albino Great Dane named Belle.

I wanted to comfort her, but you can imagine the commotion a dozen ladies can make—the energy was palpable, confusing, and distracting. But there was no time for that because the program leader announced, "Okay everyone, you have some tools in a bucket, and this is what I want you to do. After a short demonstration, I want you to take turns grooming the horse, picking its feet, and then taking it on a walk around the pen." Jill and I looked at each other, eyes the size of saucers, with that familiar "what-the-hell?" look we had shared so many times in college. We were both calculating whether to run for the hills or start protesting. With great hesitation, we decided to give it a Girl Scout try, knowing we both had each other's backs if at any time we wanted to bail, regardless of how silly it might look.

Then the leader barked out, "And don't forget to do both sides, which means you will need to walk behind your horse with your arm on its rear and your body close, touching its hind end." Honestly, I have no idea what she said after that because I was sweating bullets with my heart pounding out of my tank top. I was fighting back the urge to puke. I just knew this was how I was going to die: with a smelly, horseshit shoe print on my forehead.

But with each task, I swallowed the lump in my throat and did what was asked of me, as did Jill. When it was all over, all the ladies gathered to discuss what had happened. It was sort of like a group therapy session. One by one, we were each asked what we had learned in our experience. One woman had just lost her husband. Another lady had recently been through a rough divorce. There were lots of tears and deep expressions of how meaningful the day had been. When it was my turn, I remember just wanting to get back to the spa, take a shower, and forget about the whole damn thing. So I said, "I guess what I learned is that I have mastered the art of sucking-it-up."

When I shared this story with Dad, I remember him snapping, "Oh Jesus Christ. You paid for that shit? Those cocksuckers took your hard-earned money for that bunch of bullshit?

"Um, Yes. Yes, I did. I was hoping I would gain some experience with a horse and could stop being afraid of them," I said, feeling like an idiot.

"Well, I'm proud of your effort, honey. But next time just find a nice cowboy to teach you the real deal—not that BS that those fuckers are selling."

Eventually, I did agree to meet Ambush's horse. He was being boarded at a beautiful barn that was owned by a very wealthy Chilean man. It was designed like a Mediterranean palace and even had a swimming pool for the horses to rehabilitate in. Each stall had a window to the outside with an arched decorative door on it. The horses would stick their heads outside to enjoy the sunshine and watch the other horses getting worked in the adjacent arenas. As gorgeous as it was, it seemed dark and cold, and I remember thinking it felt like a beautiful prison. Her buckskin gelding, Willy, had a stall in the aisle with all the other quarter horses. The barn was also full of high-end Arabians and other top-notch breeds trained for a variety of performance disciplines.

Surprisingly, I really enjoyed spending time with the horses, even though I wasn't completely comfortable around them. After frequent visits, I noticed the sorrel quarter horse named Peppy, next to Willy's stall, never had any visitors. I was told his owner didn't come to Scottsdale very often. She had several homes around the country and spent most of her time in other places. I felt sad for Peppy, so I started bringing him treats and giving him some pats on the nose. A few months after consistently visiting the barn, Ambush told me that the trainer was willing to allow me to come and groom Peppy. It felt scary, but I accepted and was given a set of grooming tools, a few pointers and full access to the barn. I had been selling a lot of real estate and working my tail off, so having some time in the mornings to hang out with a horse seemed like something that might help with the stress, even if I was totally afraid of him. I'd made up my mind that I didn't want to be scared anymore, and I'd push myself outside of my comfort zone. I started getting up at six in the morning before work just to have time to groom and hang out with Peppy. He was a smart horse—he put up with my adrenaline rushes and nerves, and I rewarded him with treats. We developed a healthy codependent relationship.

On May 7, 2017, Uncle Joe texted me a photo of himself with my Uncle Ty and Dad. They had met for lunch again in Toledo. I stared at the photo in disbelief. Terry looked frail and white as a ghost. I called Uncle Joe to get his take and he said, "He seemed good. Tired maybe, but he had a long drive. I think he's doing okay." I felt in my gut something wasn't right, but both Dad and Joe were saying the opposite.

In June, Ambush approached me with an opportunity. One of her friends owned two horses and was spending the summer in Colorado. She could only take one of her horses with her; she was leaving her other horse in Scottsdale. Ambush suggested I lease her horse for three months; it would be kept in the stall across from Peppy. He was a beautiful golden palomino named Sosa. I'd been grooming Peppy for eight months, but I had not even come close to sitting on a horse, let alone being responsible for one. There was a hefty financial requirement, but it would include the trainer giving me riding lessons. And she would have the primary responsibility of making any decisions about the care of the horse. Both Dad and John were totally supportive, and they felt that it was an investment in my mental health.

"Honey, I know you'll be careful. I'm just tickled to shit that you're doing something for yourself. I'm really proud of you for trying something new, too. That horse doesn't know it yet, but he just hit the jackpot with you taking care of him," Terry said.

Life seemed like it was getting back on track. I was busy working, taking riding lessons, and grooming both Sosa and Peppy most mornings. Dad had made his annual Fourth of July trip to see Par and Brian. On July 7, they all drove from Alpena over to the middle of the mitten to meet up with Uncle Ty and his kids at Spike's Keg O'Nails in Grayling. Uncle Joe texted me a photo of the group all together with arms around each other's necks. Dad looked a little better than the last photo I had received, but he still looked underweight. It was a good sign that he felt well enough for an outing.

I had spent nearly every day for five months spoiling horses and loving it. I never totally got over my fear of all horses, but I learned to trust Sosa and loped around the arena after only eight lessons. When his owner returned, I took a small break from being a wannabe cowgirl so John and I could take a vacation. I had always wanted to take an RV trip with the dogs, and I'd regretted not doing it when Bailey was still alive. Mulligan loved the car, so I knew he would enjoy a good road trip. John continued to have health issues and had started using a cane to get around. It seemed a road trip was a good way to get him out for some fun without requiring too much activity. We both had Monument Valley on our bucket lists, so for my forty-ninth birthday, we loaded up the sexy Cruise America RV and took off north.

Dad turned sixty-nine years old. I felt a release. Every year I would hold my breath, fearing that we wouldn't celebrate our birthdays together. His doctors were monitoring some small nodules on the exterior of his lungs and had performed another biopsy. He underwent a few more radiation treatments to reduce the small cancerous masses that seemed to appear out of nowhere. The doctors were confident that he didn't need to worry—they had nipped it in the bud. Even with that going on, his blood work seemed mostly normal, so they kept him on a six-month follow-up schedule.

Terry had started complaining that his rib cage hurt after the radiation treatment. He was having a hard time sleeping and generally felt like crap. I wanted to go visit him and check things out for myself, but I was shot down again.

After Sosa's owner returned, we made an arrangement for me to continue leasing the horse. Before I had gone on vacation, I noticed that Sosa didn't seem right when I rode him. I felt like his back legs were not as engaged, which made for a bumpier ride. I didn't know enough about horses to describe it well, but I definitely noticed a change in him physically. I kept a close eye on it, but because I was a neophyte, my opinion wasn't given much credence. One day in November, I met the owner at the performance horse barn out in Rio Verde where she was keeping her horses. We were planning on riding, but when I went to get Sosa out of his pen, he was dragging both of his back legs, one at a time, slowly as he tried to walk toward me. I called the owner over, and we noted Sosa's back left leg was swollen and stiff, and he had swelling in his left rump area, too.

After the vet came to evaluate what was going on, it was determined that he must have injured his leg somehow, either by getting it stuck in his pen, or perhaps a nearby horse could have kicked him. I wasn't convinced, because his leg didn't have a wound on it, and his pen didn't look as though a horse had been thrashing around in it. He didn't have any scratches on his face, which are common for horses that get "cast" or stuck against the walls of their stalls. I did some research and was convinced he had a cancerous mass. He wasn't my horse, so I went along with the narrative; I followed the vet's protocol.

Sosa's owner and I continued taking turns checking on him every day. Each time I would see him, he looked worse. He looked like he was in more pain and was swollen, sweaty, and irritable. On November 19, the owner called me early in the morning and told me that Sosa was down in his stall and wouldn't get up. We both raced to the barn to find the trainer, workers and barn manager doing everything they could to get Sosa on his feet. I had never experienced the mania of desperately trying to save a really large soul in a very small space. It was overwhelming and devastating to watch the fruitless efforts. After several hours, the net result was that Sosa had to be euthanized. I'd spent nearly every day for more than six months with that horse, and his passing broke my heart. Ultimately, the vet concluded that Sosa, in all likelihood, had a ruptured cancerous tumor.

I decided not to call Terry until I could speak about Sosa without crying. When I finally told him, he said, "I had a feeling you were going to fall in love with that horse. You've always had a thing for animals, honey. I'm so, so sorry, Honey Babe. I wish I was there to give you a hug. He knew you loved him, and he was lucky to have you."

◆

Later in the month of November, Mulligan wasn't feeling well. One of the other horse owners at the fancy barn was a small-animal vet. When I arrived at her clinic, I told her that Mulligan seemed like he had something wrong with his lower back. I explained that when pressure was placed on his hip area, his legs seemed to give out. As soon as I said that, Mulligan jumped up on the vet and licked her face.

"Well if he had a back problem, he wouldn't be doing that. Let's do some blood work."

"In my experience, both my previous wheatens had perfect bloodwork even when they had major liver issues. Can you do x-rays instead?" I asked.

"Sure. I don't think we'll find anything, but I'd be happy to start there if that's what you'd prefer."

About thirty minutes later she brought Mulligan back into the room. She said, "Well, the good news is that I don't see any issues with his spine. The bad news is that he has a pretty large mass in his abdomen. It's likely a Hemangiosarcoma."

I was stunned that I was dealing with cancer, again. I couldn't hold my tears.

"Hey, I don't know that this will affect him short term. He might live a really long time with this. We just don't know. You don't have to do anything right now."

On the ride home with my sweet, furry boy by my side, his head resting over my shoulder from the back seat, I made a conscious decision to refocus on being grateful for what I still had. I promised Mulligan that we would spend as much time together as possible, and I would never, ever let him suffer. I was grateful that Gram, who had just turned ninety-six years old that same month, was still alive. Dad, John, Mully, and Payson were still with me, and I was still sane—which was the biggest miracle of all.

CHAPTER TWENTY-TWO

Gift Horse

The new year would bring more of the same with Dad declining and refusing to see his doctor. John was having difficulty walking, experiencing leg numbness and loads of pain. Mulligan was slowing down, and I was working seven days a week selling real estate and trying my best to stay positive.

On January 16, 2018, I received a call from my Gram's phone number. She needed some extra care and had been staying at my aunt's trailer in town, so I knew it probably wasn't Gram calling. I froze while I stared at the phone, watching it ring with the word "Gram" displayed on the screen. My aunt's voice in my voicemail instructed me to call her back at Gram's house. I gathered my strength and dialed her number. After saying hello, she got right to the point.

"Gram died."

She went on to tell me that she'd actually died on the thirteenth. I felt faint as I held back the raging fit that was welling up inside of me. I struggled to wrap my head around the idea that Gram had been dead for three days and no one could be bothered to call me. My aunt went on to say that everyone in her household had contracted the flu over Christmas and had passed it on to Gram. She took her to the emergency room but was told to take her home because they couldn't do anything. Since my aunt was a nurse, she chose to have hospice services come to her house. She rambled detailing the difficulty she had getting a comfort package; she recounted the miserable days and events leading up to Gram's passing. I sat there stunned and couldn't believe this was the first I had heard of her illness; I was deeply disturbed hearing of Gram's suffering. I took notes because I knew the shock wouldn't allow me to remember the conversation well. When I hung up the phone, I cried harder than I had ever cried in my entire life.

It had been difficult to communicate with my grandmother in her later years because she was basically deaf. I started writing her more and calling less because it would frustrate her that she couldn't hear me. I didn't want to make her feel bad, so I stopped making her try to talk to me. I had spent nearly fifty years with Gram on this earth, and now she was gone. The world felt lonelier all of a sudden.

Once I gained my composure, I called Dad. After some small talk, I said, "Well, Daddy, I have some sad news. Gram died." Dad was silent for a moment and then said, "Oh Honey Babe, I'm so sorry. I know how much you loved her. When did she pass?"

"Apparently she passed three days ago, but I just got the news."

After I told him the whole story, he said, "Well, she was a great lady. I really loved her, too. I have great memories of her. I can't believe you weren't called when she got sick so you could say goodbye. Calling you three days after Margaret died is fucking ridiculous. Well, honey, I really didn't think there could be a bigger cunt than your mother, but I was wrong. Did Margaret know I was sick with lung cancer?"

"No Dad, she always asked about you every time we spoke, and I just told her you were great. I knew it would've made her worry about you, and I didn't see the point."

"That's good honey. That's perfect," he said, sounding pleased.

◆

Sometime in March, I received a phone call from a friend. She explained that a dear friend of hers had to rehome his horse and she thought of me. His horse was a quarter horse gelding, palomino, just like Sosa. He also had a four-letter Spanish name: Peso. It seemed too good to be true, almost like a sign. After the loss of Gram, I could use a big hairy guy's shoulder to cry on.

I asked Dad about Peso. I told him it was a once-in-a-lifetime opportunity, but I was concerned that I didn't have enough experience to own a horse. I also admitted that there's no such thing as a free horse. Terry listened intently and then blurted out, "Well how old is the nag?"

"He's nineteen," I said, laughing.

"Perfect! That's a nice age."

"You don't think it's a bad idea for a novice to get a horse?"

"Oh, fuck no! You can handle it."

"What about all the money I'll need to spend on it?"

"Let me ask you this: Did your husband give two fucks about how much it cost when he joined the country club and played golf five days a week?"

"No," I answered as I followed his logic.

"This horse won't cost you a third of what you guys spent at the country club. Get the damn horse and enjoy yourself. You deserve it, and I know Sonny Boy would agree with me."

"You're right about John; he thinks it would be good for me. But you don't think I'm doing Peso a disservice because I don't have a lot of experience with a horse?"

"Fuck no. If those barn bimbos can handle a horse, you sure as hell can."

On April 24, with John's support and after hearing my father's little pep talk, Peso's owner, Rocco, delivered him to me at the same barn where Sosa had passed. Terrified and excited, at forty-nine years old, I had a new thousand-pound kid running my life.

Something about a horse forces one to stay in the moment. Being around Peso made me acutely aware of each minute and how dangerous it is not to stay focused. With John not feeling well, Dad being ill, and Mully having a cancerous mass, it felt like they were all in a race to leave me. Thinking too far ahead was a recipe for a panic attack, so for the first time in my life, I didn't think about the future.

Terry's demeanor began to change. With each passing month, he became more withdrawn and quiet. He didn't call me as much as he used to, and when I did speak to him, he seemed extremely unhappy. I used his medical portal and noticed that he had missed a few appointments with his doctors. Each time I asked him about it he blew me off and promised he would reschedule the appointment when he felt strong enough to drive himself. He deflected my concern with, "I'm fine honey. Don't you worry about me, you've got enough on your plate."

I used to send him food and other stuff that he needed, but I knew that wasn't enough. John and I offered to hire a nurse for him; he declined. Finally, his friend Sarah asked her sister Kay, who lived nearby in Salem, to help him; luckily, she accepted the job.

By August, John had been continuing to struggle to walk and started to use a walker when he wasn't strong enough to use a cane. After meeting with his neurosurgeon, we were told that he needed a four-level cervical fusion. If he didn't have the surgery, he could end up paralyzed. If something went wrong in the surgery, he could end up paralyzed, or *worse*. When we were leaving the doctor's office, his surgeon said, "Don't worry, we'll take good care of you. Between now and the surgery, don't do anything crazy and don't get into a car accident, either." Seemed like good advice, but now I had to wrap John in cotton.

Life was getting a little crazy with work, taking care of my horse, two dogs, John, and the house. To keep myself sane I began jogging ten miles a week and hiking up mountain trails. I also took on a big landscape design job with a new client who had heard about me through their landscaper. The job was scheduled for the middle of

September, so I could squeeze it in before John's surgery in October. It seemed being busy kept the stress at bay.

On September 1, Mulligan started to get finicky at mealtime. I had sensed he was slowing down on our walks, but he still wanted to play with Payson and seemed alert. I made him some homemade food and he ate it up without a problem, so I was relieved. The next day it was more of the same, except it took more coaxing to get him to eat. Later that night, Mulligan was feisty and initiating play with Payson. He fetched his ball and let his little sister knock him to the ground and jump all over his face. Mully had the sweetest soul. His forty-eight-pound body could have crushed thirteen-pound Payson, but he never, ever hurt her. In fact, she used to hurt him when she chewed on his ears too much, but he let her do it anyway.

I said to John, "Oh my gosh, look at Mully. He's seems better. He's playing again. Maybe he's okay?" John didn't respond. His expression quickly reminded me of his theory. I slept all night spooning Mulligan, holding him as tight as I could and praying for more time. But I also remembered my promise.

The next day was Labor Day, September 3. Mulligan woke up and went outside to do his business, but then went right back to bed. A few hours later, I tried to get him to eat some food, but he didn't want anything. He just wanted to lie on the tile. Payson curled up inside his legs, pressed against his belly, and never left his side. I told John that if Mully didn't eat dinner, we'd have to take him to the emergency vet because our normal vet was closed. Unfortunately, Mulligan passed on dinner, too. So I allowed Payson to spend a few minutes with her brother. She'd never been left alone in the house for her entire five years of life.

I loaded John and Mully into the car and drove to the vet located down the street. It took all my strength not to turn around and go back home. I kept repeating, "I will do this right. I will not let him suffer. Do this right." The vet tech ushered us to a room in the back. When the veterinarian came in, we explained that Mully had been diagnosed with a Hemangiosarcoma ten months prior. We also detailed his decline over the past couple of days. After a thorough examination, he asked us what we wanted to do. Everything in my being wanted to take our baby home.

"We don't want him to suffer. I'm worried that he will if we're not careful," I said.

"It's your job to make sure he doesn't suffer. Euthanasia is your decision, but what I tell people is that it's better to be a day too early, than a second too late."

The vet stepped out of the room to prepare for the procedure. I dropped to the floor, wrapped my arms around Mully's head, and buried my face in his fluffy ears. John stroked his back while we told him he was the best boy and sweetest wheatie. He was calm and ready when the doctor returned. After he started the injection, I began repeating, "I love you Mully. I love you Mully. I love you Mully. I love you Mulligan Bradford." I wanted his last second on this earth to be filled with my voice telling him he was loved. I feared that any silence would leave him thinking he was alone, and I couldn't stand that thought.

"He's gone. You did the right thing. I'll give you some time with him," the vet assured us.

As John and I sat there, we could feel his spirit was no longer in his body.

"I can't sit here. I know he's gone. I have to leave, but I can't leave him alone. I can't walk away unless I know he's not alone." I said to the vet tech.

"It's okay, I've got him," she said with a hug.

Four days later would have been Mulligan's fourteenth birthday. I spent it thinking about all the sweet memories we'd made with him. He used to enjoy long car rides and especially going to our cabin. John would always take him to the local grocery store to buy a cup of their terrible coffee that was so strong he had to water it down. He used to say, "Mully, wanna go get some woffee?" That was John's nickname for the terrible brew he would somehow come to revere. Mulligan would jump into the SUV and hang his head out the window looking for elk and deer along the way. He brought us total joy. He was easy, gentle, loving, and never asked us for anything. As difficult as our goodbye was, I realized that this was the first time I felt like I had done it right. I had so many regrets with past losses that haunted me. So many things I wish I had done better. There was comfort that I kept my promise to sweet Mulligan.

The next day, I realized I had to get my head back into work. My landscape design meeting was coming up, so I asked John to go to Kinko's to get my client's plat map copied. It was a large schematic, so we needed a professional printer. He jumped at the chance to get out of the house and think about something else. About forty-five minutes after John left, he called and said calmly: "I've been in a car accident. I'm at Thompson Peak and Hayden. Come find me."

"Are you okay?"

"I'm not sure. The ambulance is here," he stammered.

When I got to the intersection, our red GMC Acadia was facing the wrong direction and was partially on the sidewalk. John was in the passenger seat with blood rolling down his face. Fire trucks, police, and ambulances were in the middle of the road; on the side was a large, black, pickup truck with a smashed-in front end, with red paint all over it.

"Are you okay?" Then I looked at the paramedic and asked, "Is he okay? Why is he in the passenger seat?"

John was driving through the intersection, on a green light, when the other driver turned left in front of him. He wasn't wearing his seat belt, and the impact of the collision threw his head into the passenger's side window. In my head, I heard his surgeon's warning and nearly passed out. John was taken to the local hospital by ambulance,

After many scans and tests, he was cleared to go home. His neurosurgeon called the next day and said he had reviewed and compared his image tests, and by some miracle, there was no new damage to John's neck. That easily could've been a fatal accident.

"Well, somebody up in heaven was watching out for me," John claimed.

"So true, and I know exactly who your angel was. Yesterday was your dad's birthday."

◆

My father was continuing to pull away, but I still spoke to him at least once a week. Our conversations were shorter, and I could tell he was becoming more depressed. I assumed the lung cancer had spread, but I didn't know for sure. Every time I asked him how he was doing, he made his best effort to say something light and divert the conversation.

When I called him about Mulligan, he said, "I'm so sorry Honey Babe. He lived a good life and he gave you so much love. I think Payson probably kept him young. Fourteen years old is a long life isn't it?"

"Daddy, it's never long enough."

After I shared with Terry the story of John's accident, and how disappointed I was that he forgot to put his seat belt on, he gave me some advice: "Well, honey, try not to chew his ass too bad. He's okay, and it's just stuff—stuff can be replaced."

"What makes you think I would chew his ass?" I asked sarcastically.

"Not to change the subject, but are you watching *Yellowstone*?"

"Yes, are you?"

"Oh yeah, I love it. I've always loved westerns. I get a big kick out his daughter, Beth—she reminds me of you."

I laughed and said, "Dad. I don't think that's a compliment."

"Well, it sure as fuck is. She's a great cunt. I love the way she rips

209

those cocksuckers a new one," he explained, laughing hard.

Most people probably thought my father was a chauvinist, but I knew to look past the language and read the message. He didn't respect weakness and neediness and loved a feisty woman. I guess I figured that out when I was a teenager because I'd been giving him hell ever since.

On October 4, I took John to downtown Scottsdale for his neck surgery. I was as nervous as I'd ever been before one of his procedures. John had been through over a dozen surgeries before, so I should have been a pro by this point. But this one was different. The stakes were as high as they get; even the surgeon shared that this would be a difficult road. In pre-op John was tense, anxious, and he shared his fears of living paralyzed. I asked the nurse if she could give him something to help calm him. I wished she could've slipped me something, too. She checked his blood pressure and agreed that it would help.

As I held his hand waiting for the process to begin, his surgeon pulled the drape back and said, "Good morning. We've got the A-team and were about ready to go. Do you have any questions for me?" After some small talk, I stepped outside the curtain and said, "Doctor, please remember, this is not just 'some man' with a jacked-up neck. You're literally about to take my whole world into your hands. I need you to treat him like he's your whole world."

"You know it. I'll will," he promised.

"Remember to be brave like Braddy, Bailey, and Mulligan. All your angels are with you. I love you. You better come back to me," I said, before kissing John.

"It's not our destiny to end like this. I love you with all my heart, Beauty," he said with a smile as they were wheeling him down the hallway.

Six hours later in the Recovery ward John woke up, smiled and said, "Hello, Beauty." I spent five nights in the hospital with him, sleeping on a hard couch listening to all the drunks partying at the nearby downtown Scottsdale bars. Night after night, I heard speakers blasting DJ voices and the sounds of wild bachelorette parties. Revelers peddled bar carts around the block until two in the morning. I didn't really mind, but I was grateful when John was able to go home.

I spent my fiftieth birthday taking care of John and spending as much time as possible with Payson and Peso. With John's surgery behind us, I took that opportunity to see if Terry would like to come out to Arizona for his seventieth birthday.

"That's sweet of you to ask honey, but I'm just not feeling up to it. I've been super cold lately. I just can't seem to get warm. Would you do me a favor and research some winter coats for me? Canadian goose down is supposed to be the best."

"Sure Dad. How 'bout John and I send you a Patagonia coat for your birthday?"

"Well that would be great. Do you think that will be warm enough? I want something warmer than this old Carhartt I've been wearing."

"You bet Daddy, I'll order it right now. What color do you want? I think you'd look so handsome in the dark gray one."

He thought for a second and said, "Well, Daddy's kind of old school, honey. I think I'd just like a black one."

He had never owned a down coat before, and when he got his birthday present, he was really impressed. We also sent him some gloves so he was all hooked up. There wasn't much I could do for him, so when he asked for something I always tried to do what I could to make it happen. Little did I know that that would be the last birthday present I ever sent him. For my birthday that year, Dad sent me a card and $50. On the inside he wrote: "Buy your horse some apples. I Love you, Daddy." And on the front there was a book marker that read: "Make your life story a book you'd want to read." At the time I remember thinking that he definitely had achieved that.

Dad made his annual trip up to Alpena to spend Thanksgiving. He left early so he could break the driving up in to two days. About a year earlier, Terry asked me to look up some old friends on the internet.

"Remember that lady, P.D. that would babysit you when I had to work and your mother wasn't around?"

"I sure do. She had really long blond hair and wore a triangular-shaped bandana on her head."

"Yeah, that's her. She and her husband Mike live in Michigan, and I was thinking about calling them."

I think her name was Patricia, but she went by her first and middle initial. I found her number, and they reconnected. Mike and P.D. were happy to hear from him and kindly offered to let Dad stay with them on his long trips up north. The last few trips he took north required a few days of travel; he couldn't pull off the seven hours straight of driving anymore. I thought it was out of character for him to stay in someone's home, but perhaps he was tying up some old loose ends.

When he called from the Price Farm, he didn't sound well. He'd picked up a bug somewhere and was lying low, feeling weak and nauseous, spending most of his visit on the couch. Uncle Joe took him Thanksgiving dinner leftovers and checked on him. Dad stayed several days longer to gain enough strength to drive himself back to Ohio. He had made such a big effort to get there, it made me wonder if my father knew that that would be his last holiday meal with his family.

◆

John and I needed life to get back to some normalcy, and we realized we weren't the only ones missing our sweet Mulligan. Payson was plastered to our sides all the time and seemed like she was getting more depressed without her brother. I could have used a vacation—instead we started searching for a puppy.

On November 14, our new baby Aussie-doodle, Parker Blue, arrived. The breeder delivered a six-pound Blue Merle bundle of joy, right to our door. We introduced Payson and had some laughs watching them run around like maniacs. When it was bedtime, Paysie jumped on the bed with John, and I placed Parker in her pen on the floor next to my bedside. As I crawled into bed I looked at John and held my breath; turned out the light. Within seconds Parker let out a big cry and a bark.

"It's okay Parker, we're right here. Go night-night," I said leaning over the edge.

This scene repeated over and over for the next hour.

"For the love of God, just put her in the bed with us; I know that's what you want anyway," John crowed.

I wasn't sure who was happier, me or Parker. I scooped her up and as I lay on my back, she settled in on top of me. She crawled up next to my ear and draped her body across my neck. I felt like I was wearing a hot, furry, turtleneck. She fell fast asleep and didn't wake up all night. I'm not sure if it was the exhaustion of having a new puppy, or the hangover we felt from the crazy year we had endured, but something about Parker joining our family made us feel hopeful and gave us something new to laugh about. She was definitely the medicine we all needed.

PART THREE

CHAPTER TWENTY-THREE

Hip to Be Square

In January of 2019, I renewed my New Year's resolution of working out and hiking. I was in the best physical shape of my life; running and hiking gave me that "high" that allowed me to release my stress. While out on a jog, I heard something pop and felt an instant pinching pain in my right hip. The pain was excruciating, and I could feel it in my back, hip, and glute. After spending some time icing and stretching, it seemed slightly better, so I stopped exercising in hopes that it would heal with a little downtime. So much for that resolution.

Jill, Glee and I decided to take a trip together to celebrate turning fifty. With everything going in my life around my birthday, our plans had to be postponed into the new year. On February 3, Jill flew into Phoenix so we could drive together to Palm Springs, where we'd met Glee at the La Quinta Resort. Before we left, I made my traditional, pre-travel call to Dad. He sounded tired but happy that I was getting time with my friends.

"You girls have some fun. Maybe get drunk a couple of times."

"Not a bad idea, Dad."

"Hey, make sure you let Jill know that if I'd had my way, I would've been her stepdaddy," he laughed with that giggle that signaled he knew he was being naughty.

"Dad, her mom was married for Chrissake," I said, laughing.

"Oh baby girl, that wasn't a problem for me," he reminded me with more laughter.

Thirty-three years after meeting Jill's beautiful mother, she still lived rent-free in Terry's rearview mirror.

Sadly, our calls stopped being light, and Dad's attitude was often agitated and negative. I called him on March 13, to acknowledge his mother's birthday. March 20, was her ten-year death anniversary. I'd been calling him each year to make sure he knew I remembered both. Terry was always the guy in the family who reminded everyone of all the important dates; he had a memory like an elephant.

"*Hell-oh.*" his deep voice answered.

"Hi, Daddy. I just wanted to call and say hi and let you know that I'm thinking about Grandma Margot today."

"My mother was a cunt!" he released with an angry snarl.

I was stunned. I was silent for a few seconds and then said, "Wow. Um, okay. Did you ever tell Uncle Joe how you felt?"

"No. We all had different relationships with her. I'll just leave it at that."

On April 1, I texted Uncle Joe to see if we could set up a time to talk about Dad. He texted back: "Can't talk. At hospital." I wasn't sure what that meant, but I knew better than to try to send him twenty questions. The next day I called Terry and asked him if he had been in contact with Par. I assumed he probably knew what was going on, but when I told him about the text, he was clueless. He said, "Let me call you back honey, I'll call Par now."

About thirty minutes later he called me back and said, "Brian's in the hospital. Par's trying to get him to the University of Michigan Hospital as quickly as possible, but he's not stable enough yet."

My cousin, Uncle Joe's youngest son, was only forty years old. Apparently he was having trouble breathing and some other serious issues. I replied, "Oh no Daddy, this is terrible. Please let me know how he's doing."

On April 5, Dad called me and said:

"Sad fucking day, Honey Babe. Brian died."

"I'm so sorry, Daddy. I know how much you loved him, and I don't even have the words to express how sad I am for Uncle Joe and Aunt Kathy," I said holding back my tears.

"Par doesn't have enough days left in this life to ever get over this. His heart is still broken over the loss of Tracy," Dad said, surrendering to that fact.

Brian had been born on February 20, 1979, which happened to be the same day as Uncle Joe's birthday. They shared the same middle name: Joseph. Uncle Joe's legal name was Theodore, but he never went by that. They lived next door to each other and worked together nearly every day in their successful business called Joe Troy and Sons. I worried about how both Dad and Uncle Joe would handle this huge loss.

Initially, I was told that there wasn't going to be a service for Brian until later in the summer. But then Terry told me on April 9, that a last-minute service was put together on April 11. Unfortunately, I had some clients flying into town, and I couldn't get to Michigan in time to attend. When I asked Dad if he was going he said, "I'm not really feeling up to the long drive, but I can't miss it. I'll do it. I have to."

The next day, I called Dad to make sure his trip went well. When he answered the phone, I immediately knew something was wrong.

"I made it to Cleveland but had to turn around. I was just too weak."

"Daddy, that's okay. Uncle Joe will understand."

"I'm so disappointed in myself!" he growled, choking back tears.

"Daddy, stop that. I know you did your best. You don't feel well. Shit happens. Nobody's mad at you," I said with empathy.

When the call was over, I knew I had confirmation that something serious was happening. I'd never heard Dad sound like that before, and he would never, ever want to let Par down after such a major loss.

♦

John and I decided to sell our Scottsdale home and capitalize on the hot real estate market. We weren't sure where we were going to live, but we thought we'd rent for a little while until we figured it out. On May 3, the house was under contract with a buyer so I started to get organized as quickly as I could. To add to the fun, I found out that my painful hip problem needed surgery. Apparently, I was born with hips that were more square than round, and each time I was working out, the pointy hip bone was tearing my hip labrum and glute muscle. I should have listened to Dad when he told me exercise was bad for my health. I needed a hip scope operation where the surgeon would dislocate my hip, shave it down, sew up my labrum tear and punch holes in my glute, so it would scar up and heal. No wonder my back and hip hurt so much.

May 11, I received a call from Dad's neighbor, Ella. As soon as I saw her name I knew something bad was going on in Ohio.

"Do you know what's happening with your dad?" she asked.

"No, I just talked to him a couple of days ago, and he said he was doing fine."

"Well honey you better come, it's bad."

"What do you mean?"

"Hasn't Kay or Sarah called you?"

"No. No they haven't. What's going on?"

"Your dad hasn't been doing well. He was in the local hospital a few days ago, and now Kay and Frank have taken him to Boardman. I wondered if they had called you, that's not right. You need to know what's going on, but please don't tell him that I called you, he'll kill me."

"Don't worry Ella, I won't say a word. I'll call him now and see if he answers his phone."

I quickly called Dad and he answered with a grumpy tone, "Hi, Honey Babe."

"Hey Dad, how's it going?"

"Not that great. I'm in the hospital and the doctors are running a bunch of tests on me."

I instantly started to cry, knowing this was not good. I said, "Okay Daddy, I'll be there as soon as I can." And then in an angry tone, sounding meaner than he'd ever been with me, he said, "Don't cry. I'm fine. You don't need to come here!"

I was immediately jolted out of my state of mind and said calmly, "I'm glad you're getting checked out Dad. Please call me when you find out more information."

Dad had sounded totally lucid, so I was unsure about the severity of the situation. I called his friend, Sarah. The first thing she said was, "Its bad Terrina, you need to come, honey." She went on to tell me that Terry had not been eating, and he was drinking a lot of beer and straight whiskey because of the pain. Earlier in the week her sister, Kay, had called an ambulance, and they took him to the local hospital. But Terry wasn't happy about being treated by "a bunch of quacks" and didn't want to stay. Apparently they gave him some pain medication and muscle relaxers and told him that if he could walk, he could leave. They put him in a cab and sent him home. When he got out of the cab, he tripped and fell to the ground in the middle of the parking lot. The cab driver carried him to his apartment. Kay told Sarah that when she found him, he couldn't stand or walk. Sarah felt horrible that she and Kay had not called me, but Dad convinced them not to because I had so much on my plate in Arizona. She went on to say that Kay witnessed him having hallucinations where he had been reaching out with his hands and talking to his dead parents.

I called the hospital and the nightshift nurse sounded clueless and told me that she couldn't interpret his test results, so I asked for someone who could. I received a call from a palliative nurse practitioner who went over the report findings. She explained that my father had tumors in his left lung, liver, and sacrum area. He also had a complete sacrum fracture. She said they would be checking his brain with an MRI.

"You do know that he has a spinal cord stimulator in his back, right?" I asked.

"Um, oh, he does?" she said, as I heard her shuffling paper around.

"Yes, so please ask the doctor to review that before he authorizes an MRI on my father. I will be there tomorrow night."

May 12, I said goodbye to John and the pups, and rushed out the door to catch my ride. Nick was a nice guy who gave people in our neighborhood rides to and from the airport. John had been having breakfast at the general store with him, and two other neighbors; when I texted him that Pops was in the hospital. I was moving through the motions, but my mind couldn't comprehend the finality that was probably waiting for me. I told myself not to focus on all the unknowns and just take it one step at a time. On the ride to the airport, I didn't want to think about my situation. As a deterrent, I asked Nick about his life. He said with his New York accent, "We're all struggling with somethin' aren't we?" Nick had been having health issues for quite some time. He was on a waiting list at Mayo for a kidney transplant. It broke my heart that someone as sweet as Nick would have to live with that kind of stress. When he dropped me off at the airport he hugged me, kissed me on the cheek and said, "Hang in there, kid."

As I turned to walk into the airport, I suddenly felt alone, and that's when it hit me. Nobody was coming to save me. I'd had this feeling before, but it'd been a while. As I entered the security line, I took a big deep breath and just kept repeating to myself, "One step at a time. Only think about what you have to do right now. Stay in the moment. One step at a time. Stay in the moment."

CHAPTER TWENTY-FOUR

Flying by the Seat of My Pants

My father would get drunk before each flight, but I was a grin-and-bear-it kind of girl. I guess mastering that art of sucking it up came in handy, but it was definitely not the easiest path. As I waited for my flight, I called Jill to let her know what was going on, and to focus on something other than the large tomb I didn't want to die in. She was headed to Hawaii the next day to celebrate her birthday. We had a few laughs and both tried to keep it light, knowing that I was nervous about what I might be walking into in Ohio. For years, Jill and I both traveled a lot for our sales jobs. We had way too many weird experiences traveling alone, so I didn't have to explain my anxiety. I wasn't thrilled that I would be arriving at night and driving on roads I didn't know. But I couldn't think about that. I had to survive the flight.

I texted Uncle Joe to let him know that I was headed to be with Dad; he called me right away and said, "Honey, I'd come meet you, but I can't. I have a flight scheduled to take my wife to Rochester, Minnesota. She's not doing well."

"Oh no. I'm so sorry Uncle Joe."

"Well, I don't care how much it costs, or where I have to take her, we'll get her better. What's going on with your dad?"

I explained everything that had been happening and that I was unsure about the real status of his health. We both had a hard time believing the story about Terry having hallucinations and conversations with his parents because he was always so lucid.

I think Uncle Joe could hear the trepidation in my voice. He said, "Well, listen honey, don't tell Terry that he was talking to my mom and dad at the same time. If he thinks they're together in heaven, he'll know there ain't no beer in heaven, and he won't go."

"Well, there's some truth," I said, bursting out laughing.

It was just the way our family was. When things are too painful to think about, just laugh. Even though Uncle Joe had more on his plate than any one person should ever have to deal with, he took the time to speak with his niece and make her feel better. I will always love him for that.

When the airline worker started the cattle-call, I realized I was in Boarding Group C. I started praying for an aisle seat to somehow still be available since I hated the window view. Thankfully, I found my way to the back of the plane and plopped in an aisle seat with two younger ladies. I introduced myself and asked them if they were headed home. One of the gals explained that they were visiting Scottsdale for a friend's bachelorette party, and they were both feeling quite hungover. I said, "Oh, were you downtown riding one of those bar carts around the block?" They both laughed and shook their heads up and down. I said, "Ouch. I hate it when you get overserved." The laughs cut the tension welling up in my guts; then I felt the plane move. I grabbed my magazine, started reading as fast as I could to forget where I was and what was happening around me. It was my coping mechanism to deal with my fear during take-off. Once the plane reached altitude, I was less hyper-focused on smacking the ground. I asked the girls some questions about the Pittsburgh airport and if I would run into any traffic. They concurred that by the time we'd arrive that night, the roads would be empty.

After we landed in Pittsburgh, I rushed to the car rental counter downstairs. I felt like I was up against the clock, if I wanted to make it to the hospital before it got dark. I took a deep breath and reminded myself to just think about the next step.

I remembered the last time I had a rental car; it broke down on me. I pushed that thought down. I asked the clerk for directions to Youngstown. I had paid extra for GPS, but I knew having local knowledge is always a good backup. Notably absent was my confidence in having Dad's directions to lean on.

"Whatever you do, don't get on the turnpike. There's a new electronic system and you'll get a ticket if you're not set up for it. Don't turn on your GPS until you are past the exit before the Turnpike, or it will dump you on it."

"Okay, that will be tricky to do while I'm driving."

She wrote: "Take 375 west toward Beaver. Take Chippewa exit—the last exit before the toll. When you get to the light make a left and follow it straight."

I stood there reading her directions and thanking her for helping me. I looked at my map quickly and said, "Wait, is it 375 or 376?"

"Oh, silly me. I'm so sorry—yes, it's 376."

Well, that was a blow to my confidence, too, but with no time to waste, I headed down I-376 trying to remember the directions written on the car rental papers. The glare of the lights made reading difficult. The highway had very little traffic, so I was speeding along quickly when all of sudden I saw a large sign that read **TOLL ROAD**. Somehow I'd missed my exit. I looked in my rearview mirror; luckily no one was behind me. I slammed on the brakes, threw it in reverse, and backed up all the way to the last exit that I had passed. I've never done that before in my entire life. I prayed it was the correct the exit, followed it to the light, made a left, and carefully turned on my GPS. I literally had no idea where I was. I followed the voice commands and quickly found myself on a country two-lane blacktop road, with nowhere to pull over. I chuckled thinking back to when my Thunderbird ran out of gas on a similar road.

It was getting darker, and it started to rain. I had to work hard at keeping my heart from jumping out of my chest as I watched for deer, knowing all too well that these kinds of roads were littered with roadkill. At one point, I was dumped onto a roundabout in the middle of nowhere. My GPS confused me; barking at me to exit a particular street, but I couldn't read any of the signs. I went around it three times as slow as I could while I watched the map and tried to pick the correct street without crashing.

Finally, at 8:45 p.m., I pulled into the hospital parking lot. I grabbed my purse and umbrella and, just as the last bit of light was leaving the sky, I ran into the emergency room entrance. I knew Dad was on the fourth floor in room 408. As I walked down the hall, I noted that the floor seemed clean, and the hospital looked to be in good repair. My heart started to jump around with the anticipation of perhaps seeing my father looking deathly ill. I peeked my head around the corner of his doorway and saw him lying on his back sleeping. I was grateful he was in a private room this time.

I quickly stepped back, found his nurse and introduced myself as Terry's daughter. She wasn't particularly friendly and gave me the impression that she was inexperienced. I brushed her insecurity aside and asked about the status of Dad. She told me she wasn't up to speed on what was going on, but she would review his chart with me. She was stumbling for words when I said, "You know he has a fractured sacrum, right?"

"He does? No, I didn't know that. I do know that they want to do a liver biopsy in the morning."

"Liver biopsy? What the hell for?"

"Well, I don't know exactly, but I guess to see what kind of cancer he has in his liver, so they can decide what chemo to use."

"Well, you can cancel the biopsy because he will never do chemo again, and there's no way he needs to be put through that."

She said she would make a note, and the doctor would decide

what to do in the morning. I said, "Jessica, let the doctor know that *my dad* will decide in the morning. Thanks." I snapped, irritated.

I paused outside the door, took a deep breath and walked right up to his bed. I stood at his bedside holding his hand and rubbing his arm until he woke up. His eyes got really big, then he blinked hard almost like he wasn't sure if I was real. Then his brow furrowed quickly and he said, "You shouldn't have come."

"Hi Dad. I love you." I said, as I leaned over his bed to give him a kiss and hug.

He sat up and shifted around quickly, while brushing his hand through his hair, like he didn't feel presentable.

"You're gorgeous," he said, trying to absorb that I was real.

"Oh Daddy, that medication they're giving you must be affecting your vision."

"The hell it is. Why did you come? You have too much on your plate."

"Dad, the plate is big enough for you."

"How did you know I was here?"

"You told me. You don't remember me calling you yesterday? You told me Frank and Kay had taken you to Boardman because Salem is full of quacks?" I answered quickly.

"No. I don't."

"Well that's okay, they're probably giving you lots of pain meds, and that can make you forget things."

I was relieved that Terry didn't look as bad as I feared. He was really thin, sporting a full beard, and he had a nasty, rattling cough. I was grateful he recognized me and was able to carry on a coherent conversation. His room had a padded bench and two chairs for guests. I pulled one of the chairs next to his bed and sat with him and held his hand. I told him about my conversation with his nurse and asked him if he was aware that they wanted to do a biopsy on his liver.

"No. What the fuck for?"

"They want to see what kind of cancer tumor it is so they can discuss chemo with you."

"Fuck that. I am never doing chemo again. Never."

"Well Daddy, if I'm not here in the morning when the doctor comes by, make sure you let him know how you feel, don't hold back, okay?"

"Okay honey, I will."

Terry asked for pain meds but was told it was too soon. The nurse explained that he would need to get through the night, but he could try again in the morning when the hospitalist did rounds. I wish I could have left knowing he was comfortable, but as the clock pushed midnight, I had to get to my hotel. John booked me at a place that the hospital had recommended a few blocks away.

When I reached the dark parking lot, I ran to my car as fast as I could. I called John and had him stay on the phone with me while I read the directions one of the nurses gave me. I drove with my interior light on; with the rain I struggled to see. I followed the two-lane road through some old industrial buildings to the four-way stop at the train tracks. Eventually, I found South Avenue and made my way to the hotel. When I pulled in, I noticed a sign on the hotel marque. It read: **TJ'S RESTAURANT AND LOUNGE.** I hung up with John and told him I'd call him once I made it to my room. I pulled my roller bag through the mud puddles as quickly as I could. I didn't look at the men standing under the front portico smoking; I made my way to the front desk. I could hear loud music, people talking, and the noise of clanging dishes coming from the bar at the back. I thought to myself, "Great. I get to stay at the hotel where the locals hang out and get drunk."

As I was checking in I had my head on a swivel. I noticed that one of the guys out front kept stepping back inside the lobby and staring at me. The clerk told me that I could buy some food from the little alcove next to his desk and charge it to my room. So I grabbed some junk food while I kept an eye on the smoker. I headed toward the elevator while over my shoulder I saw the man at the door quickly toss his cigarette out; he briskly walked toward me. After I got on the elevator, he rushed to jump in, too. The hair on the back of my neck stood up, and my heart started beating faster, these were familiar signs. I grabbed the closing doors and said, "Oh shoot. I forgot something." I hustled back to the desk and asked the employee a few more questions. The man was holding the door open with his boot but was standing deep into the elevator where I could only see part of his ankle and foot. I pulled out my phone and pretended to ignore him.

After a few minutes, he must have given up, because I saw the doors close. I wondered if he would be waiting on my floor, since I had selected the second-floor button before he jumped on. When the elevator arrived at my floor, I put my luggage in between the doors so they couldn't close while I looked in both directions for any weirdos. It seemed clear, so I ran as fast as I could to room 207 and quickly locked the door.

Once inside, I called John and he said, "Your gut is never wrong. I'm so glad you didn't stay on that elevator."

Jill called, and I told her about what a crazy person I was after I got in the room—checking under the beds and in the closet. We laughed about it, and she said, "I know that feeling. It sucks, because now you're all jacked up and can't sleep." We reminisced about some of the nutjobs we'd encountered in the past, and laughed until we cried, breaking up the tension of the day.

The next morning I rushed back to the hospital, but I had missed the hospitalist that came around at 6:30. Dad said that he told them that he would never have chemo treatments again, so they canceled the biopsy but decided to proceed with the scan of his brain. Terry seemed agitated and was in severe pain. He kept asking for more medicine; finally the nurse called in a palliative administrator. She was a physician assistant and explained that she would be in charge of the pain management protocol. After she made her recommendations, she asked Dad what he thought.

"Well, I'll tell you right now, that ain't gonna do shit. I can take a lot more than that."

She was taken aback and looked at me to save her.

"Daddy, why don't you tell her what you've been taking for pain at home for the last few months."

"Well let's see. I've been taking three Percocet and a half bottle of whiskey, twice a day."

Her eyes got big, and she stood there silent for a few seconds.

"Well, alrighty then. I guess I don't need to start you out slowly. Based on that I'll order the maximum right now."

Most of the day was spent waiting around for tests and doctors. Sarah had come to visit Terry, and that was the first time I'd ever met her. She gave me a big hug and seemed like a sweet and kind person who genuinely cared about Terry. She sat at his bedside and held his hand while I went to the cafeteria. Later that night, Kay came by and brought his mail and other items he'd requested. She was also caring, just like her sister.

About nine that night I said, "Dad, I'm probably going to leave soon. Is there anything you need?"

"Yeah, I need some more pain meds, and can you get my wallet out of my black coat? It's in the front right pocket."

"Sure, I'd be happy to."

I walked over to the closet where the black Patagonia coat was hanging. I noticed it reeked of cigarette smoke, as I reached into his pocket and pulled out his thick wallet and something else. With my back to Dad, I looked at what I was holding: it was an open bank envelope, about an inch thick and full of cash. I quickly shoved it back into his coat, while I tried to figure out what to say to him. He opened his three-section wallet and started looking through all the papers and cards like it was a Rolodex. He'd perforate the end of cigarette cartons, which were roughly the size of business cards, and use them to write important contact information on. His wallet was bursting with this type of stuff, but it didn't have any cash in it. I stood there practically shaking at the thought of him having all that money sitting in the closet at the hospital. I decided I had to say something to him because I wouldn't sleep a wink that night if I didn't.

"Hey Dad, I noticed you have quite a bit of cash in your coat pocket. I'm not trying to be nosey, but I'm really concerned that someone might steal from you."

"Well, get it out and make sure it's all there. There should be $6,850."

I just about threw up in my mouth. I said, "Are you kidding me?"

"No, go get it," he urged.

I brought it over to his tray table and pulled the privacy curtain around us. As I counted it out, there was exactly $6,850.

"Dad, this is too much money to have lyin' around. We have to do something with it."

"Okay, what do you suggest?"

"Well, I guess I'll have to take it back to the hotel with me and put it in the bank tomorrow."

"No, no, I don't have a bank account."

"Well, I figured that. I guess I'll have to put it in my account until you need it."

He didn't say anything for a minute and looked agitated and confused. He said, "Where's my fucking pain meds?"

"Let's push the button for the nurse after I put this money away."

So after the nurse came in and gave Dad some drugs, I looked at him and said, "Daddy, I will give you any amount of the money you want, any time you want it. You trust me, right?"

He swung his head around to face me with a furrowed brow and raised his left hand like he was about to backhand me. He snapped, "I oughta!"

I let out a laugh and said, "Really Dad? Get a grip. I know you're hurting, but this is ridiculous."

Once he realized what he had done, I saw his regret.

"Of course, I trust you. Just take it with you, but hang on to $250 of it; I'll need it. Go ahead and deposit the rest into your account and keep track of what I spend."

"Okay, Dad. No problem."

Then he handed me a business card he had pulled out of his wallet and said, "Honey will you please call my doctor at the Cleveland Clinic? He's the only doctor that I trust. I just want to speak with him about what's going on with me."

"Sure, Dad. I'll call him tomorrow as soon as they open."

I called John complaining, "I can't even believe I have to walk into that dingy hotel carrying all this cash on me. It's dark and I can't find a close parking spot."

"I'll stay on the phone with you, Beauty, it'll be ok. You can take it to the bank in the morning. Hey, I'm sorry he did that with his hand. But remember, those drugs make people act mean sometimes." He was right; it was good counsel.

Tuesday, May 14, I drove to the bank to get rid of the cash and then rushed to the hospital. The kidney doctor was expected to visit. The nurses, case workers, and other admin people were hustling in and out of Terry's room. Sarah had come to visit again and was sitting in the chair next to his bed.

"Your kidneys are not doing that bad, but your sodium levels are low. You should focus on eating more and drinking less fluids, so we're going to limit your fluids," the kidney doctor explained.

Dad didn't say anything; the doctor walked out of the room. As soon as he left, another doctor showed up. He was a short man with dark hair and dark eyes. He had a thick accent that sounded like he was from India or at least vaguely South Asian. He didn't introduce himself as he walked over to the computer located behind the bed.

He started explaining everything that he could see on the scans and then announced, "So you will need to start chemo and radiation immediately." Dad turned his head and looked at me like he was about to explode.

"Will you please show me on the scans what you are talking about?" I asked as I approached the doctor.

When he pulled up the scan that showed the sacrum fracture, I felt faint. The cancer had metastasized to his spine and completely deteriorated it. My poor father had such a large lower back fracture that even a layman could see his back was broken. No wonder he couldn't walk. I could hear from behind me that Dad had tuned us out and was quietly talking to Sarah.

"Would you please tell me what kind of doctor you are?" I asked.

"I'm a radiation oncologist," he snapped, like I was interrogating him.

"Okay, can you please tell me what the prognosis is?"

He looked at me with darting eyes and said, "I don't know. I don't know."

"Well you've seen a lot of patients in this type of situation, correct?"

"Yes, but I don't have a crystal ball. Um, um, if I had to guess I'd say, um, three to six months."

I snapped at him while I lowered my voice, "Have you seen my father? Have you even looked at him? How can you say that when you haven't even properly introduced yourself and done an assessment?"

He looked embarrassed and agitated, and then glanced over at Dad and softly mumbled, "Three months. Maybe. I don't know."

He switched his attention away from me and said, "Mr. Troy do you want to do radiation?" Dad perked up and said, "Will it help? I'll do it if you think it will help."

The asshole doctor snapped, "No, no, I explained it to you before; this is for pain management only. You cannot be cured."

Terry didn't answer.

"I've never heard of radiation helping for a fracture. I thought radiation could cause fractures," I stated.

"No. Not this type. It will help and we can do the first treatment today if he wants to try it."

"Dad, I'm not sure about this, but it's up to you. What do you want to do?"

"If it will help me, I'll try it."

The doctor took his paperwork and walked out without saying a word. I wondered how Terry could process what had just happened. I couldn't wrap my head around it. Then Dad looked at me and Sarah and said,

"Well, I guess I'm fucked. The way I'm figuring it, I guess I have about three to six months. Is that right, honey?"

I stood there unable to speak. I just slowly shook my head up and down. Dad's face lost all color, and his eyes became big. Sarah started to cry, but I had my marching orders—no crying. I'd never seen anyone receive this type of news before. I felt the familiar feeling of nearly blacking out. I held the chair to steady myself. I grew angrier at the way this was all rolling out. Why didn't someone explain the situation to my father in a gentle, sensitive way? Why did I have to be the one to confirm what that shithead doctor said?

We sat silent with only Sarah's sniffles filling the air. A few minutes later Terry stared at the TV and said, "Well honey, I'm not going to my grave without telling you I never quit smoking."

"I knew that, Dad. It doesn't matter."

"What? How did you know?"

"Because when we talked on the phone, I could hear you lighting and smoking cigarettes. I also knew because if you had quit, you would've been telling me how many days you had gone without smoking."

He sounded embarrassed. "Well, I tried to quit." Then his voice changed like he was ashamed. "I just couldn't do it. I tried, and I just couldn't do it."

"Daddy, none of that matters. It's okay."

He sat quietly for a minute and asked, "Why didn't you ever say anything to me about it?"

"Because everybody has the right to live and die the way they choose. You get to be in charge of your life, and I get to be in charge of mine. That's just how I feel."

"Well, you're not like most people, Honey Babe. You're special," he said with surprise.

"You taught me that lesson, Dad. If I'm special, it's because of you."

A younger lady came in and asked me to step out to the hall. She introduced herself as a hospice care coordinator and explained that Terry was going to need a hospice facility. He was being discharged soon and we needed to choose where they would take him.

"I don't have a clue about any of this, I'm not even from around here," I said.

She highly recommended a facility that was affiliated with the hospital. It was located a few minutes away, had only sixteen beds, and there was an opening for a new patient.

"Is it nice? Or do you just have to say it's nice?"

"I promise you, if this were my dad, this is where I would send him."

"Okay, but can you answer a question for me?"

"Sure, I'll do my best."

"Why hasn't anyone explained to us what is going on? How long do you think he really has?"

She looked at me and started to lower her voice and whispered, "I really don't think your dad has more than two weeks. I'm sorry to tell you that, but I've seen a lot of patients and I totally disagree with the doctor. But I don't want to get into trouble, so please don't tell anyone I said that."

"I won't say anything," I said as I tried to absorb her message.

"Before he leaves the hospital, there will be a doctor that stops in to explain the next steps, but I'll be honest, he doesn't communicate very well. So I'll tell you what I know. He will go to the first radiology treatment while you get him checked in at hospice, and then an ambulance will deliver him to you. Any future radiation treatments will get coordinated with an ambulance to pick him up from hospice care; they'll return him each time."

I stood there, stunned. "Two weeks" still banging around my head. Could that be right? I wasn't sure because mentally he was sharp as a tack. But she seemed confident.

The doctor that she mentioned walked into Terry's room, so I excused myself and followed him in. He sat down next to the bed, crossed his legs, and started rambling. I could not believe my ears; I honestly thought I was being pranked. It's hard to describe what was happening because it was so bizarre. Dad looked at me like he was about to throw the guy out of the room. I was hoping that finally someone was going to tell Dad the truth. But it didn't happen. Eventually after about five minutes of listening to this guy talk in circles and make absolutely no sense, Dad cut him off and said, "I guess what you're saying is, I'm fucked. Right?" The doctor stammered, said something stupid, stood up, shook Terry's hand, and left.

Such a pathetic scene. Dad never cried. He didn't throw a pity party. He just looked at me and said, "Well Honey Babe, they're pitchin' and I'm catchin'."

CHAPTER TWENTY-FIVE

Kay

May 14, was a long day, but we were finally starting to get some answers and a plan on how to proceed. While Dad was getting his first radiation treatment, I was given directions to the hospice center and was told to go there immediately.

I was pleasantly surprised the facility didn't look like a medical building. The facade was built with red bricks, a giant portico, and circular driveway. White blooms smothered the trees, and purple lilac bushes were everywhere. The grass was neat and freshly cut, with picnic tables, walking paths, and a large forest wrapped behind the entire building. As I approached the front door I glanced at an angel statue located in the landscaping. When I stepped inside, I was on the top mezzanine-type floor with stairs leading to the lower level. It felt spiritual, almost like an airy church. I took a deep breath and was thrilled that it didn't smell like pee. Kay arrived and we walked downstairs together where we were greeted by workers at the nurse's station, which felt more like a hotel lobby.

We were introduced to an attractive young blond woman. She announced, "Hi, I'm Sarah. I'll be your dad's nurse. I'll give you a quick tour while we wait for him to arrive." She showed us the small kitchen, library, and vending machines next to the laundry room and small bathroom with a shower for family and guests. There were two long hallways with eight rooms in each. Past all the rooms, at the end was a beautiful lounge with a craftsman-style sofa, chair, and a fireplace. I was drawn to the French doors and windows that overlooked the wooded area in the back. I noted a shelf next to the fireplace displaying a large clock with a cement baby angel draped over the top. It had a memorial plaque designating that it'd been donated in honor of a husband-wife couple, a subtle reminder that this was not a hotel. Sarah led us into room number 101 where I did another quick smell test. I was ever so grateful for the absence of stench. The large room was painted a medium gray color with a wallpaper border around the top. The wood chair rail halfway up the wall matched the cherry wood nightstands, armoire, and window trim. The carpet looked tight and brand new. There was a hospital bed, tray table, and a private bathroom next to the bed and appeared spotless. I took a moment to look out the windows and remember thinking it was such a beautiful view of green grass, trees, shrubs, and a nice bird feeder on a pole. Under the window were two arm-less, upholstered dining chairs with a small table placed to overlook the scenery. I felt good about the facility; I hoped the staff would be just as great.

The ambulance drivers arrived with Dad on a stretcher. He was moaning and groaning as they picked up his body wrapped in a blanket and transferred him into his bed. I jumped up from the chair and said, "Don't forget his back is fractured. Please be gentle." The nurse helped get him comfortable with extra pillows and a throw blanket. I placed his things that I had brought from the hospital in the armoire, after I handed him his phone and his eyeglasses.

"Hi Mr. Troy, I'm Sarah. I'll be taking care of you tonight."

"*Oh*-kay, but call me Terry; Mr. Troy is dead."

"No problem, is there anything I can get you, Terry?"

"Do you want to get naked?"

"Dad! What the hell is wrong with you? Jesus," I stood up and snapped.

"I'm so sorry, Sarah," I said, wondering if I had an attorney on speed dial.

"It's fine. I've heard it all," she said, as she brushed it off and walked into the bathroom.

I flashed Dad a look like he better shape up, and he said, "She's kinda built like Peggy."

"Dad, she's right there. Knock it off," I growled in a lowered voice.

People were coming and going, doing their jobs and being extremely friendly. A sweet little old lady came into the room and told us that she was ninety-six years young and loved to volunteer there. She offered us some homemade cookies and a dinner menu. She said, "Wayne is the cook here, and he makes all of the food himself. It's amazing."

"Dad, the menu looks great, are you hungry?"

"No, thanks honey, I'm good."

"Daddy, how 'bout I order you a nice cheeseburger. I bet a home-cooked meal would be nice."

He looked at me like he just wanted to appease me and said, "Okay, honey that would be fine. Thank you."

About thirty minutes later, Wayne hand-delivered his meal. He introduced himself and said, "It's so nice to meet you, Terry. If there's anything you need, please don't hesitate to ask."

"That goes for you, too, dear. Call me anytime; if you place your order by eleven, I'll bring a lunch for you as well. You can order and pay for it at the nurse's station."

As he walked out the door, I was grateful that Dad might actually get some decent food. I said, "Daddy that looks so good, almost as good as what you make on the grill."

He grabbed the burger, took several large bites, and gulped it down. It broke my heart to watch him eat it. It looked like he was starving and hadn't had a good meal in a really long time. He ate every bite and didn't stop until it was gone.

"Was it good? It sure looked good."

"Well, it was a lot better than that shit they serve at the hospital. I wouldn't feed that to your dog."

He was a stickler when it came to cooking, but that day he was happy and that's the most I could ask for. I sat at his bedside in the hard dining chair. My hip was killing me, and I had a severe earache. Before I left Arizona, my doctor had burned off some pre-cancerous lesions near my left ear. In the process, the burning device malfunctioned and burned a painful hole on my ear cartilage. But after watching Dad with a broken back and cancer, I felt ashamed even thinking about my issues.

Terry had perked up after eating his meal and started taking charge. He asked me to find him some Hershey candy bars and then asked if his doctor from Cleveland Clinic had called me yet. I explained that I had called him multiple times, but they said he was too busy to take my call. What I didn't tell him was that I literally begged several different people at his doctor's office to please just let my dad have a short conversation with the only doctor that he trusted. But they refused and said that if the doctor can't see him in person, then he would not be able to comment on my father's condition.

Then he asked Kay to get some paperwork that was on his kitchen counter and bring it to him when she returned the next day.

"No problem, Terry, but I'm gonna need some more gas money."

"You already blew through the hundred dollars I gave you?" Dad asked looking annoyed.

"Yes. I've been driving back and forth to the hospital every day and checking on your apartment, too."

"Honey Babe, give her a hundred bucks outta that cash I gave you."

"Daddy, is there anything you need before I head back to the hotel?"

"Is there any way you could get someone to wash my hair? I hate how dirty it feels."

"Sure Dad, let me find out who the new nighttime nurse is."

Just then a larger lady walked in the door. I asked her if it was possible to clip Dad's nails and wash his hair. A second woman joined us, a nurses' assistant, also quite big.

"Sure, no problem, we'll go get our supplies." the nurse kindly replied.

"I don't want them touching me," Dad snarled after they left the room.

"Dad, stop it. What's the matter with you?"

"I can't stand fat people; you know that about me."

"Well, I'm fat."

"Bullshit! You are not fat. These people are killing themselves with a knife and fork."

"Dad, this is the best I can do for you. I'm sorry but I can't control what nurse you get. Let's just be grateful that they are going to take care of you. By the way, they're not judging you, so maybe you should consider not judging them."

He looked defeated and angry, and he quickly mumbled, "I just want to go home. Take me home. Why can't I go home?"

Honestly, I didn't understand what he considered to be fat. None of his girlfriends had been skinny, and they didn't seem to be a problem. Despite his bad behavior, I did feel sad that I couldn't honor his request to take him home. I kept thinking about how much Gram had suffered. There was no way I was equipped to help him in a home setting.

When the two ladies returned, I excused myself and walked to the end of the hallway where I could get good cell reception. I wanted to call Jill because she was leaving for Hawaii in the morning.

"How's it going, Terrina?" Jill asked.

"Jill, he is being such a bastard. I can't even tell you how difficult this is," I answered while trying not to cry.

"I know it's hard, but try and remember, he's on some pretty heavy medication, and he's not smoking or getting his alcohol fix. Those meds alone can make people act really mean."

She was right. Cancer had stolen my father's sense of humor. I hadn't heard him laugh since the joke he made about Jill's mom, three months earlier.

I was exhausted so I said goodbye to Dad and told him I'd see him in the morning. Before I left he said, "Did you call Par?"

"Yes, Dad, he knows you're here, but he had to take Aunt Kathy to Minnesota for medical care, so he can't come."

"What's wrong with Kathy?" he asked as he tried to sit up.

"I don't know, but Uncle Joe is pretty worried."

"I'll call Par now."

I grabbed some food at Panera on my way back to Youngstown. I could feel myself stacking on the pounds, but I shoved the comfort food in my mouth anyway. Wayne had been making me the most amazing grilled-cheese croissants; doesn't get more comforting than that.

I called John to give him an update and find out what was happening in his world. I felt like I was on a different planet, disconnected from everything familiar to me.

"Bie, I can't get a clear gauge on how sick Dad is because you should have seen him eat today. He gulped-down a huge homemade cheeseburger, and his mind is clear as a bell. Who knows, maybe he's rallying."

Then there was total silence. He didn't say a word.

Wednesday May 15, I woke up early still hurting. My doctor in Arizona called in a burn cream prescription for my ear and instructed me to take Advil for my hip and back pain. I went to Walgreens about five minutes away to fill my script and get Dad the candy bars he wanted. The clerk told me it would be about twenty minutes, so I stood in the store and surfed the MLS listings for rental homes in Scottsdale. I found four that met our criteria, emailed them to John, and asked him to go check them out. We only had a few weeks before we had to move out of our house, and not only did we not have a place to go yet, I still had not packed one single box. I asked John to put a deposit down on the best one that had a pool, didn't stink, and had a yard for the dogs. Not gonna lie, life was starting to feel a bit like a pressure cooker.

I hustled to Dad's room and found a female doctor checking on Terry. I introduced myself and asked if I could ask her some questions in the hall. She agreed and started to walk toward the nurse's area, so I followed next to her.

"Thanks for taking care of my dad. I know you probably can't give me a definitive answer, but I'm trying to manage a few things. I just sold my house, and I might need to leave to pack and then come back. I could use some help figuring out what to do. Do you know how long we have?"

She seemed like she was in a rush because she simply said, "No. I get that question all the time and I just don't know."

After I returned to the room, I was met at the door by a short lady with a blond bob. She had a soft, calm, voice and she said, "Hi, I'm Donna. I'm a social worker. Could you join me in the lounge just for a few minutes?"

I agreed and followed her down the hallway where we both sat on the sofa. She started asking me details about Terry. I can't remember everything she asked, but I do remember her telling me that I would need to start thinking about where Dad should go if he got discharged.

"I don't understand."

She went on to explain that the staff, including the doctors and nurses meet each morning to determine if a patient will stay or get transferred out. I asked her what criteria were being used to make that decision.

"If your father's pain gets under control, then the insurance

243

company will not pay anymore, and he'll have to go to a long-term care facility or go home."

"Well, he's not going home, that's for sure. He can't even walk."

"I'll be in to see him after he gets back from the radiation treatment."

"Please let me know the daily rate in case I need to pay cash, because I can't imagine a better place than this—I don't want him moved."

I returned to Dad's room and handed him his candy bars. He opened one immediately and devoured half of it.

"Dad, would you like me to ask your nurse for a nicotine patch for you?

"Okay," he mumbled.

A slim, tall, dark-haired nurse named Amanda, was happy to help. She also let us know that the ambulance was there to get Terry for his second radiation treatment.

When the stretcher returned with Dad, he was really hurting.

"Goddamn, my back hurts. Those motherfuckin' ambulance drivers tossed me around and hit every fuckin' bump they could. They didn't have to be that rough."

"I'm so sorry Daddy, that's horrible. Let's see if Amanda will get you some more pain meds."

After I pushed the help button, I said, "Dad, I want to tell you something. The social worker is going to come in here in a little bit to meet you. She told me that they evaluate you every morning to see if you can stay another day. If your pain is under control, you will need to get transferred to a nursing home."

"So if my pain is not under control, they keep me. Is that what you're saying?"

"Exactly."

"Got it," he answered, nodding his head up and down.

When the nurse arrived, Dad said:

"Amanda, my goddamn back hurts so bad. Can I have some more pain killers, please?"

"Sure Terry, I'll be right back with some more."

"I'm glad you asked for help Daddy. It doesn't pay to be a tough guy, so make sure you're honest when they come in the morning."

He looked at me with a little twinkle in his eye and said, "I sure will, Honey Babe."

The social worker knocked on the door and said, "Can I come in for a minute?"

"Sure," I answered.

She sat down near the end of the bed, so she could face Terry. I was sitting at the table, so I could see them both. Dad sat up in bed and tried to focus on what she was saying. She was a sweet lady, but her voice was really soft and mousy. After a few sentences, Dad blurted out:

"If you're going to talk to me, you're gonna have to fuckin' speak up, cuz I can't understand a word you're saying."

She looked a little taken aback and quickly raised her voice a little and said, "Oh, okay, I'll try to talk louder."

She began asking questions about my father's life. Things like: Are you retired? What did you used to do for work? How long did you do it? After answering several of her questions, he interrupted her and yelled: "What the hell is this about? Why are you asking me this stuff?"

"Daddy, she's just getting to know you, she's not from the IRS," I said trying to diffuse the hornet's nest.

"I see your daughter is here. How many children do you have?" she asked.

"Two. My daughter, and I have a son," he snapped.

"Oh how nice, what's his name?"

"His name is Ted, and that's all I'm going to say about that," he sternly responded.

Donna got the hint that Terry wasn't in the mood for a chat. She politely excused herself and walked toward the door. She waved at me to join her in the hallway.

"I forgot to ask you. It's for my records. Do you need me to arrange for a clergyman visit?

Without even thinking, I said, "No. That won't be needed." I knew the way Terry felt about his Catholic upbringing, so I was confident that he did not want to deal with that.

While we waited for Kay, Dad was still focused on wrapping up loose ends. He asked if I wanted his GMC truck, or just the cash.

"Daddy, I want what you want."

"Well, I'll leave Frank a message and ask him to go get it and find out how much it's worth."

After he left a voicemail for Frank, I said, "I can look-up your truck on Kelley Blue Book on my phone if you want. I'd just need you to tell me what the features are."

"Okay, let's do that."

So I asked him all the questions listed and walked him through the process. When it came to the section about condition, I asked him, "Did you ever smoke in your truck?"

"No," he said, avoiding eye contact.

"No? Seriously, you never smoked in your truck?"

"No. I *didn't*."

"Okay, well, here's what Kelly says," I said, flashing him my phone.

"Fine. That's fine."

Kay came by with the paperwork Dad requested. I was sitting next to his bed when he handed it to me. It was a receipt for a headstone with a computer drawing of the order.

"I bought my dad a new headstone. I had P.D. help me arrange it in Michigan, and they supposedly delivered it to St. Patrick Cemetery in Parnell, but I've never seen it."

"Wow, Dad, it's beautiful."

I texted John a photo of the receipt and asked him to call the granite company in Lowell, Michigan, to find out if they had a photo of it installed. Twenty minutes later, my grandfather's headstone appeared on my phone. It read: **TSGT ROBERT F TROY**, located above the words: **30 MISSIONS IN A B-17 BOMBER**. Then his dates were listed and the words: **LOVING FATHER OF FIVE**.

"Where'd you get that?" he asked, staring at it intently.

"Sonny boy called Michigan and got it for you."

"His old stone looked terrible. I thought it was a damn shame, so I had this one made. Please thank John for me," he said, looking pleased.

"I love the black granite, and the flag on the corner is beautiful, you did a great job, Dad. Did you ever tell Uncle Joe about this?"

"No. He can see it when he goes there."

Terry asked Kay to find his title to his truck and a notary that would come to the hospice center. He also asked for the $550 in cash he had paper-clipped to his car insurance bill and wanted me to deposit it in my account. I asked the social worker if she could help us with a power of attorney, last will and testament, and any other documents that might be helpful.

"Dad, where do you keep all of your important papers?"

"Everything you need will be in that pink tub. Everything else in the apartment you can get rid of. I don't have anything nice there."

Since we were discussing this kind of stuff, I took the calculated risk of asking something I had never asked him before.

"Daddy, do you owe anyone any money that I should know about?"

"No, I don't owe anyone shit," he quickly assured me.

And then he paused for a second and looked at me and said, "Except you. I never paid you for the Ford you gave me."

I hadn't thought about that transaction in over twenty years. I was stunned, but I didn't want to get into that with him; I quickly switched gears.

"So nobody is going to come to me and tell me that you owed them money, right?"

"Well, if they do, you can tell them to go fuck themselves, because I don't."

"Okay, well since we're on the subject of money, do you still have money in Frank's shop safe?"

"No, that money was spent a long time ago."

Terry had only spoken with Frank once when he was first admitted to hospice, he hadn't been by to visit, and he never returned Dad's call about his pickup. I called Frank's wife and she said that both she and Frank were planning on coming by for a visit soon.

Thursday May 16, I spent the day sitting quietly with Terry. He was mostly sleeping or staring at the TV. I didn't want to make him talk, so I stayed quiet and wrote in my journal while we waited for Kay to come.

Donna, the social worker came by and said, "Do you think your dad will be getting his radiation treatment today? You know he doesn't have to do those treatments."

"Do a lot of people get these? They said it would help his pain."

"Nobody does these. It's up to him, but I need to cancel the ambulance if he doesn't want to go."

"Dad, what do you want to do? Do you want your next radiation treatment?"

"No. It hurts too much to get banged around in that damn ambulance."

"Okay, I'll cancel it for you," said Donna.

"When can I go home? I just want to go home," Dad blurted out.

Donna looked at me and didn't say a word. So I said, "Daddy, you can go home, but you have to be able to walk. If you can walk, I'll take you home."

"So if I can walk, I can leave?" he asked, looking at Donna.

Donna gave me a nervous look and then slowly shook her head up and down.

"Okay," he softly replied.

Later that night, Kay showed up with Denise, the apartment manager from Dad's complex. A lady named Barb also joined them. Kay had enlisted Barb a few weeks prior to sleep at Terry's apartment. She was afraid he would burn down the entire complex because he insisted on always having a cigarette lit, even when he was falling asleep.

When they arrived, he was alert enough to still recognize everyone, and he tried to carry on a conversation, but it was definitely uncomfortable. After about twenty minutes, Terry said, "Honey give me $50 out of that cash I gave you." Then Denise walked over to the bed. Dad handed the money to her and said, "Happy Birthday, Denise." She smiled, thanked him and made more small talk, before she said she needed to get going—it was getting late.

Denise and Barb walked out into the hall, Dad slumped deeper into his bed. Kay sat on the side of his bed and put her face really close to his while holding his hands. I decided to step out and make a quick phone call, but as I was walking by the bed I heard Kay quietly say, "Terry, I want to see you in heaven. All you have to do is accept Jesus Christ as your Lord and Savior, and you will go to heaven." I was sort of shocked, but I kept on walking toward the hall. I knew even with pain meds, it was unlikely he was going to welcome that conversation.

After they all left, I returned to the room and said, "Hey Dad, I'm here to help you in any way that I can. I want you to spend your time, the way you want. Do you want me to say something to Kay about not discussing that stuff with you?"

"No. I took care of that," he quickly answered.

He wasn't upset. He didn't seem agitated at all. Strangely, he was the calmest I'd seen him since I'd arrived in Ohio.

On Friday, May 17, I checked out of the hotel and started sleeping in Dad's room. The staff placed a cot for me next to the armoire near the foot of the bed.

"Daddy, I'll be staying here now. Is there anything I can do to help you feel more settled?" I asked.

"I just want this paperwork done. I don't want you to get fucked over, and I damn sure don't want anything going to probate."

"Don't worry, we'll get it handled," I assured him.

"Have you heard from Frank?" Dad asked.

"No, Dad I haven't."

"I tried to call him. Left him a voicemail. But he hasn't called me back."

"Daddy, do you want me to call Uncle Ty?"

"No."

"Okay, do you want me to call Michelle?"

"Absolutely not. If something does happen to me, make sure you call P.D. But not now."

Later that night I said something that prompted Dad to make a comment that I will never forget. It finally brought some clarity.

"I thought Frank was coming by to see you, but something must have come up."

"That's okay. It's better this way. I don't want him to see me like this. I want him to remember me as the strong man I used to be," he calmly answered, staring toward the window.

It finally all made sense to me. He valued being a strong man so much more than I had ever understood. His pride was deeply rooted in his physical strength and independence. That's why he didn't want me to come. And that's why he didn't want his brothers and Frank to visit. It broke my heart that he felt betrayed by his body, but I certainly understood the feeling.

I texted Frank's wife and told her what Terry had said. She responded, "Well that's probably better because Frank really couldn't bring himself to say goodbye."

The social worker gave us the legal documents we asked for, and Kay found an eighty-eight-year-old notary named Betty she'd met at church. Right before Kay arrived, his nurse Kelly had given him some more pain medication. Kay brought Barb and Betty, so there was a lot of talking and commotion that Terry wasn't used to, and he started to become agitated. I didn't want to waste Betty's time, so I quickly got out the paperwork, and she told me where to have Terry sign. As the signing dragged on, Kay and I noticed Dad became quiet and withdrawn, and he was having difficulty using the pen, but thankfully he managed to get his signatures down. I sensed something had changed the second he was done signing.

"Daddy are you okay?"

"Honey, who are all these people in my room?"

I looked at Kay and motioned for her to get everyone out. I thanked Betty and tried to pay her, but she refused to take any money. It concerned me that he didn't recognize Barb, especially because she had spent so much time with him in his apartment.

"It's okay Dad, they're leaving," I answered, trying to comfort him.

On her way out, Kay said, "I'm glad you're staying here, I didn't understand why you were staying at a hotel."

"Because my back and hip are killing me, and I didn't want to sleep on this shitty cot. But I'm here now."

"Well, I'm glad because that hotel's in a shady part of town."

Every morning around seven a doctor would check on Terry's status. On Saturday, May 18, it was a tall woman with short graying hair. She looked at Dad's feet and legs. Then she noticed his right arm was curled up with his hand close to his face. She tried to pull it back down, but Dad let out a wail and gave her an angry look. She said, "He's getting really stiff. We'll see how he's doing tomorrow."

Terry was withdrawn and quiet all day. Other than the candy, he hadn't eaten a meal since the cheeseburger, days before. Later in the day, his friend Sarah and her boyfriend stopped by. I met them in the hallway, so they didn't get caught off guard. I explained that Terry wasn't doing well and that he was having a hard time recognizing people like Kay and Barb. Sarah understood; her visit was short.

A few hours after they left, Terry no longer wanted to sit up and could only find a comfortable position on his back. The nurses wanted to keep moving him so he wouldn't get bedsores, but he couldn't tolerate being placed on his side. That night I tried to catch some sleep at the foot of his bed, but the room was filled with the sound of him gasping for air every three seconds. His eyes were closed and his mouth was wide open, with his breath rattling in and out.

"I love you Daddy. I'm still here," I said, as I crawled onto the cot watching him breathe.

"I love you, Honey Babe," he answered, lying still with his eyes closed.

On Sunday, May 19, Dad had stopped opening his eyes or speaking. I sat at his bedside thinking about how lucky I was, that even when he didn't recognize anyone else, he still knew who I was. The last words he ever spoke left zero doubt; it seemed like he'd made a conscious decision to let me know.

I sat at his bedside holding his left hand. His fingers were curled into his hand so I cupped my fingers around his, so our thumbs were next to each other's. I realized in that moment that I would never hear his deep voice again. I held his hand all day and told him over and over, "I'm here Dad. I'm here."

On Monday, May 20, the same doctor from the day before came in. She noted that his arm was no longer curled up. She said, "He seems more relaxed now. I think he's in the beginning of the 'active dying' phase."

"How long does this take now?" I asked.

"We don't know. We'll have to see how much he fights it."

That day was also Jill and her father Fred's birthday, so I thought perhaps that was a sign.

His nurse Amanda came in and asked, "Is there anything you need?"

"I need to run to the store and get some products. But I'm curious. Why are there no birds at the birdfeeders?"

"There've been some budget cuts so we haven't had any birdseed for a really long time."

"That's a shame, I think my dad would have really enjoyed listening to them."

Later that day I drove to the bank and I noticed an ACE Hardware across the street. For some strange reason, I felt drawn there to purchase some birdseed. I walked into the feed aisle and said to the guy behind the register, "Can you help me load up all of your birdseed?"

"All of it?" he asked with a dumbfounded look.

"Yeah, I want to donate it to hospice."

He loaded my trunk; I could barely get the lid closed. I called the hospice staff on my way back, and they agreed to have someone meet me to unload it. After the nice worker emptied my trunk, I said, "Would you mind filling up the bird feeder outside my father's window as soon as possible?" She agreed, and by the time I parked my car and got back to his room, it was already done.

A new man in the room across the hall had arrived a few days before. He used his walker to shuffle from his bed, to his chair, and back again. He liked to sit and stare at me through the open doors. The way my chair was positioned, I could see him when I was sitting next to Dad's bed. The entire time he was there, I never saw any visitors come to see him. I vowed Dad would always know he wasn't alone.

Donna told me that she needed to know about Dad's burial wishes right away. It caught me off guard because I'd been there for days, and now all of a sudden it was an urgent matter. I remembered he'd mentioned on several occasions that he had pre-paid for his cremation, and his ashes would be shipped to me in the mail. He never gave me the details because he always said, "You don't have to worry about anything. Frank went with me, and he has all the information."

I quickly called Frank, and luckily he answered the phone at his shop. I asked him to get the cremation information, and he acted like he didn't know what I was talking about. After several minutes of trying to prod him, he said, "Well honey, I think it was somewhere in Youngstown, but we were pretty drunk that day and I don't really remember."

I tried not to panic, but I needed to do everything exactly the way Dad wanted it. I called John and asked him to start calling around to all of the funeral homes in the area.

"Do you know how many there are? Hundreds! Let's just find a local place and pay for it ourselves," John said.

"No. It has to be done the way he wanted it. He will be so pissed if I screw this up."

John was sweet and called over twenty places, but he didn't find anyone that had Terry's information on file. I started searching the internet for anything that might look like something Dad would have been drawn to. Within a few clicks, *bingo!* I found a local place in Austintown that advertised "affordable, quick and easy cremations," or something like that. The guy's name was Gary, and the building on their website resembled a warehouse. I sent the info to John, and about five minutes later he called and said: "You were right. Gary remembers Pops because he tried to pay with cash about two months after he had just opened his business."

Later that night, I remembered that I should have looked in Dad's wallet. When I did, Gary's business card was filed right behind his car insurance company.

Jill, Glee, Uncle Joe, and John had all been texting me trying to be as supportive as possible. I did my best to keep everyone in the loop, but I mostly focused on staying with Dad. I took a quick shower and did a load of laundry, but otherwise I sat at his bedside. His nighttime nurse, Mary Jo, was one of my favorites and she'd just arrived. I told her that I noticed he was rubbing his eyes a lot and was concerned there was a problem. I don't think he could move his fingers anymore, so he used his thumb and first finger, cupped together to rub at his face.

"He's probably got some dry eyes. Let me get him some eye drops to see if that will help," Mary Jo said in a sweet tone.

She leaned over the bed and got really close to his face.

"Okay, Terry, its Mary Jo here. I'm going to put some eye drops in your eyes, sweetie," she quietly explained.

I was so impressed with her gentleness. Nothing I asked from her was ever a problem. Sleeping was impossible. Terry had been gasping for air every three seconds, non-stop, for days. I felt like I was stuck in Edgar Allan Poe's "The Tell-Tale Heart." It was agonizing to watch him suffer like a fish out of water, gasping over and over, day after day. Even opening the windows couldn't clear the room of its stale smell of liquid morphine.

I hadn't said anything to him about leaving, I was conscious not to pressure. He was ultimately the one deciding obviously, but I wanted to start helping if I could. In a calm, strong voice I said, "Daddy, I want you to know that you have done everything right. You've taken care of everything, and I know exactly what you want me to do. I'm so proud of you for being so strong through all of this horrible pain. It's all going to be okay, Daddy. I will be okay. I remember you told me I could call Uncle Joe if I needed help with anything. We will all be okay. I know that Brian and your dad are waiting for you. Daddy, it's okay to go. Really, it's okay to go. I will be there with you in the blink of an eye. I know we'll be together again—I just know it."

I felt like I did that day forty years ago, when I asked my dad to leave the mudroom door. For his own good, I needed him to go. The last thing I really wanted was for him to be gone, but it hurt so much watching him struggle. Absolutely unbearable.

I sat next to his bed most of the night holding his hand and calling Mary Jo any time I felt he was uncomfortable. She would dab sponges loaded with liquid morphine in his mouth to help with his pain. I prayed and asked that all of his loved ones that had already crossed over, please come and get him.

Early in the morning, as Mary Jo's shift was about to end, I thought about all the strangers that had helped me, each time I had a great loss in my life. I vowed to be that stranger when it was my turn.

She said goodbye to Terry and then hugged me.

"My shifts are over for a few days. I doubt I will see you when I return. Hang in there, you've been an amazing daughter," Mary Jo said.

"Thank you, but I'm the lucky one."

CHAPTER TWENTY-SIX

Janine

On Tuesday, May 21, I'd been awake all night long, holding Dad's hand and talking to him. A stocky, strong looking woman I'd never seen before walked into the room.

"Hi, I'm Janine. I'll be your dad's nurse today."

Something about Janine felt comfortable and safe, like we'd met before. Her energy and demeanor felt like family. She had a presence and power about her that led me to believe that she was a "closer" of sorts. It was the weirdest thought, but that's what popped into my head.

Something in my gut made me feel that this might be the day that he would leave me. The sun was beginning to rise and shine into the room. As I gazed toward the window I said, "We put birdseed in the feeder, but not one bird has shown up."

"Well, they'll find it eventually. Is there anything I can bring you?"

"Nah, I'm okay for now, thanks."

"I'll be back to check on you."

I sat on the bed, and I lightly rubbed Dad's struggling chest. I continued to repeat, "Please Daddy, it's okay to go. It's okay to go. I'll be right here. I want you to know that I'm so grateful that you were my dad. I never doubted that you loved me. I never wondered if you were proud of me. I am so lucky to have you as my dad. You're still so handsome and strong. I want you to know I will be okay; I promise

I will be okay. I have your strength and you have taught me so well. I love you, Daddy."

I stayed with him all morning, making sure he knew I was there. His eyes were closed, and his body hadn't moved in days. I could see only his chest moving and hear him gasping for air, but otherwise he was calm and still. Around 10:15, Janine came back.

"I think I'm going to try to suction him to see if I can help him along," she stated.

"Okay, whatever you think," I said through my brain fog.

"But I'll need you to step out because I don't want you to see this."

I didn't know exactly what she meant, but I had learned to trust in the great care that the hospice nurses had been giving him.

"Okay, Janine, I'll go get some tea and wait for you."

I felt like a zombie as I walked down the short hall where I mindlessly stepped into the library. I grabbed some tea and wandered in a daze, looking at all of the book titles. I was so exhausted at this point, that I felt nauseous. The only thing that was keeping me going was pure adrenaline. I had my back to the door while I was looking for something in the vending machine that might calm my stomach. And then I heard a loud voice.

"Terrina!"

It jolted me out of my stupor, and I snapped my head around to see Janine in the doorway. I had not heard someone say my actual name in so long, it startled me. People would call me sweetie or honey, or not use a name at all, but nobody in all the time that I had been there, had called me Terrina.

I walked over to her, and she said, "I just wanted to tell you that I don't know if it's going to be twenty minutes or two hours, but it's going to be today."

I could tell by her energy that something had changed. I rushed past her and ran back to his room. When I stepped inside his doorway, I could see his back and noticed that she had placed him on his left side facing my chair and the windows. In that split second I wondered why she would do that, considering it hurt him to lie on his side. As I walked around to the left to sit in the chair, I was completely horrified. Whatever she had done to him had caused him to open his eyes really wide, and his expression was one of terror. His eye color had completely faded, and his pupils looked weird, almost like snake eyes. His mouth was stiff and wide open. The only thing moving was his chest; his breathing had slowed. He was still taking long, intermittent breaths, but nothing else moved. I tried not to let him know that I was scared. I grabbed his hand, sat in the chair and didn't allow myself to look away. What if he could still see? I knew I couldn't cry. I pushed it back and told myself to be there for him. Be in the moment. Don't think about anything else.

"Daddy, I'm here. I am right here with you. It's just you and me Dad, just like it's always been."

He continued to take deep breaths about every five seconds. I could sense that this was the end.

"I love you, Dad. I'm never going to leave you. It's okay to go. Daddy it's okay to go."

I calmly repeated, "I love you, I love you, I love you, Daddy."

Just like I had with Braddy, Bailey, and Mulligan. I didn't want him to have one second on this earth where he felt he was alone.

"I love you Dad, I'm here." And then his next breath wasn't coming.

I didn't look away, and said, "Dad? Dad? Are you still here, Dad? I love you."

And then he took one more raspy breath, and I just knew he was gone. My body started to shake as I fought to hold back my tears—just in case he was still alive. After about twenty seconds, I could feel the room felt cold and empty. I let go of his hand and started to slowly walk around his bed, not taking my eyes off of him. I pushed the call button and a voice said, "Do you need something?"

I started to slowly hyperventilate as I choked back tears. I searched for the words.

"I. need. Janine."

"She'll be right there," the voice rushed to say.

I turned around and started to walk back around the end of the bed. Janine must have been nearby because she ran into the room before I was able to get back to my chair. She grabbed me with her right arm and pulled my face into her chest, while she used her other hand to pull her stethoscope off her neck.

"I think he's gone," I stated, as I started to cry.

"Let me have a listen," she said, as she squeezed me tight. "Yes, sweetie, he has passed."

Within seconds of her saying those words, I heard some chaotic noise and felt a tremendous energy coming from the window. I pulled my head away from Janine and said, "Oh my God, Janine! The birds! Look at the birds!"

We both just stood there in shock as we watched the birdfeeder. It was teeming with birds. There must have been at least twenty-five of them. Some would land and others would fly away, and then more would land. They were chirping loudly and jumping up a few inches and then landing again. Without even knowing it was about to come out of my mouth I said, "Our family came to get him."

Exactly four years after his first lung biopsy, the father that I had adored for over fifty years, was gone. The second he took his last breath, I wanted him back.

CHAPTER TWENTY-SEVEN

Cardinals Rule

I watched the birds until they seemed to find peace and became quiet. I told Janine that I was going to step outside to make some phone calls.

"Sounds good. I'll get him ready for when the funeral guy gets here."

I walked to the end of the hallway and stepped outside to get some fresh air. I could hear the sound of the Ohio Turnpike off in the distance; I remember thinking it sounded like there was a tunnel on the other side of the woods. I gathered up my strength and called Uncle Joe. He didn't answer, so I left him a voicemail.

I knew that John was still asleep back in Arizona, so I called Glee next. Even though it was early, she answered quickly, almost as if she expected the call. After I told her about how Dad had departed, she said,

"I'm so sorry Treen. I'm so sorry you were alone," she said, trying not to cry.

"Well, Glee, this is my life. Maybe in my next one I'll have a dozen siblings, but not in this one."

"How are you doing?" she asked.

As I choked back my tears, I answered without thinking, "I just wanted to get it right, Glee."

"Of course. Of course you did. You did everything right, Treen."

I'll never forget that conversation. Because it was in that moment I realized how I truly felt. The responsibility of my role felt intense and enormous. I had one shot to get it right. Even in death, my father was still teaching me how to push my fear aside, and to choose bravery instead.

I stood with my back to the building, staring at the forest. I was conscious of the cool breeze blowing through the leaves on the trees. I wondered if Dad was being a smart-ass, laughing again with his dad and Gram in heaven.

All of sudden, I felt this strange energy force coming from behind me, almost like I could sense I was about to get run over by a train. My entire body got warm, and I started to tremble. I slowly turned my head around, bracing myself. A large, bright, red cardinal was flying straight at me. I froze and it felt like time was moving in slow motion. Its wings were flapping gently, then the bird was gliding, then flapping some more, heading straight toward me. It looked like it didn't have a care in the world. Floating, free and happy. Then, a few feet away from my face, it slowly turned, drifted into the woods, and completely disappeared. My emotions changed without my permission. I was drained of sadness, settling into a weird sense of relief. I got the message. I just knew. I knew that my father was in a better place; free from all of his pain and all of his struggles. And he was happy.

I felt a sense of calm wash over me. There was absolutely no doubt in my mind that Terry was letting me know he was on his way. When the cardinal disappeared into the woods, I kept looking for it. I never saw it land. It was almost like it was sucked into the distant noise. Perhaps you have to take the Ohio Turnpike to get to heaven. One thing was for sure, nobody would question Dad's directions. I wondered if I was crazy and had just imagined it all. But then I stopped myself and fully accepted it as the gift that it truly was.

Epilogue

On December 5, 2021, I finally opened the box that was delivered shortly after Dad passed. Inside I found a plastic, square container with a hinged lid. I carefully placed it into my backpack along with the last two cigarettes that my father had left in his coat pocket.

I wanted to place him at the highest point of my most favorite mountain. I hadn't been hiking since before my hip surgery, and I worried about the climb, carrying fifteen pounds on my back. I parked my car and took a deep breath. I put the backpack on, looked toward the top and said out loud, "Okay, Dad, it's just you and me again. Let's do this."

I focused on taking one step at a time. I could feel not only the weight of the backpack, but the weight of the task. With each step, I heard my father's voice encouraging me. As I passed the other hikers, I could hear many of them sharing their personal struggles. I thought perhaps the mountain brings that out of people. Maybe we climb and challenge ourselves so we learn it's okay to try and fail. Or possibly to remind ourselves that it's also okay to push limits and succeed.

As I continued to hike I noticed that I wasn't getting tired but actually getting stronger with each step. When I reached the first viewing station, I knew I would make it to the top because it wasn't much farther. I stopped for a moment and took in the view. I contemplated the great memories I had made with Dad. I worked at not feeling sad—I knew that's not what he wanted. I wouldn't allow myself to cry.

I took another deep breath and continued up the trail. A few minutes later I saw the orange sign that stated I had reached the highest point. I looked around and took in the amazing view; it felt right. I found a large boulder next to a tree, just off the side of the trail, and sat down. I pulled the backpack off my shoulder and placed it on the ground, as I watched the other hikers pass by. I waited for a quiet moment. I wasn't sure if I was breaking the law, but I knew I wasn't leaving without completing the mission. So when things looked clear, I nervously pulled out the container and popped open the lid. I could feel myself shaking; also feeling silly because no one was there to bear witness to my simple ceremony. Inside was a thick, plastic bag with a name tag tightly tied to the top. Suddenly, I realized that I hadn't come prepared with scissors or a knife, so I started to panic. I didn't want the next hiker to come by while I was in the middle of dispersing his ashes. I grabbed the bag, with both hands, pulling and ripping a hole in the plastic. I pulled too hard, and the entire bag exploded all over my black pants and black, long-sleeved shirt. I was covered in gray dust. I tried to wipe it off, but that only made it worse. I quickly emptied the rest onto the ground and shoved the container back into my backpack. I sat down on the boulder and laughed out loud.

I could hear Dad's voice saying, "Honey Babe, stop being nervous. Fuck 'em *all but six*, save those for pallbearers."

I took out the two cigarettes and crumbled them over his ashes. I remembered all the times I had bummed a smoke from him when we had grabbed a drink at a bar, and thought it was apropos that he had left exactly two.

After sitting with him, I knew I had to let him rest, but I struggled to leave. I walked to the other side of the trail and took pictures of the exact location, so I would never forget. And then I slowly walked a few feet away. I still couldn't leave, so I allowed myself to stand there looking at his view. I noticed off in the distance there were two people, one younger, one older. They were getting ready to rappel down the steep mountain. It was obvious that the younger person was learning and was scared. It took about five minutes for the first few steps, but eventually the older person coached him down. I thought about how many times Dad had "coached me down."

I turned and started down the path. I didn't look back, for fear I wouldn't be able to leave. With each slow step I took, I could feel the heaviness of the day drifting away. I passed a mother and daughter who looked to be struggling and lost. I stopped and said, "Are you guys okay? Do you need some help?" The daughter said, "My mom is really scared of heights, and she doesn't know if she can keep going. Does the trail get tighter? Where does it go?" I smiled at the mom and said, "I promise you the worst is behind you. Just a few more steps and you'll be able to say you reached the highest point. Don't stop now; it's just gettin' good." She thanked me and kept going up the trail. I replied, "Enjoy the view, it's heavenly."

At that exact second, I felt the "peace" and the "piece." The peace that I knew my father would always be with me, and the piece of him that lived on in me, as I carried on teaching others what he had taught me.

Feeling light and free, I decided to test out the hip, and I ran the entire way down the mountain. When I got to the bottom, I had a great epiphany. I'd finally learned that just because my father had died, it didn't mean the relationship was over. I was totally convinced that goodbye is not the end. Perhaps that's why I never said it.

I've obviously thought a lot about Terry's life and his accomplishments. I contemplated the definition of a successful life. I ultimately concluded that when I leave this earth, if there's one person who thinks about me every day, misses me and loves me, as much as I do my father, I will have reached the pinnacle, too.

People often say that it's lonely at the top. I disagree. I know who's waiting for me.

(NOT) THE END

Conclusion

My wish for this book is to help others who have been through a similar experience, heal, even if it's just a little. If you can't put into words how you feel, let mine speak for you, and please know you are not alone.

And to those who may be faced with a comparable heartbreak, hopefully this story will help you prepare to be an organized, focused advocate for your loved one.

One of the driving forces behind writing this book was feeling traumatized by what I witnessed during my father's passing. I share my experiences, lessons, and a piece of my heart and soul, all in a true effort to help others have a less painful journey to the other side.

I also hope that by being totally honest and sharing my authentic story, the great lessons that I learned will touch others, and become a gift that keeps on giving—through which my father will live on.

Acknowledgments

First and foremost, I'd like to thank Dad for passing on to me his strength and determination, without which I could not have relived these experiences and written this book. I feel you with me when I laugh, when I look at my eyes in the mirror, and every day I brush these ridiculous cowlicks. I love you Daddy with all my heart, and I am so grateful that you were my father. I would pick you over, and over, again. I truly feel so blessed to have had you in my life. I only wish you hadn't had to leave so soon.

A very special thank you to my husband and Woobie, John. I'm so appreciative that you always believed in me and never doubted that I could put pen to paper honestly and effectively, without bowing to political correctness. Thank you for your love and unwavering encouragement, and for enduring all the crazy stories. Your unconditional love means everything to me.

My life would not have been the same without all my fur-babies. I am truly blessed to have had the privilege of being your mom. Thank you for all the lessons you taught me. To my loves: Braddy, Bailey, Mulligan, Peso, Payson, and Parker—you all make my heart want to explode. I love you all completely.

A huge serving of gratitude to all my friends that supported me through one of the worst times in my life—especially my lifelong soul sisters: Glee, Jill, and Holly. Without you being there during the madness and afterward, listening and caring, there's a pretty good chance I would have lost my shit. I love you! Girl Power!

I also want to acknowledge one of my favorite humans ever: Uncle Joe. As he was enduring some of the worst of times in his own life, he reached out to me, offered support, and even managed to make me laugh. I will never forget your love and kindness. I love you and miss you, more than you'll ever know. I'll see you in the blink of an eye. Rest in peace.

A special thank you to my Uncle Ty for being a positive connection and caring about me after the loss of Dad and Uncle Joe. I Love you for including me in your life—you're my only "Ty" to my family.

I'm so grateful to Aunt Donna for reading my manuscript, enduring all my typos, and being an awesome cheerleader. Thank you! You're amazing. I love you.

Jordy, thanks for the support and advice on the artwork. I hope you're proud. I love your sweet soul.

Thank you to Dad's friends who helped me throughout my time in Ohio. I will always be grateful to those who stepped up and offered true kindness. Thank you Kay, Ella, Sarah, Frank, Ruth Ann, Jeff, Bill, and Linda. I promise to pay it forward.

And finally, to all the hospice nurses, doctors, and staff who provide comfort to the dying on a daily basis, I applaud you. You are all truly the most amazing people I have ever met—particularly my father's care team of nurses. You've earned your place in heaven. I am eternally grateful. Janine, I will never, ever, forget you!

BRITTA VAN VRANKEN

About the Author

TERRINA TROY is a writer, designer, artist, serial
entrepreneur, challenge seeker, and wannabe cowgirl.
She, her husband, and their two sweet dogs,
Payson and Parker, live in beautiful Arizona.
All But Six is her first book.

terrinatroy.com
Facebook.com/TerrinaTroy
Substack.com/@terrinatroy

www.ingramcontent.com/pod-product-compliance
Lightning Source LLC
Chambersburg PA
CBHW030407130626
46549CB00004B/1670